Tibet
OF THE WORLD...
MT. EVEREST
High and cold
PASHPATTI
Very holy
KHATMANDU
BHATGAON
PATAN
CHANDRAGIRI Pass
SISAGARHI Pass
The TERAI
ELEPHANTS and TIGERS here
MT. KINCHINJUNGA
MT. KUBRA
SIKKIM
BHUTAN
DARJEELING
Where the tourists see the Himalayas
NEPÁL
The
PATNA
SACRED RIVER
GANGES
The BRAHMAPUTRA RIVER
India
A Nepalese Lady
CALCUTTA
Low and Hot
The BAY OF BENGAL

THE LAST HOME OF MYSTERY

THE PALM-FRINGED SHORES OF CEYLON

The fronds of the slanting cocoa-palms, etched in indigo against the carmine evening sky, stir in the languid breeze like the feathered bonnets of Indian warriors

A STAR BOOK

THE LAST HOME OF MYSTERY

BY

E. ALEXANDER POWELL

Adventures in Nepal together with accounts of Ceylon, British India, the Native States, the Persian Gulf, the Overland Desert Mail and the Baghdad Railway. Illustrated with a Map and with many Photographs by the Author

GARDEN CITY PUBLISHING COMPANY, INC.

GARDEN CITY, NEW YORK

PRINTED IN U. S. A.

TO

SIR THEODORE ANDREA COOK

EDITOR OF "THE FIELD"

A GREAT SPORTSMAN AND A

STAUNCH FRIEND

AN ACKNOWLEDGMENT

WHEN Sir Theodore Cook, a friend of many years, learned that I was once more heading for the East, he lost no time in setting the cables a-hum. To his influence and kindly interest I am indebted, therefore, for the countless courtesies shown my cousin Colonel Gallowhur and myself by the Government of India and by the Indian princes.

My gratitude is due in almost equal measure to his Highness the Nawab of Bhopal, whose guests we were both at his camp at New Delhi and at his capital, Bhopal City. His cordiality, the magnificent fashion in which he entertained us, the trouble to which he put himself on our account, showed me to what lengths hospitality can be carried.

I am likewise deeply grateful to the nawab's mother, her Highness the Begum, that remarkable woman who for many years ruled Bhopal wisely and well; to Colonel Amir Ahmed, military secretary to his Highness, who was guide, counselor and friend in one; and to the nawab's private physician, Dr. Rahman, who attended me when I was ill.

The pleasure and interest of our sojourn in the Native States were immensely increased by the hospitality of his Highness the Maharajah of Patiala and his Highness the Maharajah of Gwalior, at whose courts we were guests. It was a source of deep regret that lack of time prevented us from accepting the cordial invitations of his Highness the Gaekwar of Baroda and of his Highness the Jam Sahib of Nawanagar.

For permitting us to visit his forbidden country, and for

the extraordinary facilities afforded us for observation and investigation, I am under great obligations to his Highness Marshal Sir Shum Shere Jung, Prime Minister and Supreme Commander-in-Chief of the Forces of Nepál.

Colonel Husband of the Indian Medical Corps was on two occasions our host at Raxaul and was of great assistance in facilitating our journey into Nepál.

Least of all have I forgotten the hospitality shown us during our stay in Khatmandu by Mr. Roy Kilburne, an English electrical engineer in the Nepálese service, and his beautiful and charming wife. Nothing that would add to our pleasure or comfort was too much trouble for them and they made us feel that their home was ours. I send them my thanks across the miles.

It is impossible for me to mention all of the British officials to whom I am indebted in various ways, but I cannot miss this opportunity of expressing my gratitude to the Honorable the Earl of Winterton, Under-Secretary of State for India; to Sir Stanley Jackson, Governor of Bengal, the officers of his staff and the officials of the Bengal Political Department. They could not have shown greater eagerness to assist us had we been old friends.

For their unfailing kindness, hospitality and assistance I am also deeply indebted to many officers of the American Foreign Service; in particular, Mason Turner, Esq., vice-consul at Colombo; Richard R. Willey, Esq., vice-consul at Calcutta; Wilbur Keblinger, Esq., consul at Bombay; John Randolph, Esq., and Wendell S. Howard, Esq., respectively consul and vice-consul at Baghdad; James H. Keeley, Esq., consul at Damascus; Paul Knabenshue, Esq., consul at Beirut; and Harry L. Troutman, Esq., consul at Aleppo. At each of their consulates I found the latch-string out and an extra place at the table.

In the preparation of this book I have consulted many

authorities on India and Nepál. Among the volumes from which I have drawn valuable material or suggestions are "India and Its Problems," by William S. Lilly, Esq.; "Cities of India," by Sir George William Forrest; "Courts and Camps in India," by Miss Yvonne Fitzroy; "India Under Curzon and After," by Lovat Fraser, Esq.; "India," by Sir Thomas Hungerford Holdich; "In India," by G. W. Steevens, Esq.; "India," by Pierre Loti; "Winter India," by Miss E. R. Scidmore; "India and the Indians," by E. F. Elwin, Esq.; "The Empire of India," by Sir J. Bampfylde Fuller; "Cults, Customs and Superstitions of India," by J. Campbell Oman, Esq.; "Indian Manners, Customs and Ceremonies," by Abbé Dubois; and "Picturesque Nepál," by Percy Brown, Esq.

I am deeply grateful to all of the above, and to many others whom I have no space to name.

E. ALEXANDER POWELL

"Journey's End,"
Chevy Chase, Maryland
February, 1929

CONTENTS

THE LAST HOME OF MYSTERY

This is India, the land of dreams and romance, of fabulous wealth, of fabulous poverty, of splendor and of rags, of palaces and hovels, of tigers and elephants. Cradle of the human race, birthplace of human speech; mother of religion; grandmother of history; great-grandmother of tradition. The land of a hundred nations and of a hundred tongues; of a thousand religions and of three million gods, and she worships them all. All other countries in religion are paupers; India is the only millionaire. The one sole land under the sun that is endowed with an imperishable interest for all men; rich and poor, bond and free; alien prince and alien peasant; all men want to see India, and having seen it once even by a glimpse, would not give up that glimpse for all the rest of the shows of the earth combined.

—MARK TWAIN

A shrewd observer, who will make numerous mistakes in describing details, will understand the general tendency of the sum total of Indian life more accurately than one who has lived so long in the country that he has ceased to see it except as a moving mass of detail.

—RAMSAY MACDONALD

THE LAST HOME OF MYSTERY

CHAPTER I

THE UTMOST INDIAN ISLE

THE monster pomegranate which was the waning sun ripened before our eyes from gold to crimson. So roseate was the glow it cast over the unruffled surface of the Indian Ocean that the *Sphinx* seemed to be cleaving her way through a sea of bright pink molten glass. The awnings stretched above the after-deck took on the same ruddy hue; the ostrich feathers curling from her bow were cerise shot through with silver.

In our wake, along the ocean's western rim, cumulus clouds assumed the fantastic forms which presage the approach of nightfall near the Line. Wisps and streamers of smoke-colored fleece drifted leisurely athwart a sky of flaming splendor to merge and rear themselves in magic mountain ranges, fairy forests, the battlements, gateways, turrets, spires of enchanted cities.

Some leagues ahead, a few points off the starboard bow, a tremendous peak, shading from pale amethyst to sullen purple, sprang abruptly from the darkening waters. At first but a dusky mass swimming nebulously in a mulberry haze, its outlines became more distinct as we forged nearer. Soon, despite the failing light, we could make out lesser peaks, then a congeries of wooded hills. At length there rose to view a low and brooding coast plain, dark with palms, bordered by the white ribbon of a sandy beach upon which combers hurled themselves to break in spray and spume. Catamarans with spidery outriggers and hibiscus-tinted sails slipped along the shore. The gentle land-breeze brought to our nostrils the subtle aroma of the spice-lands. Ceylon!

There was no particular reason why we should have chosen Ceylon to land in, except that, for the outward-bound steamers of the Messageries Maritimes, Colombo is the first Asiatic port of call. Moreover, my companion, Colonel Gallowhur, who is also my cousin, had never been there—indeed, had never been east of Suez before. And from Colombo it is only a step across the straits to India. While up through India, from the Coromandel coast right away to the northeast frontier, led the road which we must follow if we were to attain our final objective. For the real goal of a journey which had brought us half-way round the world was Nepál, the mysterious and inaccessible kingdom which lies hidden behind the curtain of the Himalayas.

Whether, upon reaching its borders, we would be permitted to enter Nepál was a matter for uneasy conjecture. For this remote buffer state, sandwiched between British India and Tibet, lying at the very feet of Everest and Kinchinjunga, is to all intents and purposes a forbidden land. Its rulers rarely grant permission to foreigners to penetrate beyond the outlying provinces of the Terai. Its warlike mountaineers, jealous of their independence, regard all Europeans with suspicion. The white men dwelling within its confines may be numbered on the fingers of a single hand. And for political reasons the Government of India discourages those travelers who seek to cross the Nepálese frontier.

But why anticipate difficulties? we asked ourselves. Closed doors are not necessarily locked. Besides, were we not at the gateway to the glittering East? There was enough to see and do even were admission to Nepál denied us. In our pockets were invitations from nawabs and maharajahs. Even the India Office had so far unbent as to recommend us to the viceroy and the British governors. Our imaginations toyed with visions of beturbaned princes and bejeweled nautch girls, of pink palaces and gilded temples, of elephants and tigers. We were foot-loose and free, ten thousand miles from home. True, we were no longer frank and twenty, but we still had faith and hope aplenty, with life and love to spare. And those seductive sirens, Mystery, Adventure, and Romance, insistently beckoned and called.

Viewed from the harbor, the capital of "the utmost Indian isle," as Ceylon was called by the ancient geographers, is extremely disappointing. The unlovely face which Colombo turns toward the visitor entering its port gives no hint of the tropical paradise to which it is the door. From the port-hole of my cabin I looked out at dawn upon a fleet of grimy cargo boats idling at anchor within the protecting arm of a concrete breakwater, a shore fringed by wharves piled high with tea-chests and copra-sacks, a line of corrugated iron godowns, and a wooden customs shed, the whole flanked by a row of monster oil-tanks and dominated by the many-galleried, tenement-like rear of the "G. O. H.," which, as every Eastern traveler knows, is the Grand Oriental Hotel.

Once out of the customs shed, however, and past the gantlet of importunate hotel runners, taxi drivers and rickshaw coolies, the visitor emerges abruptly into a clean, well built and bustling city, a city with a population of nearly a quarter of a million, the broad asphalted thoroughfares of its business district lined by modern stores and office buildings. But, despite its up-to-date habiliments, curious and colorful contrasts are observable on every hand, for

Colombo stands at one of the world's cross-roads, a half-way house on the road to Farther Asia.

Here West meets East. Here white and brown and yellow men rub shoulders. The city's population represents a medley of races and a variety of religions—Europeans, Singhalese, Tamils, Malays, Chinese and Arabs; Christians, Buddhists, Hindus, Parsees, Confucians and Moslems.

Perspiring tourists from a round-the-world-cruise ship in the harbor haggle with suave Parsee merchants over Japanese kimonos, Chinese ivories, Indian silks, Persian shawls, Syrian embroideries. Half-naked brown men in flaming head-cloths and skirts of gaudily striped cotton lounge before huge emporiums behind whose plate-glass windows are displayed radio sets, typewriters, Paris millinery, Scotch whisky, office furniture, electric refrigerators, the latest fiction. A few steps from the towering office building whose elevators shoot one up to the American consulate, Singhalese sentries in slouch hats and shorts pace before the crested gates of Queen's House, the low white residency, almost hidden by tropical foliage, which is the seat of British rule. In the very heart of the city, as though at the intersection of Fifth Avenue and Forty-second Street, yet visible far out at sea, stands a lofty campanile which serves the dual purpose of the principal lighthouse of the port and a city clock-tower.

Trim little policemen, as dignified and imperturbable as London bobbies, cope efficiently with a river of traffic composed of so bewildering a variety of vehicles that they might have come from a transportation museum. Lordly Rolls-Royces, agleam with nickel and varnish, shoulder aside ramshackle rickshaws with sweating coolies between the shafts. The drivers of Packards, Cadillacs, Buicks and Fords cursingly jam on their brakes while a ponderous, palm-roofed cart, hauled by a yoke of humpbacked zebus, creaks past with exasperating slowness. White trotting-bullocks, harnessed to hooded tongas, obstruct the progress of impatient young Englishmen astride of spluttering motorcycles. Satin-coated polo ponies, ridden by syces with bundles of polo mallets under their arms, snort contemptuously at their less fortunate fellow-equines which have sunk to the ignoble status of drawing *gharries*, those rattletrap vehicles, second cousins to our old-time hacks, which are being rapidly shoved from the streets of Oriental cities by the ubiquitous motor-car. Darting in and out amid the jam, like minnows among a school of larger fish, are native bicyclists, thousands of them, whose reckless riding and insistent bells add to the prevailing bedlam. Yet the diminutive brown policemen untangle the snarls and keep the traffic moving with perfect competency and unruffled calm. Scarcely five feet tall, yet every European motorist, Singhalese cyclist and Tamil bullock-driver respects their admonitory hands, for they personify the majesty of the white man's law.

When a resident of Colombo tells his wife that he is going to run down to the Fort he means that he is going down-town, for the business district of the city occupies the site of the extensive fortifications which were erected in the sixteenth century by the Portuguese, reconstructed in the seventeenth by the Dutch and demolished in the nineteenth by the British. It is a singular fact, by the way, that though the rule of Holland in Ceylon endured for upward of a century and a half, or somewhat longer than that of Portugal, the language of the Dutch, the use of which they sought to make compulsory by imprisonment or fines, is no longer spoken even by their direct descendants, whereas a corrupted Portuguese is to this day the vernacular of the lower classes in every town of importance. The Dutch have almost ceased to be remembered by the islanders, but the chiefs of the south and west cling with pride to the title of Dom, accorded them by their first European conquerors, and still prefix to their curious ancestral cognomens the sonorous Christian names of the Portuguese.

Five minutes beyond the Fort by motor or fifteen by rickshaw—and on the smooth red roads about Colombo the little man-drawn buggies provide by far the pleasantest means of getting about—is a ramiform sheet of fresh water known as "the Lake," which has become the center of a highly successful scheme of landscape-gardening, its irregular, bayou-indented shores being banked with masses of tropical shrubbery and flowers. The narrow isthmus between this lagoon and the sea is called Galle Face. In order to save the visitor from embarrassment, I might remark that the first word is pronounced to rhyme with "fall." The coolest spot in Colombo, even on the most torrid day usually swept by at least a hint of breeze, it is appropriately given over to promenades and playing-fields, a huge tourist hotel and one of the most luxurious and exclusive clubs east of the canal. The club bartender, by the way, is an adept at mixing a highly potent short drink known as a "gimlet," which is guaranteed to pierce anything short of armor-plate.

Still farther out is the romantically beautiful suburb known as the Cinnamon Gardens. In Dutch days a reserve for the cultivation of the spice which we use on buns, toast and milk-shakes, it is now the fashionable residential quarter for Europeans. The branches of stately tropical trees interlace in leafy canopies over roads of brick-red sand; nestling amid blazing gardens are vine-smothered bungalows whose green jalousies inclose deep, inviting verandas. The whole district is, indeed, a vast botanical garden, a horticulturist's delight, aflame with poinsettia, hibiscus and bougainvillea, redolent with the fragrance of lilies, gardenias and jasmine. I should earn the eternal gratitude of the local chamber of commerce, while taking no liberties with the truth, were I to assert that in the Cinnamon Gardens Colombo has the most beautiful residential suburb of any city in the world.

Like praise cannot be bestowed upon its climate, however, which, owing to Colombo's situation on the margin of a hot, low-lying plain, is peculiarly trying, as those who are condemned to remain there for any length of time will readily testify. In the dry season the air is as close and enervating as the atmosphere of an orchid-house; so excessive is the humidity during the period of the monsoons that one might as well be living in the steam-room of a Turkish bath. This is good for the vegetation and for the laundry business, but it is hard on the white man, particularly if his duties prevent him from making frequent visits to the hills.

Numerous attempts have been made to induce the Department of State at Washington to classify the Colombo consulate as an unhealthy post and shorten the term of its incumbent accordingly. But as the consular inspectors during their brief periodic visits usually sleep at the club and do their work within the cooling radius of an electric fan, their reports have thus far failed to contain the suggested recommendation. Incidentally, life in Colombo, as in most Eastern cities, is extremely expensive for the European. How the representative of the richest nation on earth manages to maintain his dignity and make ends meet on the salary of a bookkeeper is a source of mystery to his colleagues and of perpetual worry to himself.

A certain measure of relief from the unremitting heat and humidity of Colombo may usually be found toward nightfall on the seaward terrace of the Galle Face Hotel.

An enchanting place, this, in which to idle away that all too brief hour of surpassing loveliness which immediately precedes darkness in these latitudes. The level rays of the setting sun, striking across the burnished surface of the Indian Ocean, bathe everything in a rosy radiance which is like an enormously intensified alpenglow. The great hotel becomes a temple built of pale red coral and even the greensward turns a clover-pink. The fronds of the slanting cocoa-palms along the shore, etched in indigo against the carmine sky, stir in the languid breeze like the feathered bonnets of Indian warriors. The servants bring out and range upon the lawn huge lounging-chairs of cane and teakwood, over whose six-foot arms the occupants drape their legs more or less gracefully, and set beside them tables bearing tall, thin glasses from which comes the pleasant sound of tinkling ice. In the gathering dusk cigarettes glow like fireflies. Here one lingers, *dolce far niente,* until the purple drop-curtain of night has fallen and it is time to go in and dress for dinner.

I have never been able wholly to overcome my aversion for Singhalese hotel servants. It makes me feel embarrassed and uncomfortable to have about me a valet who wears a skirt instead of trousers, and whose long hair is twisted into a knot on top of his head and held in place by a tortoise-shell comb. It is all a matter of taste, of course, but I prefer to be waited on by servants who look more like men and less like hermaphrodites. The long hair and the combs, survivals of an ancient island custom, are looked on with disdain by the younger generation of Singhalese, however, and in a few years more will be as obsolete, I imagine, as the pigtail is in China and the fez in Turkey.

The European who wishes to travel comfortably in the Orient will exercise great care in the selection of his bearer, which is the Anglo-Indian term for a personal servant. A bearer is, at least in theory, a sort of factotum—a courier, valet, messenger, house-boy and butler in one. He purchases your tickets, reserves accommodations on trains and at hotels, acts as guide and interpreter, cares for your clothes, polishes your shoes, and, if the necessity arises, cooks and waits on table. An efficient bearer can relieve his employer of all responsibility and make life one grand, sweet song; a lazy or dishonest one can make traveling the saddest of all pleasures.

As we had been invited to visit at the courts of several of the Indian princes, and were planning furthermore to penetrate into certain remote and savage regions beyond the Indian frontier, we required a servant of exceptional reliability, resourcefulness and experience. Within a few hours after our arrival in Colombo it became known that we were looking for a bearer and we were besieged by applicants. We finally whittled them down to a slim brown fellow, very trim and neat in his white cotton suit and pipe-clayed sun-hat.

"What is your name?" I asked him.

"Julius."

"An odd name for a Singhalese," I commented.

"That my great-grandfather's name," Julius explained. "He one Dutch soldier. My great-grandmother she fall in love with him. She ver' careless. We keep his name in fam'ly ever since."

"So long as you attend to your duties," I told him, "I'm willing to overlook your great-grandmother's indiscretion."

"I ver' high-class bearer," he asserted modestly. "Can do ever'thing. Marster look at my chits?"

He tendered for our inspection an imposing sheaf of recommendations from former employers. Most of them bore the signatures of princes, dukes and earls, though once, during an off-season in the tourist business, he had condescended to enter the service of a mere baronet. If his chits were to be taken at their face value Julius was a paragon, a combination of all the virtues, a Singhalese edition of the Admirable Crichton.

"Very well," I told him. "You are engaged."

Had Julius dreamed of the experiences which were in store for him amid the passes of the Himalayas, however, he would have resigned on the spot.

Julius was one of those soft-spoken, soft-footed, gentle-mannered souls who have the knack of getting other people to do their work for them. Though he described himself as a bearer, he had an inherent antipathy to anything in the nature of a burden. But he was on friendly terms with every station master, railway guard and hotel porter from Nuwara Eliya to Srinagar, and when it came to securing compartments in crowded trains or desirable rooms in hotels that were already full, he was worth all we paid him. He invariably addressed us as "Marster," which tended to give us a pleasant proprietorial feeling, as though we were slave-holding plantation owners in the days of "Uncle Tom's Cabin."

In the East one either inherits a servant from a friend who is going home or engages one on the strength of his "chits." Chit, in Asiatic phraseology, means a note, a letter, a bill, a voucher, a recommendation—indeed, almost anything written on paper. You send a chit to invite a lady to dinner or a friend to play golf. The chit which you receive from your tailor is the local euphemism for a bill. When you have a drink at your club you scrawl your name on the chit tendered you by the bar-boy. And when a servant leaves your employ he asks you for a chit of commendation which he can show when looking for another job. In a land where servants are so numerous that they fairly fall over each other the inditing of chits frequently threatens to bring on writer's cramp.

It does not take long for the heat and hurly-burly of Colombo to get upon one's nerves. We were glad to escape from it and seek the coolness and quietude of the Kandyan hills. Kandy, which is near the center of the island, four-score miles from Colombo as the motor goes, is one of the most enchanting little towns in all Asia. Because of its accessibility from Colombo it is much frequented by those Europeans who cannot spare the time to go to the higher and colder Nuwara Eliya; it is beautifully clean, with some good shops, two excellent hotels, a fine golf-course, and miles and miles of shady, winding roads. Owing to its elevation, seventeen hundred feet above sea-level, it escapes the heat and humidity of the lowlands, while possessing an even greater wealth and variety of vegetation.

The town is built round the margin of an artificial lake, constructed by the last of the Kandy kings, its limpid waters mirroring a curiously wrought balustrade of lichened stone, dense banks of ferns and a row of slender palms. In the soft gray haze of early morning, and again at dusk, this lake is strongly reminiscent of Japan, perhaps because of the rickshaws which flit silently along the shore.

Rising from the sea of greenery are the sculptured walls and gilded spires of Buddhist temples; amid the groves of sacred bo-trees are innumerable white dagobas, the curious, onion-shaped structures in which sacred relics are enshrined. Here and there one glimpses a stately pillared portico which recalls those of the old Dutch mansions along the Hudson, a reminder of the days when Holland ruled Ceylon. Fascinating little bungalows, festooned with roses and bougainvillea, are tucked away in miniature forests of banyans, mangoes, palms. For sheer, intoxicating loveliness I know of nothing comparable to the perfumed gardens beside the lake of Kandy by moonlight . . . but *my* companion was a man!

Until the early part of the last century Kandy was the capital of a native kingdom, the impenetrable forests and precipitous mountain ranges which hedged it in having enabled its people to maintain their independence against the Portuguese and Dutch in turn. In 1803 the British, having ousted the Dutch from Ceylon, sought to extend their rule over Kandyan territory, but the expedition, decimated by disease and desertion, failed of success. The cruelty and oppression of the king, Sri Vikrama Raja Sinha, now became so intolerable that not even by the infliction of the most horrible punishments could he repress the rapidly spreading disaffection among his own subjects. Conditions finally became so impossible that, at the urgent request of the native chiefs, the British despatched a second expedition against the tyrant, who was captured near Kandy in 1815 and ended his days in exile. With him ended a long line of sovereigns whose pedigrees may be traced through upward of two thousand years. Some of his descendants still live in the vicinity of Kandy, being accorded a certain deference by the natives by virtue of their rank as chiefs. Paunchy, unimpressive men, ordinarily clad in the single cotton garment which comprises the costume of a Singhalese, there is nothing about them to suggest that they are the tailings of a dynasty whose rule endured for more than twenty centuries. On ceremonial occasions, however, such as the Festival of the Tooth, they turn out in all their ancient finery. Singular figures they are in their quaint little bolero jackets with puffed sleeves, exactly like those which were the mode in America in the late nineties, their voluminous trousers girded with embroidered surcingles and terminating in frills, the whole fantastic outfit topped off by triangular, gold-incrusted bonnets bearing a vague resemblance to the headgear of the Continental Minute Men. Thus splendiferously appareled, atop of gorgeously caparisoned and painted elephants, they make a pompous progress through the capital of their ancestors.

A good many years ago, during my first visit to Ceylon, I had the good fortune to be in Kandy during the Festival of the Tooth. It should be mentioned, by way of explanation, that one of Gautama Buddha's teeth is enshrined in the Dalada Malagawa, the molar—though it may be an incisor or a bicuspid—being preserved in a jeweled reliquary in that temple's holy of holies. How a tooth of the Great Teacher, who never traveled far from his birthplace in the Terai of Nepál, found its way to a hill-town in Ceylon is a matter for speculation, but there it is, and on one day a year, in the early spring, it is displayed amid much pomp and ceremony for the consolation of the pious, tens of thousands of pilgrims flocking to Kandy for the occasion from all parts of the Buddhist world.

On this day the ordinarily tranquil streets of the ancient capital are jammed with milling throngs, clad in every color and shade which can be produced by the dye-maker. The procession which marks the climax of the day's ceremonies is worth making a long journey to witness, whether viewed merely as a spectacle or as a reminder of Ceylon's one-time splendor. Bands of native musicians torture the tympanums of the spectators with the wailing of their weird instruments. The air pulses to the thunder-roll of drums. Masked devil-dancers in grotesque costumes caper like lunatics, leaping and whirling, shrieking and yowling. Groups of Buddhist priests with shaven polls, their saffron robes leaving bare one arm and shoulder, chant their eternal *Om mani padme hum* and twirl their prayer-wheels. Pikemen, swordsmen, musketeers swagger by in the comic-opera uniforms of old-time warriors. Then, amid a forest of standards and banners, of flaunting flags and feathered fans, the elephants come. Streaked and spangled with ocher and vermilion, they roll along beneath their gold-and-velvet housings, the Kandyan chieftains and the great religious dignitaries looking none too comfortable in the swaying silver howdahs. Even the late Phineas T. Barnum, great showman that he was, never staged a spectacle half so colorful and glittering.

Two thirds of the inhabitants of Ceylon profess the Buddhist faith, its temples, shrines and monasteries dotting the whole island. Many of the Buddhist temples, particularly those in the Kandyan country, are, like the abbeys of mediæval England, immensely rich in lands, most of which are held by hereditary tenants who pay their rentals by rendering services of one form or another to the church. These lands were apportioned with much care in order to provide all that was necessary for the maintenance of the temples and the monasteries connected with them. Thus, some tenants rendered service as carpenters, blacksmiths, masons, while others were required to provide the priests and monks with food. Another class had to assist at the numerous ceremonies and festivals, to prepare the decorations, to carry lamps and banners, to furnish the music, if music it can be called. The British authorities looked with disfavor on a system under which the rent of lands was paid for by hereditary service, and in the course of time there arose an agitation for reforms. Accordingly, a government commission was appointed with a view to abolishing the alleged abuses, but an investigation developed the fact that the services were not onerous and that almost without an exception the tenants favored the retention of the ancient system.

The ease and comfort of the ecclesiastical life make a strong appeal to the indolent Singhalese, and, as a consequence, the island swarms with priests and monks, some of the theological schools being enormous institutions with hundreds of neophytes. The members of the priestly class are readily distinguishable by their shaven heads, as bare as billiard balls, and by their marigold-colored garments, the dye for which is obtained from the fruit of a sacred tree. The Buddhist clergy are supposed to lead lives of austerity and poverty, sternly renouncing all worldly luxuries. But some of them, at least, indulge in expensive tastes, for in a shop in Kandy I saw a monk, barefooted, shaven-headed, clad in the single cotton garment permitted to members of his order, pay the equivalent of twenty dollars for a silk umbrella.

Wild elephants are still fairly numerous in the highlands of Ceylon. Once every two or three years a great "kraal" is held for the purpose of replenishing the supply of domesticated animals, thousands of beaters being employed to drive the beasts into a stockade, or kraal. Once within, they are roped, shackled to trained elephants—which seem to enjoy the proceeding hugely—and conducted, with much balking and trumpeting, to the studs, where they are tamed and trained for service. Far more docile and sagacious than their African cousins, they learn with surprising rapidity to make themselves of economic use. The elephant is to the Singhalese a tractor, a truck and a portable derrick in one, being employed in the forests and lumber-yards for moving heavy timbers, in road construction, for draft purposes on the plantations, and, of course, in the religious processions. The government maintains a stud of several hundred elephants; others are owned by the temples and the chieftains.

Because the big pachyderms have as much fascination for me now as they had when I was a boy and they lumbered through the streets of my home town in the annual circus parades, I suggested to my cousin that we drive out to a secluded reach of the river, not far from Kandy, where the elephants are bathed and watered in the late afternoon. In the old days the grooming of the elephants was a routine affair and no one save an occasional visitor paid it much attention. But all that has been changed by the coming to Ceylon of the great cruising steamers with their hordes of tourists. The canny Singhalese, with an eye out for the main chance, have capitalized the elephants' bathing-hour by turning it into a sort of exhibition and charging admission. Now a screen of bamboo has been erected along the river bank, there is a ticket office (one rupee, please), and within is a thatched pavilion before which the beasts perform a few commonplace circus tricks. What was formerly a picturesque aspect of island life has, like the performances of the devil-dancers, become as commercialized as a professional base-ball game.

The only redeeming feature of the show was provided by a young American couple, evidently on their honeymoon, who insisted on mounting the largest elephant in order to have their photograph taken for the benefit of the folks at home. The bride was a slim and very pretty girl with shapely Chippendale legs, which she displayed so shamelessly that even the elephant became restive. And when, oblivious of the spectators and their cameras, she and her husband indulged in a rapturous and prolonged osculation, the scandalized animal, overcome by embarrassment, gave a groan of disapproval and sank slowly to the ground. He was a very old animal, the mahout explained apologetically, brought up in the Victorian tradition, and could not reconcile himself to the goings-on of the younger generation.

A sensational murder case was tried during our stay in Kandy. As it promised an opportunity to observe the workings of Anglo-Singhalese justice, which is based on Roman-Dutch law, we dropped in and were given seats within the inclosure reserved for members of the bar. A Singhalese agriculturist was on trial for shooting his wife and her paramour—a *crime passionel,* as the French would term it. He had not intended to kill his wife, it developed, but he had caught the pair in *flagrante delicto* and one slug from his muzzle-loader had done for them both.

The trial was held in the ancient hall of justice of the Kandy kings, which is utilized for the same purpose by the British administration. It is an apartment of impressive size and great dignity, the lofty roof supported by richly carved teakwood columns. The interior, once gay with gilt and colors, is now dimmed by age. There are no walls, the room being inclosed by wooden blinds which can be readily removed, thus making it comfortable even in the sultriest weather. It is a setting such as would delight the heart of David Belasco. At times it was difficult to follow the proceedings, however, owing to the pandemonium of horns and tom-toms which arose at intervals from the adjacent temple, where some sort of religious ceremony was in progress.

The accused, a sullen-eyed fellow clad in a single length of cotton which left the upper half of his body bare, his long hair gathered on the top of his head in a Psyche knot which gave him a curiously feminine appearance, leaned negligently on the rail of the prisoner's box, guarded by two constables in smart blue uniforms and pillbox caps.

He was defended by a very youthful native lawyer who, judging from his halting speech and obvious embarrassment, had only recently been admitted to practice. The English barrister who represented the Crown was a typical prosecutor—sarcastic, hard-boiled, eager for the defendant's scalp. The jury was composed of both natives and Europeans, most of them merchants or planters. The one vivid note of color in the great somber room was struck by the presiding justice, an imposing figure in his full gray wig and voluminous scarlet robes. Enthroned beneath the gilded arms of Britain, aloof, inexorable, majestic, he was the very personification of British law. But the eyes, though shrewd and penetrating, twinkled with good humor, and in the crisp, incisive voice there was an undertone of good humor too.

I have not attended many murder trials, for they are not a form of recreation which appeals to me, and consequently I cannot speak on the subject with authority. It seemed to me, however, that in no country in the world could a case involving capital punishment be conducted with greater fairness, dignity and despatch. There were none of those appeals to sympathy, passion or prejudice which so frequently thwart the ends of justice in America. From beginning to end the proceedings were as precise and unemotional as the workings of a calculating-machine. Every native present knew that the ruddy-faced man in the red robes and powdered wig, alien though he was, stood for the square deal, and that the defendant would get just that, nothing less and nothing more. It was no place for a Clarence Darrow to exercise his talents.

Here were none of the reporters, special writers, sob-sisters, photographers, artists, alienists, psychologists and finger-print experts who are part and parcel of a murder trial at home. It was all as matter-of-fact and businesslike as a directors' meeting of the Steel Corporation. Native witnesses, speaking through an interpreter, gave their evidence with the naïve candor of untutored peoples, never hesitating to call a spade by its vulgar name. An alert young medical inspector briefly described the nature of the wounds. The blood-stained garments of the victims were exhibited, as was the leaden slug and the six-feet-of-gas-pipe gun with which the deed was done. The trial began at nine o'clock. By eleven thirty the evidence was all in and the lawyers had completed their summations. At five minutes to twelve the jury returned a verdict of manslaughter, whereupon the judge sentenced the prisoner to eight years of penal servitude. And before the great bell of the Dalada Malagawa had finished booming out the hour of noon every one was filing out of the court-room, the murderer—who did not appear particularly downcast—on his way to prison; the rest of us on our way to tiffin.

Prior to the British occupation of the Kandyan territory in 1815 the towns and villages were connected only by footpaths through the forests, for the Portuguese made no attempt to open up the country below the hills and the Dutch confined their efforts to the improvement of the inland waterways. But the British authorities saw from the outset the necessity of making roads into the interior, at first for military purposes, and later in order to aid the planters in getting their products down to the coast. As a consequence, the whole of the hill country is now covered by a network of fine highways, every male inhabitant of Ceylon (save only Buddhist priests and British soldiers) being required to contribute six days' labor annually on the roads or the equivalent in money.

To leave Ceylon without seeing the mountain country would be equivalent to visiting California without seeing the redwoods or the Yosemite. High up in the hills is Nuwara Eliya, 6200 feet above sea-level and one hundred and sixty miles from Colombo as the motor goes. With the possible exception of the trip from Surabaya to Bromo, in eastern Java, I can recall no journey of like distance which is so enchanting. In a distance scarcely greater than that from New York to Albany one passes, in effect, from the torrid to the temperate zone, from July to late October, from the tropics to a region that is truly alpine. Leaving the steaming beaches of the Indian Ocean after a late breakfast, one can have tea on the chilly slopes of Pedrotallagalla, whose cloud-wreathed peak soars nearly 8300 feet into the blue.

For the first half-hundred miles one is in a land of eternal summer, the smooth white road leading past fields of rice, cinnamon and cacao, through rubber and cocoanut plantations. The villages and even the smaller towns are in great measure concealed by the abundant and abiding verdure, their presence being betrayed only by their fields and palm-groves. The cultivated areas are but islands in a sea of cocoanut-palms, of which there are said to be twenty million in Ceylon. In fact, the wealth of a Singhalese is estimated by the number of these trees which he owns, there being on record a lawsuit brought in a district court by a native to establish his claim to the 2520th part of ten of these precious palms.

Small wonder that the Singhalese places a high value on the *Cocos nucifera,* for it is to him what the camel is to the Bedouin, providing him with all, or nearly all, that he requires from the cradle to the grave. Its fruit, when green, furnishes him with food and drink; when dried into the copra of commerce it yields the oil used in the manufacture of soap, of most toilet preparations and of candles. Enveloping the husk is the fiber known as coir, from which are fabricated ropes, fishing-nets, brushes, door-mats and matting. The young bud cut from the top of the tree makes the "heart of palm" salad for which New York restaurants charge a dollar a portion. From the juice of the unopened flower are distilled two highly potent native drinks: toddy, which can be boiled down to sugar, and arrack, a sort of Singhalese "white mule." From the leaves are made fans, baskets, the thatched roofs of houses; when dried they are used as torches; the large leaf stalks as garden fences. The trunk of the tree, sawn up, is employed for every conceivable purpose, from knife-handles to chairs; hollowed out, it is equally serviceable as a canoe or a coffin.

In the Kandyan hills the tropical vegetation of the coast plain still persists, but from here on it is found blended with plants which are characteristically European, violets, pansies, geraniums and buttercups thriving side by side with magnolias, gardenias, acacias and orchids. Higher up, on the cool, moist plains of Nuwara Eliya, the tropical flora almost disappears, being replaced by that of the temperate zone, the flowers, vegetables and grains native to northern latitudes here flourishing as they do at home. Indeed, so great is the range of Ceylon's soil and climate that even grapes are grown successfully in parts of the island. The vines were introduced by the Dutch, the most skilful of all horticulturists, who overcame the difficulty of perpetual summer by the ingenious expedient of exposing the roots, thereby giving the plants in effect an artificial winter.

By the time we had reached an altitude of four thousand feet the trees as well as the herbage had assumed an altered character. On the uplands the trees attain a height unknown in the hot low country and the leaves are larger and darker. I could now understand how fitting was the name given to Ceylon by the ancients—Taprobane, the island of dusky leaves. For the upper slopes of the mountains are still densely covered with the virgin forest which clothed the whole country before the white man came, the masses of dark green foliage producing a peculiarly somber effect, particularly when enveloped in the heavy mists which are common to these altitudes.

Above Kandy, right away to the foot of the highest mountains, the whole aspect of the country-side has been changed by the ax and energy of the European. Over hundreds of thousands of acres the forest has been ruthlessly cut away to make space for the tea plantations for which Ceylon is famous. For from the low green bushes whose serried rows cover the chocolate-colored hill-slopes comes the leaf which is used in a quarter of the teacups of the world. Every plantation has its factory, the methods which are now employed for withering, rolling and firing being so rapid that within forty-eight hours after the leaves have been plucked they are sealed in leaden boxes, ready for shipment, sale and an excuse for gossip.

In Ceylon tea-picking goes on nearly the whole year round, the pickers, with their children and bedding and cooking utensils, moving from plantation to plantation, like hop-pickers at home. Even in Ceylon, where Nature has outdone herself in making life easy for the natives, the employers are not free from labor troubles, for bolshevism has made its appearance in a mild form. It is dealt with energetically by the planters, however, for we met along the road several large groups of pickers who, having shown signs of becoming obstreperous, had been discharged en masse.

At one plantation, reputed to have the most up-to-date

factory in the island, we stopped to give the tea industry the once-over. The young Englishman who showed us around looked like a planter of fiction in his double-terai hat, flannel shirt open at the neck, and shorts. (Why is it, I wonder, that one always gets a little thrill of satisfaction upon encountering a person who looks and dresses like the pictures in the magazines?)

"I suppose most of these plantations belong to Lipton," I remarked, by way of making conversation.

"To *whom?*" he asked blankly.

"To Lipton—Sir Thomas Lipton, you know. The tea king."

Our cicerone laughed.

"You mean the chap whose name is plastered on all the buses and tube stations in London? He owns only a few small plantations in Ceylon. He buys nearly all his tea from the big planters. But he does a lot of advertising."

And I, in my ignorance had always thought that in Ceylon the yachtsman-baronet was regarded as a sort of tea tycoon.

But men whom the public at home associate with certain regions are seldom regarded with enthusiasm by those who live on the spot. I once spoke admiringly of Colonel Lawrence to a British official who had spent the better part of his life in Arabia.

"Lawrence?" he repeated. "Oh, yes. He's quite a clever fellow and did some rather useful work out here during the war. But I can name half a dozen men who have forgotten more about the Arab than he ever knew—yet the public back in England has never so much as heard of *them.*"

I asked the planter if the practice which prevails in parts of China of having the coolies urinate on the half-dried tea leaves was followed in Ceylon. (I believe that certain brands of Orange Pekoe are thus treated, but I am not certain.) He said no, that it was not necessary, as Ceylon tea has a taste and aroma of its own.

For the last twenty miles before reaching Nuwara Eliya the road is steep and narrow, in places a mere shelf bordered by dizzy precipices, with an infinity of hair-raising corners and hairpin turns. Cautious driving is imperative, for around the next shoulder of the cliff one is as likely as not to encounter an elephant, or a string of bullock carts, or a drove of buffaloes.

The air grew steadily more chilly as the car panted upward, and long ere the upper levels had been reached we were glad to don our overcoats and draw the rug over our knees. A dense mist now rolled down upon us, shutting off the landscape as with a wet gray blanket and making it impossible to see the road for more than a score of yards ahead. It was distinctly comforting to have a skilful driver at the wheel, for the excessive moisture had made the road in spots as slippery as glass, and the big car occasionally skidded until its outer hubs overhung the precipice's brim. It is not a drive which I should recommend for pleasure during the monsoons.

But at length we topped the final rise and emerged upon a vast plateau. The chill wind that blows upon these lofty table-lands had swept the fog away and, though there was still a thick stratum of gray fleece immediately below us, we could see beyond its edges the island world, outspread like a map in bas-relief. Their upper flanks dark green with forest or bright green with tea plantations, the ranges which we had so toilsomely ascended went sweeping downward in a bewilderment of hills and valleys, of rock-strewn watercourses and leafy glens, to the palm-smothered coast-plain and the sea.

Nestling amid evergreens and rhododendrons at the foot of Pedrotallagalla, the highest mountain in the island, Nuwara Eliya is the sort of place where I could have settled down quite contentedly for a lengthy stay. In spite of being only six degrees from the equator, it has one of the finest all-the-year-round climates in the world, for climate is, after all, a matter of altitude rather than latitude, and the little town stands 6240 feet above the level of the sea. It has one large hotel and several less pretentious ones; numerous attractive bungalows; a huge park dotted with venerable trees; a race course; and one of the most beautiful golf-courses I have ever seen. Meandering through the latter is a mountain stream, apparently designed by Nature to penalize the player who is prone to slice or hook; the greens are hedged about by masses of rhododendrons, which here attain enormous size; and, owing to the prevailing moisture, the fairways are strips of bright green plush.

Though Nuwara Eliya has an average shade temperature of only 58 degrees, and a top-coat is by no means uncomfortable when one is not in the sun, the English insist that to venture out-of-doors between nine and four without a topée is to invite sunstroke. This shibboleth of the sun-hat is a thing which I have never been able to understand. Why is it that the Englishman in Ceylon deems it necessary to protect his head with an inch of cork every time he steps off the veranda, whereas the American in the Philippines, which are in the same latitude, contents himself with a covering of felt or straw, such as he wears at home, and the sun lets him pass? Kenya in East Africa and Ecuador in South America are both traversed by the equator, and their ranges of temperature are approximately the same, yet in the former country the white man frequently supplements his helmet with a spine-pad, while in the latter he successfully defies the sun with a Panama.

In British Asia, particularly in Ceylon and India, the status of the European can be deduced with a considerable degree of accuracy from his head-covering. If a man sports one of those round, white, hard-finished helmets such as are displayed in the hatters' windows in Old Bond Street, the chances are a hundred to one that he is a tourist, fresh from home. Should he wear a high-crowned, mushroom-shaped affair coming far down over his ears, however, it is almost a certainty that he is a French colonial en route to Indo-China. The low pith hat, wound with a silk pugree, very light and comfortable but affording no great protection, is almost invariably the distinguishing mark of an official, a member of "the Government House set." Sportsmen, engineers and others who spend much time in the open wear a large, thick headpiece covered with quilted khaki and with a strap over the top, while planters, more often than not, do not wear a helmet at all, preferring the softer and equally protective "double-terai," which consists of two slouch hats of heavy felt, one drawn over the other so as to leave an air space between.

Occupying the table next to ours in the dining-room of the hotel at Nuwara Eliya was a group which aroused my curiosity. One of the party was a girl, in her early twenties I judged, tall, slim, dark, obviously American; there was an elderly woman, also American; and there were two men who, from the swarthiness of their skins, might have been Indians. One was quite evidently a secretary; the other, a short, dark-complexioned man thin almost to emaciation was, judging from the deference paid him by his companions and the servants, a person of rank. My at-

THE KANDY KINGS

Paunchy little men in three-cornered hats, bolero jackets with leg-of-mutton sleeves. and enormous trousers terminating in ruffles

CARDBOARD GIANTS

Fifteen feet in height, swayed and tottered ludicrously as the men within their lower extremities capered along in the great religious procession which escorted Siva and Paravati to the Teppa Kulam

tention was attracted to him at first by the peculiar quality of his eyes, which were as green and glittering as those of a serpent, and later, when he and his companions left the room, because every one else abruptly stopped talking and stared at them.

"You know who that chap is, I suppose?" asked an Englishman whom I met in the smoking-room.

"Meaning the coffee-colored fellow with the snake's eyes? No. Who is he?"

"That's the ex-Maharajah of Indore, Sir Tokaji Rao Holkar. And the girl with him is his fiancée, Miss Nancy Ann Miller. A compatriot of yours, I believe. I wonder if she knows what she's in for. Holkar, you remember, was mixed up in the Mumtaz Begum affair. Mumtaz, who was his favorite dancing-girl, eloped from the palace with some of the crown jewels and a rich Indian. The latter didn't have long to enjoy her, however, for he got a knife blade between his shoulders a few days later, whereupon the Government of India, which has to draw the line somewhere, forced the maharajah to abdicate in favor of his son. Why a white woman should consent to take a chance with a fellow of Holkar's reputation passes my comprehension."

I looked at the oddly mated pair with added interest, for the whole East was buzzing with the story of the dethroned prince who was adding an American girl to his zenana, and of the curious purification ceremonies to which she must submit before she could marry him according to the rites of the Hindu religion. It struck me that it was the ex-maharajah who needed purifying. Here was a quiet, almost a timid girl, yet to the friends who had pleaded with her, to the American consuls and British officials who had sought to point out the unwisdom of such a union, she had been adamantine. She didn't look like a girl who would be dazzled by the prospect of life in an Oriental palace and the title of maharanee. Perhaps she was marrying this man because she loved him. Oh, well, there is no accounting for tastes.

Not far from Nuwara Eliya is a garden which you should not fail to see, for it is one of the most enchanting spots in all the world. I don't recall the name of it at the moment (which is of no importance), but it is only half an hour or so by motor from the town, tucked away in an obscure and sheltered valley with the forest-clothed mountains rising steeply all around. It is a government botanical garden, like the much larger and more celebrated one at Peradeniya, outside of Kandy, but it is a thousand times more beautiful, to my way of thinking. Unlike Peradeniya, there are no throngs of chattering tourists, no obtrusive guides, no formal flower-beds and manicured lawns, comparatively few evidences, in fact, of the handiwork of man. But there are palms in infinite variety, a perfect wilderness of them, and orchids and creepers and masses of giant rhododendrons; there is a water-garden with aquatic plants of every kind; and a great elliptical pergola, festooned with bougainvillea, inclosing a sort of floral amphitheater where roses and lilies bloom in unbelievable profusion. Everywhere are alluring little footpaths which meander irresponsibly into the greenery, playing hide-and-seek with one another amid the thickets of bamboo and tree-ferns. The air is heavy with the fragrance of flowers and filled with the music of birds and falling water. And from the encircling heights the tropic forest, dark, silent, mysterious, sweeps down like the folds of a vast velvet curtain. It is my conception of the Garden of Eden. To make it perfect only an Eve was lacking.

In order to catch at a way station the night mail from Colombo to Manaar, where a ferry plies between Ceylon and the Indian mainland, we took our departure from Nuwara Eliya shortly after tiffin. Julius we had left in Colombo with instructions to secure a compartment and meet us on the train. It is a night's run from Colombo to Manaar, at the northern end of the island, and another two hours by steamer across the narrow Pamban Passage to the Indian railhead at Rameswaram. A coral reef, known as Adam's Bridge, all but connects the peninsula with the island, and plans are now under consideration for the construction across it of an Indo-Ceylon railway, government engineers having pronounced the project entirely feasible.

Never to be forgotten was that drive down the mountains in the waning afternoon. The mist which had veiled the higher levels on the up-journey had completely disappeared and the great peaks now revealed themselves in all their purple majesty, standing out sharp and clear against the cloudless sky. During the first portion of the trip the air was as exhilarating as champagne, but upon dropping down into the lowlands we were greeted by a wave of heat and humidity which served to remind us that we were still in the tropics. For the last fifty miles the road led through the jungle, the vegetation rising in high walls of green on either side. Night had long since come; native camp-fires twinkled amid the forest, and the moon, a plate of burnished silver, rode high above the feathered tops of the palms. Our powerful headlights bored twin holes in the velvety darkness and in their glare we caught fleeting glimpses of thatched huts in lonely forest clearings, of sleeping villages, of interminable strings of hooded ox-carts market bound, and of occasional late-faring natives, their brown skins gleaming like bronzes in a museum.

At Kurunegalla we learned that the train was late and that we had an hour or so to spare, so, as one can always eat when there is nothing else to do, we employed the time by having a late supper in the rest-house which is maintained by a thoughtful government for the convenience of travelers. Afterward we lounged in cane chairs on the veranda, while myriads of bats flitted overhead, and smoked furiously in order to hold at bay the legions of man-eating mosquitos, which would have driven us out altogether had they had an insect Foch to lead them. At ten minutes to midnight the train came roaring in and there was the gentle Julius leaning anxiously from the window of a reserved compartment. We swung ourselves aboard, our luggage was tossed in after us, lanterns waved along the platform, the locomotive shrieked as though in pain, and we slid into the night, India-bound.

CHAPTER II

IDOLS AND IDYLS

JULIUS awakened us at the crack of dawn, just when slumber is sweetest, for *chota hazri,* the tea and toast, served in bed, with which every European in the East deems it necessary to start the day. It is a pernicious custom, and one of which we broke Julius later on, for food at that hour is an affront to sleep and an insult to breakfast. On this occasion it made no particular difference, however, for half an hour later the train rumbled out upon the quay at Manaar. Tied up alongside was the small and none too comfortable steamer which was to bear us across the straits to India.

Approached from Ceylon, one's first sight of Hindustan is distinctly disappointing—a treeless, white-hot spit of sand thrusting itself seaward, a cluster of warehouses whose corrugated iron roofs crackle in the heat, numerous strings of freight cars, and a waiting passenger train, the Madras Mail, its blue glass windows closely shuttered against the intolerable glare of the sun. An alert young sergeant of police scrutinized our passports, for the British authorities are keeping a sharp eye out for the emissaries of bolshevism; a horde of half-naked porters swarmed over the rail and descended upon our luggage, and we filed down the gangplank onto India's coral strand.

On the steamer we had made the acquaintance of two very charming and distinctly pretty girls who were making a leisurely tour of the world in go-as-you-please fashion. They were so well-bred and poised and sure of themselves that it was gratifying to find that they were Americans. Bound by no set itinerary, they bothered themselves not at all about railway time-tables and steamship sailings. Eight months out of the Golden Gate, they had visited Hawaii, the South Sea Islands, Australia, New Zealand, Ceylon, and after seeing India they planned to continue to Europe by the overland route. Whenever they came to a place which took their fancy they stopped off, rented a bungalow and remained until the spirit urged them to move on. Which is, of course, the most intelligent way to see the world, and the most amusing. They were in quest of the unusual, the little known, so when I suggested half-jokingly that in order to round out their journey properly they should return from Europe to America via Iceland they seized upon the idea with enthusiasm.

Julius, who displayed excellent judgment on occasion, had managed to secure us a compartment next to that occupied by our pretty countrywomen and ere long the four of us were playing bridge on a table extemporized from a couple of kit-bags and a suit-case and, between rubbers, discovering mutual friends. So, despite the heat and the dust and the monotony of the South Indian landscape, it turned out to be a very enjoyable journey after all.

An English automobile salesman whom we had met in Nuwara Eliya had boasted of the luxury of the Indian trains, but he was either suffering from patriotic myopia or had a deplorable disregard for the truth, for the sole superiority they can claim over our own is the spaciousness of the first-class compartments, which are fully double the size of the drawing-rooms in American Pullmans.

Running along either side of each compartment is a low, broad seat, a sort of divan. The similarity ends there, however, for the leather cushions, judging from their rugged and unyielding surface, might be stuffed with bricks. The seats have no springs and no backs, unless one chooses to lean against the rattling window-panes, which lift by a strap like the windows of old-fashioned taxicabs. So clumsy are the metal fittings that they might have been made by a village blacksmith. And in the dry season the dust enters in such suffocating clouds that the railway companies ought to provide the passengers with gas-masks, just as steamship companies provide theirs with life-preservers. Opening from each compartment is a lavatory, usually provided with a shower-bath, but after a single experience I refrained from using the latter, refreshing though it was, because the sudden deluge stirred into activity armies of giant cockroaches, almost as large as mice.

Barring these minor annoyances, however, two persons can make themselves tolerably comfortable in a compartment with the aid of the quilts, blankets, sheets and pillows which every traveler carries with him in a huge canvas roll, for bedding is not provided on Indian trains. But when the traffic is heavy and the compartment is invaded by two other travelers, with their impedimenta, who take possession of the two narrow and slippery swinging shelves which can be lowered to form upper berths, the place becomes an inferno on wheels, for the new-comers invariably proceed to turn off the electric fans, which are directly above them, leaving the unfortunate occupants of the lowers gasping for breath. Experienced travelers can usually prevent such intrusions, however, by tipping the guard munificently, locking the doors, drawing up all the blinds, and, when passengers at way stations clamor for admittance, answering their appeals with stertorous snores. I knew one young Englishman who, when other travelers sought admittance to his compartment, gave a most convincing imitation of an infant squalling with colic. He assured me that he had never failed to obtain privacy when he employed this ingenious stratagem.

Weeks later, when we were starting north from Delhi to visit one of the ruling princes of Rajputana, a young Indian, unable to obtain admittance to our compartment, made such a row that the guard, whom we had taken the precaution of subsidizing, was compelled to unlock the door and let him in, together with a ton or so of hand luggage. We took no pains to conceal our irritation at the intrusion; in fact, though it was a sweltering night, the atmosphere in the compartment was distinctly chilly. The next day, lunching at the palace with the maharajah, we were somewhat embarrassed to find ourselves seated opposite our unwelcome fellow-traveler, who was now resplendent in a pale blue cavalry uniform and an orange turban. He was our host's younger brother.

The native servants of Europeans hold third-class tickets and are supposed to travel in third-class carriages, which are invariably packed with perspiring and odoriferous humanity to the point of suffocation. But Julius, to whom we intrusted the bestowing of largesse, by his vicarious generosity to the guards usually managed to secure an entire second-class compartment for himself.

"Third-class carriage not proper place for gentleman's gentlemen," he explained naïvely. "Too much coolie in third-class. Ver' common folks. Plenty smell, plenty dirt, plenty bugs, plenty people sick."

His objections to third-class travel were tragically sustained a little farther on, for a few stations up the line we saw the corpse of a young girl taken with scant ceremony from an overcrowded native carriage. She had died on the train from cholera or plague—I forget which. Her thumbs had been tied together, as had her big toes, so that the body could be slung from a bamboo pole, no stretcher being handy. It was dumped on the platform like a sack of meal, covered with a soiled sheet to keep off the flies, and left there until the local health officer should find time to remove it. I wondered how many other passengers in that crowded compartment would contract the disease from which the girl had died, for there was no attempt to fumigate it, but no one else appeared to give the matter a second thought. Human life is the cheapest thing there is in India. Death is only an incident.

The train, gradually veering inland, jogged leisurely northward across a flat, monotonous country dotted here and there with bamboo clumps or solitary palms. Away to the northwestward the level horizon was broken by a low range of tawny hills—the Eastern Ghats. Fields of rice shared the land with millet, producing a vast checkerboard of green and yellow, and in the vicinity of the villages were numerous garden patches, irrigated at the cost of enormous toil. Coming from the amazingly luxuriant vegetation of Ceylon, which is one of the most verdant spots on earth, these Coromandel coast plains, though productive enough when cultivated and watered, seemed sterile and discouraged-looking.

The backwardness of agriculture in India is due not so much to the poverty of the soil as to the religious and social prejudices, the indolence and superstition of the people. Most religions glorify agriculture, but the Hindu Scriptures condemn it as a degrading pursuit which should be avoided by the truly pious. This is all the more astonishing in a land which is periodically swept by famine. Manu, the Hindu lawgiver, whose writings have exercised, and still exercise, enormous influence upon Indian ideas, customs and religion, discountenances agriculture and places farmers in one of the lower castes, because tilling the soil inflicts pain on draft-bullocks and causes the death of insects. As a consequence of this inhibition, very few men of the two highest castes—the priestly Brahmans and the warrior Rajputs—will so much as lay hands upon a plow, the large areas which many of them hold being cultivated for them in slovenly fashion by hired labor. Superstition also plays its part in retarding the country's agricultural development, many peasants refusing to sow lentils, for example, because their gentle souls are agonized by the color of the grain, which reminds them of blood! And finally, those who do engage in agriculture are handicapped by their inherent laziness, as exemplified by the fact that the Hindu farmer leaves to his women-folk the laborious task of transplanting the young rice shoots, on the ingenuous plea that stooping causes more fatigue to men than to women.

The towns at which the train halted were for the most part depressing-looking places, their broad, sun-baked thoroughfares, inches deep in yellow dust, lined by small and tawdry shops, open to the street; stuccoed houses with ramshackle wooden balconies and flat roofs; and miserable hovels of mud and thatch. The natives who crowded the station platforms—for all India seemed to be upon the move—were all too frequently gaunt and hollow-eyed. They looked, and probably were, underfed. They were amazingly picturesque, however, for their cheap cotton garments were often of gorgeous colors and always gracefully draped; their foreheads dotted and streaked with the white, ocher or vermilion caste-marks which are the crests and ciphers of the Hindu's creed.

At one station the train was boarded by a local chieftain, a fat, greasy-looking little man with garlands of marigold-blossoms festooned about his neck. He was accompanied by half-a-dozen women and a score or more of servants and retainers, evidently being a person of some importance, for half the village had come down to see him off. He and his zenana were boosted by willing hands into a compartment and the servants pushed in after them an incredible amount of luggage—bales, bundles, bedding-rolls, sleeping-mats, flowered quilts, wash-basins, brass ewers, jars of drinking-water, dishes of rice and fruits, bouquets of flowers, numerous umbrellas, a couple of gilt swords and several brace of live and squawking fowls. It was a hot day, and as soon as he was inside his compartment the head of the family proceeded to divest himself of all his clothing save only a pair of cotton drawers. Thus comfortably attired, he stood in the doorway chatting with his friends until the train pulled out.

Toward nightfall, while approaching the outskirts of what appeared to be a town of considerable size, I glimpsed a group of lofty and most singular shaped towers which rose from behind a distant screen of palms. Neither square nor cylindrical, I am at a loss to describe them, for I have never seen their like. The best I can do is to say that they looked like immensely steep, rectangular pyramids which had been sliced off near the top. Even from that distance I could discern that they consisted of solid masses of carvings, thus vaguely suggesting without in any way resembling the celebrated pyramid at Boroboedor in Java. Their enormous height accentuated by the low flat roofed houses which huddled at their feet, they glowed like rosy coral under the rays of the setting sun. In the failing light there was something peculiarly mysterious and intriguing about these mighty monuments which reared themselves so abruptly from the dusty Indian plain.

"Those are the *gopuras* of the great temple of Madura," explained an English fellow-passenger when I called his attention to them. "A most extraordinary place. There is nothing like it in all India, or, so far as I know, in the world. On no account should you miss it. It is well worth twenty-four hours of any one's time."

We had planned to go straight through to Madras, but the man's enthusiasm, plus my own curiosity, caused me to hesitate.

"How about it?" I asked my cousin. "Shall we stop off here for the night and give the place the once-over?"

"Sure thing," he agreed promptly. "I've traveled halfway round the world to get here and all I've seen thus far is sun, sand and some filthy-looking natives. If there's anything worth while in Madura we might as well take it in."

So, when the train jolted to a halt with squealing brakes, I leaned out of the window and shouted for Julius, who came a-running. Our luggage was hastily tossed out upon the station platform, the whistle shrieked and the train moved on. That is the way I like to do things—impulsively, on the spur of the moment, without debating them in my mind. As it turned out, I was glad that we stopped off at Madura. Otherwise I should have missed one of the most curious and interesting experiences of my life.

There is no hotel in Madura, but for the convenience of travelers the government maintains a dâk-bungalow where visitors who do not insist on luxuries can make themselves comfortable enough. Opening on a deep vine-embowered veranda, tolerably cool even in the hottest weather, were half-a-dozen stone-floored, scantily furnished rooms, each containing a pair of mosquito-curtained iron beds. Swung from the ceiling above each pair of beds was an enormous *punkah,* operated by a cord which ran through a pulley set in a hole in the outer wall. For a few annas we were able to obtain the services of a native urchin, who, lying flat on his back on the veranda, one foot thrust through a loop at the end of the cord, kept the *punkah* swinging and a faint breeze stirring all night long. Toward dawn, sleepless from the heat, I went out on the veranda to get a breath of air. Our human dynamo was fast asleep, but his foot was moving up and down, up and down, with the regularity of a pendulum.

The only other guests at the rest-house were the two American girls who had been our fellow-passengers from Manaar. I might have known that they would have stopped at a place as alluring as Madura. Four Americans thus thrown together in a strange land, we soon felt as though we were old friends. That evening we had a delightful little dinner on the terrace overlooking the town. The inevitable chicken was like leather and most of the other food came out of tins, but I dug up the ingredients for cocktails, though there was no ice, and Julius, who had a nose for such things, discovered in the cellar a couple of bottles of champagne of a famous brand and year, doubtless brought there by some luxury-loving traveler and then forgotten. We brought them to a moderate degree of coolness by wrapping them in a wet blanket and hanging them in a draft—a trick which I had learned in Persia years before.

The girls had put on filmy evening gowns for the occasion, my cousin and I had exchanged our dusty traveling clothes for the white mess kit of the tropics, and Julius, with the Singhalese's love for flowers, had strewn the candle-lighted table with heavy-scented gardenias and crimson hibiscus blossoms. In the shadows the servants of the rest-house, their long white garments set off by scarlet cummerbunds and turbans, moved like ghosts on naked, noiseless feet. With nightfall a gentle breeze sprang up; the air was heavy with the fragrance of flowers; from a grove of palms hard by came the plaintive tootling of a native flute; and above our heads, spangled with a million stars, arched the purple canopy of the Indian sky. It was quite a festive little affair and one which I like to look back upon—a white mile-post on the road of memory.

Like the Taj Mahal, the temple of Madura should be seen for the first time, if possible, by moonlight. And, by the time dinner was over, the moon had accommodatingly appeared—a great silver platter, swung so low in the heavens that its rim seemed to touch the palms. Beneath its radiance the sordid town became a place enchanted. The plastered houses, garish enough by day, now seemed to be built of snowy marble; their recessed doorways and deep verandas, cloaked in blue-black shadows, became centers of mystery. The moon's pale rays, filtering through the thin branches and delicate foliage of the mimosas, the serrated fronds of the palms, transformed the dusty street into an avenue of frosted silver, a road to fairyland.

In order not to spoil the picture, we refused to avail ourselves of the *gharries,* whose drivers had been confidently counting on our patronage ever since the arrival of the train; declined to use the town's one and only taxi, a decrepit Ford; and insisted—all foreigners are more or less insane!—on driving out to the temple in two-wheeled carts drawn by humpbacked, milk-white bullocks. The carts were covered with arched hoods of plaited palm-leaves, beneath which we crawled to recline, none too comfortably it must be confessed, on mattresses laid upon the floors, which were tilted at such an angle that it was with difficulty that we prevented ourselves from sliding out. Julius, secretly scandalized by the unseemly conveyances chosen by his "marsters" and the *mem-sahibs,* followed in lonely dignity in a hack. The way to the temple led through the most congested quarter of the town, through narrow streets teeming with dark-skinned folk in garments of white or flaming colors, where languorous-eyed women peered curiously down at us from tottering wooden balconies (why is it, I wonder, that a woman leaning upon the rail of a balcony is so alluring?), where guttering tallow lamps and flaring torches half-illumined the interiors of shops and dwellings, affording us fleeting but intimate glimpses of the life within.

It was not a friendly crowd through which our creaking bullock carts slowly made their way, for the arrival of the Simon commission at Bombay the day before had evoked a rebellious rumbling whose reverberations had rolled across the whole breadth of the peninsula. On that same day, indeed, in Madras, several persons were killed or wounded as the result of an anti-English demonstration which had to be suppressed by the troops. But we were not molested, though we encountered occasional scowls, and the demeanor of the people was uncomfortably sullen. Frankly, I should have welcomed a glimpse of a white face —preferably under a soldier's helmet—in that sea of brown ones. But if there were other Europeans in Madura, we did not see them.

St. Christopher, the patron saint of travelers—or is it St. Anthony?—has always been kind to me, for on numberless occasions I have arrived in distant cities just in time to witness some interesting festival, ceremony or celebration. And my run of luck in this respect held good in Madura, for we found that our arrival coincided with the beginning of the greatest feast in the Hindu calendar—the Sivaratri, or Night of Siva. Throughout the twenty-four hours which it lasts the faithful may not eat or drink nor even sleep, and at three-hour intervals during the day and night *puja* is offered to the god. Consequently, the temple, ordinarily almost deserted after nightfall, was packed with worshipers, and we witnessed many curious sights and ceremonies which we would have missed on any other day of the year.

Pierre Loti said of the great temple of Madura that it "is larger than the Louvre and much more elaborately sculptured, and contains perhaps as many marvels." It is large enough, heaven knows—it covers an area of fifteen acres, if that conveys anything to you—and the number of sculptured figures which adorn it inside and out is beyond computation. But Loti's "marvels" might, to my way of thinking, more aptly be described as horrors, the effluvia of diseased brains and a debased religion. A vast chamber of horrors. That is what it amounts to, when all is said and done. Yet it is enormously worth seeing, for it is unique. Though its grotesqueries and obscenities recall certain other temples in Siam and Nepál, though in its construction there is a strong suggestion of those everlasting edifices at Thebes and Memphis and Angkor over which time has no control, there is nothing exactly like it anywhere else in the world.

The massive and lofty wall which surrounds the temple is broken, north, east, south and west, by four monumental gate towers known as *gopuras,* the tallest 152 feet in height, it being these which we had seen from the train. They are difficult to describe because I can think of nothing with which to compare them. In this respect I am in the embarrassing position of the missionary in the Arctic who failed lamentably in his attempt to describe a tree to his Eskimo parishioners, who could conceive of no other landscapes than those of snow and ice. But why waste words when my readers can turn to the accompanying illustration?

The base of each *gopura* is pierced by a tunnel-like passage, resembling the sally-port of a mediæval fortress, which gives access to the temple courtyard. Every square foot of these tremendous towers, from ground to summit, is covered with sculpturing: course upon course of carved gods and goddesses, elephants, lions, bulls, horses, monkeys, peacocks, serpents and mythological monsters, together with a bewilderment of symbolical ornament, all colored and gilded, which gradually diminish with distance, the stone *trisul* at the top resembling the most delicate golden filigree. No matter how long and how carefully one studies them, one is always discovering new figures, new beauties, so amazing is the wealth of detail; seen from a distance, they look like stupendous examples of Chinese ivory carving. We were fortunate, as I have already remarked, in being in Madura on the eve of a great religious festival, and the *gopuras* as well as the temple itself were outlined by myriads of colored lamps, red, blue, green, yellow, thousands and thousands of them.

The temple inclosure contains two sanctuaries. The larger is dedicated to Siva, [1] "the Blessed One"; the other to his wife Paravati, the goddess with the fish's eyes. Why Siva, with all the goddesses of Hindu mythology to choose from, should have selected as his consort a lady whose bulging optics suggest that she is suffering from an advanced stage of goiter, passes my comprehension. Separating the two sanctuaries is a huge tank, or artificial pool, the Pond of the Golden Lily. It is surrounded by a colonnaded loggia, broad flights of granite steps enabling the pious to bathe in and drink the green-scummed water. We were informed that this water is so holy that fish cannot live in it, which suggests that fish are more fastidious than the human beings whom we saw gulping the nauseous slime.

Julius, being a Buddhist, either could not or would not set foot within the temple, so he procured for us as guide a sleek and slick Babu of the Brahman caste, who devised so many ways of separating us from our money that he

[1] Pronounced Sheeva.

would have been invaluable as the manager of a charity bazaar. I suspect that after we had taken our departure he made the innumerable priests and holy men on whom we had bestowed alms at his suggestion divvy up with him.

The inner precincts of the temple are gained through a sort of vestibule lined by stalls where flowers, fruits, grain, ghee, lamps, perfumes, incense and other articles used by the Hindus to win the favor of their gods are sold. Most numerous were the venders of garlands made of marigolds and narcissus, whose heavy, sickish scent filled the air.

Ignoring the importunities of the hucksters, we pushed our way through the milling throng in the vestibule and plunged into a seemingly endless labyrinth of gloomy aisles and dimly lighted chambers. Despite an attempt to illumine the place by a multitude of lamps—cheap affairs of colored glass containing rags dipped in grease—everything was mingled and obscured by the pervading gloom: saffron-robed priests whose shaven heads were as hairless as billiard balls; holy men whose naked bodies were smeared with cow-dung, and other men who were equally filthy but not at all holy; wild-eyed, wild-haired *gurus* who stretched themselves upon beds of spikes or thrust into their mouths the heads of living serpents; whining mendicants with loathsome sores, dreadful mutilations, faces eaten by leprosy; worshipers whose foreheads were painted like Sioux warriors; sinuous temple girls with jewels in their nostrils and clanking bangles on ankle and wrist; carved horses and sacred cattle; leering idols and grinning monsters; gods with the heads of elephants and gods with the heads of monkeys; gods with too many arms and gods with too many faces; goddesses in postures which would make the keeper of a brothel blush.

It is a vast and echoing city, this house of Siva, its

gloomy galleries peopled by countless thousands of stone images. These sculptures assume an infinite variety of forms. There are serried ranks of prancing horses whose forefeet beat the air; an endless vista of carved and colored elephants; rows of repulsive gods that die away in the dim distance in lines of fading perspective; the Hall of a Thousand Columns, which is a forest of chiseled stone.

The ceilings are for the most part flat, composed of enormous slabs of stone laid by master masons who have been dust for centuries; the antiquity of the massive columns which support them may be gaged from the polish which they have attained as the result of contact with men and animals for generations beyond reckoning. Save only the floors, no spot has escaped the sculptor's chisel or the painter's brush. The columns, the capitals, the cornices are so overburdened with carvings, so bedecked with gilt and glaring colors, that the eyes grow weary and the senses reel.

In the very heart of the enormous structure, beneath a great gilt cupola, is the holy of holies, which is forbidden to all unbelievers and may be entered only by the higher members of the priesthood. Here, behind ponderous silver doors, jealously guarded, are consummated the secret rites of Hinduism. One of the girls unwittingly approached the outer portal of this chamber of mystery, whereupon a dozen priests and worshipers, their eyes aflame with fanaticism, made as though to fling themselves upon her, but I shouted a warning and she turned away in time. She said that she had no desire to go further. She had seen enough. She felt as though she had been contaminated and wanted to go back to the bungalow and take a bath.

Notwithstanding its absorbing interest, which amounted almost to an uncanny fascination, there was something ominous and sinister about the place; it stank of unclean things. Every few paces there loomed before us out of the semi-darkness obscene or repulsive images of Hindu deities, half-devils and half-gods, mainly of Siva in his various incarnations, of the elephant-headed Ganesha, of Paravati, the woman with the eyes of a fish. Certain of the figures were smeared with some scarlet substance to simulate blood; most of them had festoons of marigolds draped about their necks; all dripped with fat. In the light of the guttering torches they cast monstrous shadows upon the walls and pavement. Heaped on the greasy, blackened altars were offerings of rice, fruits, flowers. Congealing on the floor were horrid pools of crimson—the blood of recent sacrifices. The smoke of incense spiraled upward to hang in gray clouds beneath the ceilings.

One monstrous figure, so outrageously lewd that we hurried our companions past it, was literally plastered with gobs of the clarified butter known as *ghee,* flung there by the devout as boys would fling snowballs. The stone pavement before it was so littered with worshipers stretched prone in adoration that it was with difficulty that we avoided treading on them in the gloom. Others abjectly dragged themselves round and round the idol on their bellies.

Mingling with the throng of worshipers were beggars suffering from advanced forms of all the loathsome maladies to which the Indian falls heir. My garments were clutched by the skinny talons of a creature whose naked body was a mass of festering ulcers. I was jostled by a leper whose little, red-rimmed eyes glared at me malevolently from what had once been a human face but now resembled a decaying cauliflower. A miserable wretch, *sans* hands, *sans* feet, *sans* eyes, ambled aimlessly about the pavement on all fours like some giant species of blind beetle. All three were caked with filth and crawling with vermin.

Sacred cows wandered about at will, dropping their dung where the worshipers were thickest. An elephant, one of a number kept by the temple for use in religious processions, rocked ponderously by, the throng parting at the shrill warning of its mahout. A pair of camels, likewise temple property, poked their supercilious faces over the shoulder of an idol to nibble the garlands of flowers about the figure's neck. Huge gray rats scuttled from crevices between the stones to seize upon the grains of rice fallen from the altars. Along the lofty ceilings flitted great vampire bats. A serpent, escaped from a conjurer's basket, wriggled its mottled length across a patch of torch-illumined pavement to disappear in a hole beneath the feet of an idol. Fantastic animals made from cardboard, employed in temple pageants, lay crumbling and rotting in the corners.

The echoing corridors were a-hum with weird chants and murmured prayers, the tinkle of unseen bells, the clatter of coins in brass begging-bowls, the wail of pipes, the roar of conch-horns, the throb of distant drums and the soft, ceaseless *shuffle-shuffle-shuffle* of thousands of naked feet.

The fitful flare of lamps and torches fell upon faces that were genuinely devout and upon other faces that were unspeakably depraved; upon vindictive, crafty eyes and eyes which gleamed with the mad light of religious fervor; upon hairless heads and hairy bodies; upon stone which had been chiseled into beautiful and into repulsive forms; upon cheap cottons and rich brocades; upon priceless jewels and the tawdriest brummagem.

The air was fetid with the mingled stenches of rotting fruits, withered flowers, stagnant water, rancid butter, fresh blood, crushed marigolds, candle grease, guttering lamps, incense, medicaments, opium, cow-dung and sweating human bodies. In that eerie setting beauty was blended with bestiality, spirituality with obscenity, magnificence with filth. It was Dante's Inferno realized. Within those walls was

> Much of Madness, and more of Sin,
> And Horror the soul of the plot.

Here, as in no other spot I have ever seen, one is brought face to face with the true significance of heathenism and idolatry. Here you may look on Hinduism in the raw, lewd and unashamed. Here are the poisonous fruits of perverted piety, of religion run amuck. One encounters here the India of the old writers and the Sunday school books, is appalled by the seeming hopelessness of the task undertaken by the British Government and the missionary, the impossibility of making any impression upon so debased a people, of coping with such abysmal ignorance and deeply rooted superstition.

In the dark crannies and gloomy galleries of that dreadful house of horror, amid the maze of columns and in the black shadows behind the leering idols, lurked the spirit of evil. The sane and wholesome outside world seemed immensely far away. I felt lost and helpless among unclean things. I was oppressed by the uneasy feeling that in these foul chambers almost anything might happen. The fingers of a fear which was not physical plucked at my heartstrings and I shuddered. A feeling of revulsion swept me, such as might be experienced by one who has peered over the rim of the Pit—a nausea of the soul. God, but it was good to get out into the open air, to smell the fragrant night-breeze, to see the stars again!

We returned to the temple the next morning to get a better look at its carvings, to visit the elephant stables and to inspect the jewels contained in its treasure-house. But even the light of day failed to dispel its repellent atmosphere, though it dissipated much of its mystery. What a pity, I thought, as I looked again at the prancing Siva and his goggle-eyed consort, at Ganesha of the elephant's head, at the lewd carvings and the blood-stained sacrificial stones and the images adrip with grease, that those American women who in their quest for new sensations toy with Hinduism, who prate of its inner beauties and occult meanings and spiritual loftiness, could not have stood beside me. They would have seen that which would have cured them—and probably sickened them as well. It is said that if you understand the Hindu religion you can understand the Hindu mind. Well, if the temple at Madura is an index to the Hindu mind, I for one have no desire to understand it. Perhaps I am over-fastidious, but I don't care for unclean things.

Later in the day we drove out to the Teppa Kulam, some two or three miles to the east of Madura. This is a tank, or artificial lake, some eight hundred yards square, dug out at enormous labor by human hands. It is bordered by a stone parapet striped like a barber's pole, and at intervals are staircases by which the faithful may descend to cleanse themselves of sin—and vermin—in its sacred waters. In the center of the lake is a square island with a little marble kiosk set at each of its corners. From amid the trees and shrubbery which cover the island peers a charming pagoda, as white and delicately fashioned as though made by a confectioner from sugar. It was high noon when we visited the Teppa Kulam, and the relentless Indian sun had turned the lake into a pool of molten brass; the stone balustrades were so hot that one could have fried eggs upon them. But toward nightfall, when the heat of the day has abated, it must be an idyllic spot in which to spend a leisure hour.

Once a year, in February, figures representing Siva and

Paravati are taken with much ceremony to the lake for a boat ride. Bedecked with jewels and seated in magnificent palanquins, escorted by elephants and camels splendidly caparisoned, by priests and musicians and banner-bearers and dancing-girls and all manner of grotesque creatures made from cardboard, they are borne in an imposing procession from the great temple to the shore of the Teppa Kulam. There they are embarked in a huge gaily decorated barge and rowed across to the pagodaed island, where certain rites, cloaked in mystery by the priesthood, are performed.

We did not witness this ceremony, for we were leaving that evening for Madras, but we saw the preparations being made for it in the temple courtyard. Half-a-dozen elephants with gilded tusks, their massive foreheads elaborately frescoed in brilliant colors, were being hung with embroidered velvet housings, atop of which were girt howdahs of gold or silver, richly carved and studded with jewels. Lying about promiscuously were a number of artificial elephants, horses and legendary creatures made of papier-maché, destined to be borne on men's shoulders. Finally, there was a group of cardboard giants, fifteen feet in height, which swayed and tottered ludicrously as the men within their lower extremities rehearsed the antics they were to perform. What with the pachyderms and the camels and the clowns, it resembled a circus getting ready for a street parade rather than the preparation for a solemn religious procession.

Our Brahman guide, who always had an eye out for the main chance and who evidently foresaw an opportunity to separate us from some more of our rupees, was insistent that we remain over and witness the performance, but so much that was novel and interesting lay ahead of us that we refused, albeit somewhat reluctantly, to yield to his persuasions. India is, after all, so rich in strange sights and colorful ceremonies that missing one now and then does not greatly matter. And with Nepál the mysterious beckoning to us, why loiter longer in Madura? The fact is that the East is so crowded with things interesting, curious, picturesque, romantic, that the visitor frequently finds himself in much the same frame of mind as the Irishman, just landed in New York, who spied a gold-piece lying on the pavement. Instinctively he bent as though to pick it up, hesitated, straightened up again. "Begorra," he remarked, continuing on his way, "why bother meself wid only wan of thim? Oi'll wait till Oi git to th' pile."

Before leaving the vicinity of the temple the Brahman took us to see two most curious equestrian figures, known respectively as the Dravidian and the Aryan gods. The gods, dressed in the costumes of ancient maharajahs, were mounted on gigantic prancing horses, fully twenty feet in height. Beneath the horses' bellies were sculptured figures of old-time warriors, and supporting the front feet of each animal was a pair of lesser deities with enormous paunches and goggle eyes. Painted in colors so vivid and poisonous that the eyes ached from looking at them, they stood quite by themselves in the middle of a sun-scorched maidan. No one seemed to know why they were there or where they had come from; only that the one on a white charger was an Aryan divinity and the one on a black war-horse a god of the Dravidians. They doubtless have their religious significance, but they looked to me as though they belonged to a titanic merry-go-round.

Julius, who had been to Madura with other employers and consequently was familiar with the city's places of interest, insisted that we should not leave without visiting the seventeenth century palace of a former maharajah, Tirumala Nayak. It is a rather imposing place, a not unpleasing mélange of Hindu and Moorish architecture; the apartments are of enormous size, and portions of the interior, particularly the ceilings, are reminiscent of the Alhambra.

One room, the loftiest of all, once the maharajah's bedchamber, had originally contained an enormous golden bed which swung by silver chains from the ceiling. When Tirumala Nayak was ready to retire for the night he was accustomed to assemble in this singular sleeping-room his wives and concubines, numbering upward of a hundred. Selecting from this beauty chorus the houri who happened to catch his fancy, he would order her to join him on the bed. All being in readiness, the chains manned by a score of slaves, the court chamberlain would give the order "Hoist away!" and the great bed with its amorous occupants would rise slowly toward the ceiling. When it was forty feet in the air the chains were locked in place and there, swinging between floor and roof, free from interruption and safe from assassination, the maharajah and his fair companion would pass the night. The arrangement, as my cousin observed, had much to recommend it, for when the ruler became ennuied by his lady friend and wished to dispense with her company, all he had to do was shove her overboard. Perhaps this was the origin of the term "Give her the air." Doubtless more than one local *Scheherazade* gossiped herself hoarse in order to avert such a fate.

The maharajah, who trusted no one, was also accustomed to take aloft with him for safe keeping the crown jewels. But one night a clever thief, a prototype of our own second-story artists, chopped a hole in the palace roof and, while the couple on the bed were engrossed in their aërial amours, slid down one of the chains, abstracted the crown jewels from beneath the royal pillow and escaped as he had come. The maharajah having issued standing orders that under penalty of death no one was to disturb him until daybreak, his calls for assistance went unheeded and he remained a prisoner in the air until morning broke, thus giving the ingenious thief ample time to make his get-away. Should you question the truth of the story, the palace guide will confute your skepticism by pointing out the hole in the roof.

The sun has sunk once more behind the western hills in its accustomed splendor. Night has come, and to this ancient land of Hindustan brings peace. The clamor of the market-place has died away. In the bazaars the merchants are putting up their shutters. One by one the flaring lights go out. Swathed and softened by the darkness are the mad excesses of color. The great *gopuras,* majestic, mysterious, alone remain, outlined in gleaming jewels against the velvet sky.

We stand upon the terrace of the dâk-bungalow in silence, looking out across the flat roofs of the houses, now silvered by the rising moon. The town below is silent and deserted, but from the distant Teppa Kulam, borne on the night-breeze, comes the moan of conches and the sullen growl of drums. The procession of the gods has started; we catch occasional snatches of strange, barbaric chants. But there is no sound close at hand save the rustle of the palm-fronds, scarcely louder than our breathing. The air is as soft as a young girl's cheek. The heavy fragrance of tropic blossoms is intoxicating. Moonlight . . . distant music . . . whispering leaves . . . the scent of flowers . . . it is an enchanted world. . . .

But all beautiful things are of brief duration. Abruptly the spell is broken. A distant rumble rises into a crescendo of sound. The darkness is pierced by a long lance of dazzling light. A raucous shriek splits the night. The north-bound mail roars in. Confusion on the platform, waving lanterns, the slam of carriage doors, an impatient hoot from the locomotive, and the train moves on, rapidly gathering momentum. We lean from its windows as it hurtles through the darkness, to bid Madura a last farewell.

It is over! It has faded—and the dance-drums throb no more,
And the glamour only lingers in our dreaming;
For other ears the plaintive songs are wafted from the shore,
For other eyes the tragic sunset's gleaming. . . .

CHAPTER III

UNCLEAN GODS

ONLY after much hesitation as to its propriety have I decided on the inclusion of this chapter, for if I am to treat the subject frankly—and it must be treated thus or not at all—it is impossible to ignore certain aspects of Hinduism, even though candid discussion of them will be offensive to decency. It is certainly not a chapter which should be read by the unsophisticated, by those who are easily shocked or by the very young; and it will prove rather strong meat, I suspect, even for those who pride themselves on their worldliness, for it stinks—a politer word will not suffice—of unspeakably foul and evil things.

The notoriously low estate of the Hindu people, physically, mentally and morally, has been attributed to many causes—to their poverty, their ignorance, their superstition, the enervating climate in which they dwell, their child-marriages, their contempt for women, their caste system. But trace these contributory factors to their common source and in every case you will come up against the bed-rock of the Hindu religion.

It has been said, and with truth, that one must understand the Hindu religion in order to understand the Hindu mind. However wholesome a faith Hinduism may have been in the beginning, however pure and lofty the conduct, thoughts and aspirations of a certain small fraction of its followers, the undeniable fact remains that it constitutes, on the whole, a spiritual cesspool in whose noxious depths every form of depravity and vice flourishes amid the slime.

It is a religion which not only tolerates but actively encourages practices which the followers of all other faiths view with abhorrence and speak of, if they speak of them at all, with a sense of shame. There are certain pagan tribes in central Africa and elsewhere, it is true, some of whose customs resemble those of the Hindus—though none, so far as I am aware, which practises all of them; but Hinduism is the only religion in the modern world which actually wallows and glories in the unnatural, the degrading and the obscene.

No less an authority than Sir Thomas Hungerford Holdich has characterized Hinduism as "the most contemptible religion in existence. . . . The rural population of India is governed through ignorance and superstition by a degenerate race of priests, and the priests are supported by the people."

"The Hindu religion is a religious chaos," says Sir Alfred Lyall. "I doubt if any one who has not lived among Hindus can adequately realize the astonishing variety of their ordinary religious beliefs, the constant changes of shape and color which their beliefs undergo, the extraordinary fecundity of the superstitious sentiment. Hinduism is a tangled jungle of disorderly superstitions, ghosts and demons, demi-gods and deified saints, household gods, tribal gods, local gods, universal gods, with their countless shrines and temples and the din of their discordant rites, deities who abhor a fly's death, and those who still delight in human victims."

"The most deplorable feature of Vishnu-worship at the present day," Dr. W. W. Hunter remarks, "is that which has covered the temple walls with indecent sculptures, and filled its innermost sanctuaries with licentious rites."

Says another famous authority, Dr. H. Julius Eggeling, in speaking of the worship of Siva's wife, whether as Kali,

Durga, Paravati or some other of her many and terrible forms, "It is probably the most degrading cult ever practiced under the pretext of religious worship."

That many of my assertions will be denied or disbelieved is, of course, to be expected. Consequently I shall confine myself in statements which are capable of substantiation, either by the Hindu Scriptures themselves or by those whose knowledge of these subjects entitles them to speak with authority—as, for example, the Abbé J. A. Dubois, a priest singularly free from prejudice and remarkably well informed, who lived among the peoples of India for nearly a third of a century. His "Hindu Manners, Customs and Ceremonies," an amazing but little known book, from which I have drawn much of the material for this chapter, is spoken of with respect and admiration wherever scholars congregate.

It will also doubtless be said by its champions that I have not presented a fair picture of Hinduism—that I have merely picked out a few sensational examples which are not characteristic. It is true that it is impossible to generalize with complete accuracy on any subject connected with Hinduism, for India is a vast country, and practices which are common in Mysore are unknown in Kashmir, and vice versa.

Moreover, owing to pressure from the British authorities and public opinion, certain of the practices I shall describe are probably much less common now than they were a generation ago and some of the worst have doubtless all but disappeared. Others, however, are so widespread that the best the apologists for Hinduism can do is to shroud them in mystery and give them esoteric interpretations. Take Sivaism, for example, a Hindu cult whose followers run into the tens of millions. It is, when all is said and done, nothing but a form of phallicism—that is, the worship paid to the generative function as symbolized by the phallus, the male organ. This obscene symbol, known in India as the *lingam*, together with its female counterpart, the *namam* or *yoni*, is as common among Hindus as the cross is among Christians, millions of Sivaites painting it on their foreheads or wearing it as an amulet about the neck.

The point I wish to make is that no religion which tolerates any of these monstrous customs, or which permits any of its sects or any of its priests to practise them, is fit to serve as a spiritual guide to more than two hundred millions of people. Until it has utterly exterminated these abominations and all lingering belief in them, Hinduism will remain an unmitigated curse to the vast population which it has spiritually enslaved and debauched.

It seems scarcely necessary for me to stress the fact that not all, or nearly all, of the inhabitants of India are Hindus. The total population of the Indian Empire is not far from 320 millions, or almost triple that of the United States. Speaking broadly, of every hundred persons in India sixty-eight are Hindus, twenty-two Mohammedans, three Buddhists, three follow the religion of their tribes, one is a Sikh and one is a Christian. Of the remaining two, one is equally likely to be a Buddhist or a Christian, and the other most probably a Jain, much less probably a Parsee, and just as possibly a Jew or a pagan.

The Hindus largely predominate in the center and south of India, and in the Madras presidency form 89 per cent. of the population. The Mohammedans monopolize the Northwest Frontier Province, Baluchistan and Kashmir and form the majority of the population in the Punjab, eastern Bengal and Sind. The Buddhists are almost entirely confined to Burma, where 85 per cent. of the inhabitants follow the doctrines of the Great Teacher. The Sikhs are localized in the Punjab, the Jains in Rajputana and the Parsees in Bombay. Only about 1½ per cent. of the total population of India are Christians, nearly three fifths of these residing in the presidency of Madras.

The whole structure of the Hindu religion rests on the caste system, without which Hinduism in its present form could not exist. The enormous complexity of the system makes it impossible to give more than the barest outline here. The usual and at the same time the most ancient classification divides the Hindus into four main castes—the Brahmans, the Kshatriyas, the Vaisyas and the Sudras. The Brahmans represent the priesthood; the Kshatriyas, the nobles and warriors; the Vaisyas, the bourgeoisie, or commercial class; the Sudras, the workers. Each of these four main castes is subdivided into many others, the number of which it is impossible to determine because they vary according to locality, but they certainly run into many hundreds, if not thousands. One authority enumerates 1429 different Hindu castes.

The Brahmans have ever represented the sacerdotal class in India, and, like the priestly clan the world over, they have directed the political destinies of the country and still exercise the most potent influence of any caste in India. The great difference between their caste and all others is that it is not hereditary, for a Brahman only becomes a Brahman after the ceremony of the triple cord. Until this essential ceremony has been performed he ranks only as a member of one of the lower castes and hence is called *Dvija*—Twice-born. His first birth gives him only his manhood; the second raises him to the exalted rank of Brahman and gives him membership in the Hindu hierarchy.

Though all priests are Brahmans, all Brahmans are not priests, but all belong to the priestly caste. Hence they exercise enormous influence throughout India, many of them holding lucrative posts in the service of the British raj or of the native princes. In fact, the prime ministers of the various maharajahs are almost always Brahmans, whereas the maharajahs themselves do not necessarily belong to the Brahman caste. Take, for example, the case of the Maharajah of Travancore. That prince applied to his priests for permission to become a Brahman. The royal request was finally granted on condition that the ruler build in gold a life-size image of a cow and publicly crawl through it. The condition was complied with, the maharajah wriggled himself through the hollow image of the sacred animal from head to tail, and was thereupon inducted by the ceremony of the triple cord into the caste whose exclusiveness he coveted. The golden cow was, of course, given to the priests as a perquisite.

According to the Hindu Scriptures, the author of the caste system was the god Brahma, who established it when he created and peopled the earth. The Brahmans were the product of his brain; the Kshatriyas issued from his shoulders; the Vaisyas from his belly; and the Sudras from his feet. It is easy to understand the allegorical significance of this legend. The Brahmans, destined to provide spiritual guidance for their fellow-men, issue from the head of the creator; the Kshatriyas, endowed with the strength required of warriors, have their origin in Brahma's shoulders; the Vaisyas, whose duty is to provide food, clothing and other necessaries of life, are born in the belly of the god; while the Sudras, whose lot is servitude and labor in the fields, come from his feet.

In addition to the four main castes I have enumerated, there are certain other castes, or rather outcastes, whose members are regarded by self-respecting Hindus as without the pale of decent society, as almost another race of beings. The best known of these outcastes is the Paraiyan, a Tamil word from which is derived the European term "pariah."

The various outcastes, taken collectively, comprise nearly a quarter of the entire Hindu population and are the most useful of all, for they perform manual labor and drudgeries of every description. Without them the other classes could not exist. Yet they live in hopeless poverty, the greater number lacking means to procure even the coarsest clothing, and they rarely have enough to eat.

The contempt and aversion with which the members of the other castes—particularly the Brahmans—threat these unfortunate victims of a pernicious system are carried to such excess that in many places their presence, or even their footprints, are considered sufficient to defile a whole neighborhood. If a Brahman, a Kshatriya, a Vaisya or even a Sudra is touched, even inadvertently, by a Pariah he is defiled and may hold no communication with any one until he has purified himself by bathing. It is contamination to eat with any members of this class, to touch food prepared by them, or even to drink water which they have drawn. In most neighborhoods they are not permitted to use the common wells, frequently being obliged to go considerable distances under a scorching sun in order to drink from wells of their own.

The servants employed by Europeans are all Pariahs, because no native of any other caste would condescend to perform menial labor—to clean shoes, to empty chamber receptacles, to collect garbage. And certainly no self-respecting Hindu could be found who for any reward whatsoever would consent to cook food for Europeans, as this would necessitate his touching beef, a flesh which all pious Hindus hold in abhorrence.

Some idea of the importance in Indian life of the Pariah element may be obtained from the figures of the last government census, which estimates the "Depressed Classes," as they are officially termed, as numbering between fifty-five and sixty millions. There has been much discussion in recent years as to the best method of alleviating their unhappy lot, but, owing to the opposition of the other castes, comparatively little has been done for these wretched beings.

In some districts there are castes which are not to be met with elsewhere and which may be distinguished by peculiarities of their own. Nowhere save in Travancore, for example, may be found the Nairs, whose women enjoy the privilege of possessing several husbands. They are not polyandrists, however, in the strict sense of that term, for a Nair woman is not permitted to entertain more than one husband at a time.

In the same state of Travancore is also found the caste called Nambudiri, the members of which, according to Abbé Dubois, an authority whose general accuracy of observation has never been impugned, are distinguished by one abominable and revolting custom.

As is the case throughout India, the girls of this caste are married when they are very young, though they do not enter into marital relations with their husbands until they have reached the age of puberty. If, however, a girl-wife dies when the signs of puberty are already apparent but before she has had intercourse with a man, caste custom rigorously demands that the corpse of the deceased shall be subjected to an unspeakably vile connection. As the bereaved husband is naturally reluctant to perform this dreadful office, the family employs a Pariah, a wretch so degenerate that nothing is beneath him, to make post-mortem amends to the dead virgin. Were not the marriage thus hideously consummated by proxy, the girl's spirit would be denied admission to the Abodes of Bliss and the members of her family would hang their heads in shame.

Preposterous and utterly incredible as this may sound to Western ears, a parallel may be found in English history. After the execution of Mary Stuart the headless body of the beautiful Queen of Scots was placed on a litter and borne into the crypt of Fotheringay Castle, where it was left for the night under the guard of a single man-at-arms.

"Then," in the words of her biographer, "occurred the most monstrous relationship in history, between a woman without a head and a man without a heart."

Some of the caste customs, Abbé Dubois tells us, while not sexually immoral, so grossly violate the most elementary rules of decency and decorum that the members of other castes, themselves none too squeamish, regard them as abhorrent and nauseating. Thus, the women of a caste in the interior of Mysore are required by custom to accompany the male members of their households whenever the latter retire in answer to the demands of nature, and to cleanse them with water afterward. This practise, though now falling into desuetude, is regarded by those who observe it as a sign of exquisite good breeding.

I might mention, à propos of the above, that the Hindus —and the same is true of the Mohammedans—consider it unpardonably filthy to use the right hand when anything dirty has to be done, such as blowing the nose or cleansing the intimate parts of the person. It is the left hand only that may be used on these occasions. Generally speaking, the right hand is employed when touching any part of the body above the navel, the left, or "unclean," hand being reserved for the lower portions of the body. All Hindus are so habituated to this that one rarely sees them using the wrong hand. That is why most Orientals consider themselves insulted when a European returns a salute, offers them anything or pours a drink with the left hand. The spectacle of a European blowing his nose on a handkerchief and then putting it in his pocket nauseates them, while the European custom of using paper for toilet purposes is looked upon by all Hindus, without exception, as an abomination. A Hindu blows his nose between his fingers and then wipes them on the wall. For cleansing his person after a visit to the latrine he uses only dirt and water.

The various classes of Sudras who dwell in the hills of the Carnatic faithfully observe the caste law which forbids them to wash their clothing. Once they have wrapped themselves in cottons fresh from the looms of the weavers they never take them off until the material actually falls apart from rottenness. One can imagine the filthiness of their garments, particularly those of the women, after they have been worn day and night for months, caked with dirt and offal, soaked with sweat, acrawl with vermin and stinking to high heaven.

Every self-respecting Hindu paints on his forehead and certain other parts of his body the curious marks—streaks, dots and circles—which are the crest and sign-manual of his creed and caste. A bare forehead is a sign of mourning or that the daily ablutions have not been performed. The paint used for this purpose—black, white, vermilion or ocher—is made into a fragrant paste by mixing it with sandalwood and rubbing the concoction on a damp stone. The followers of Siva smear their foreheads and their private parts with the ashes of cow-dung or with ashes taken from the places where the dead are burned. Most of them also wear a sectarial mark consisting of two red perpendicular lines, meeting in a semicircle at the base of the nose, and having a round red spot painted between them—the sign of the *lingam*. The Bairagis, a sect whose members go about stark naked, paint on their buttocks an emblem symbolical of the female generative organ. Even the private parts of small children have their own particular adornments. Little girls often wear nothing save a gold or silver shield or cod-piece on which is graven an indecent picture. A boy's ornament, also of gold or silver, is an exact copy of that member which it pretends to conceal.

The Hindus acknowledge three principal divinities—Brahma, the Creator; Vishnu, the Preserver; Siva, the Destroyer. These three, known collectively as the Trimurti, are worshiped generally by all Hindus. In some of the Puranas it is related that the Trimurti sprang from a female source called Adi-Sakti, who gave birth to these three divinities united in a single body, like the Siamese twins, and it is added that after having brought them into the world she fell so desperately in love with them that she committed incest with all three. This passage, it might be mentioned, is one of the least indecent of the doings of the gods as chronicled in the sacred writings of Hinduism. Each of these gods had a wife, Brahma being wedded to Sarasvati, Vishnu to Lakshmi, and Siva to Paravati, though each of these goddesses is worshiped in numerous forms and under many names.

One hears comparatively little about Brahma, however, who, having played his part in the mundane evolution by his original creation of the universe, has retired into the background, where he remains a mere figurehead so far as the worship of the people is concerned. The majority of Hindus pay equal honor to the other two great divinities of the Trimurti—Vishnu and Siva—in whose honor temples and idols have been raised everywhere. There are, however, vast numbers of sectarians who specialize, as it were, confining themselves to the worship of one or the other. The members of one of these sects are known as Vishnu-bhaktas, or votaries of Vishnu; the others as Siva-bhaktas, or disciples of Siva.

It is impossible to conceive of anything more obscene than the symbols, known as the *lingam* and the *namam,* which are worn in one form or another by the followers of Siva and Vishnu respectively. The emblem of the Siva-ites, as I have already mentioned, is the *lingam* or, to put it baldly, the phallus. They paint it on their foreheads, but more often they wear it in the hair, round the arm or hanging from the neck inclosed in a little silver tube. The *namam,* often called the *yoni,* represents the entrance to the genital parts of a woman and is the distinguishing device of those who worship Vishnu.

The *lingam* is an object of the deepest veneration throughout India. The origin of this obscene emblem, as described in several of the Puranas, was as follows: Brahma, Vishnu and Vasishta, accompanied by a numerous following, repaired one day to Kailasa, the particular paradise of Siva, to pay a visit to the god. Having neglected to inform him of their coming, they entered his abode to find him in the act of intercourse with his wife. The illustrious visitors were somewhat disconcerted by this contretemps and hastily withdrew, but Siva, far from being embarrassed, continued to indulge in the gratification of his sexual desires. His shameless behavior was due, so it is explained in the Puranas, to the fact that he was drunk and consequently in no condition to appreciate the indecency of his conduct.

He seems to have had a vague realization, however, that something of an unseemly nature had occurred, for when he had sobered up he summoned his guards and demanded that they relate exactly what had happened. This they did, omitting no detail. So overwhelmed were the god and goddess by the disgrace which had overtaken them that they died in the same amorous posture in which their fellow-deities had surprised them, and in which they are depicted in countless Hindu temples to-day. Before he expired, however, Siva ordained that the act which had shamed him unto death should be perpetuated and celebrated by the devout.

"My shame," he said, "has killed me; but it has also given me new life and a new shape, which is that of my lingam. Yes, the lingam is I, myself, and I ordain that men shall offer to it henceforth their sacrifices and worship. Those who make images of it with earth or cow-dung shall be rewarded; those who make it in stone shall receive seven times more reward; those who make it in gold shall be seven times more meritorious still. Let my priests go and teach these truths to men and compel them to embrace the worship of my lingam."

That is why one sees representations of the *lingam* painted on the foreheads of the Sivaites, or in amulets about their necks, or, wrought in enormous proportions in metal or stone, in the temples dedicated to Siva, along the highroads, in public places and other frequented spots. There is, indeed, scant difference save in name between Sivaism as practised by millions of Hindus and the phallic rites which shocked Jewish writers in connection with the worship of Baal and Aphrodite.

What I have just said of the *lingam* also applies to the *namam,* or *yoni,* representing the female vulva, which is adored by the followers of Vishnu. At Malabar Point, a few miles outside of Bombay, there rises from the shore a cleft rock which bears a fancied resemblance to the *namam.* In the belief that they will secure physical regeneration thousands of Vishnuites make pilgrimages to the spot each year for the purpose of squeezing themselves through the sacred hole.

It is difficult to believe that in inventing these vile superstitions the religious teachers of the Hindus intended that the people should render direct worship to objects whose very names are rarely spoken among decent people of civilized nations. There can be little doubt, indeed, that these obscene symbols originally had allegorical meanings and typified the reproductive forces of nature. But the Hindu priests soon learned that by perverting the original meaning of these symbols, they could keep a tighter grip on the people by pandering to their passions. As might be expected, centuries of these pernicious teachings have produced among the Hindus a state of sexual excitation which the devotional exercises of other religions tend to repress.

One does not need to remain long in India, or to inspect many of its temples, to realize that carnal intercourse in every form is uppermost in the Hindu mind. Many of the Hindu religious ceremonies are, as a consequence, unspeakably obscene and degrading.

At Mogur, a village in southern Mysore, a great festival is celebrated each year in honor of a female divinity named Tipamma. An image of the goddess, entirely nude, is borne through the streets in a magnificently decorated palanquin. Facing her is the figure of another divinity, a male, likewise naked, the two being placed in close juxtaposition. By means of an ingenious mechanism the two idols are caused to give a lifelike imitation of sexual intercourse, their amatory motions continuing as long as the procession lasts, to the huge delight of the onlookers. The effect on the children who witness this sort of spectacle can be imagined. Nor is this all. Walking beside the palanquin is a Pariah who has made a special study of all the filthy expressions to be found in the Hindu language, which is rich in them, the lascivious goddess being supposed to speak through him. Consequently, the spectators are treated to a liberal education in obscenity, Tipamma's human mouthpiece having all the foulest expressions in the Hindu lexicon of lewdity at his tongue's end.

In certain isolated places may be found temples where the most disgusting debauchery is considered the only form of service agreeable to the presiding gods. The priests, speaking for the deities they serve, promise children to barren women who will consent to lay aside every vestige of clothing and modesty and yield themselves to all comers indiscriminately. At the very gates of the temples, therefore, ordinarily respectable women grant their favors to any one who asks for them. The authority of Indian husbands over their wives is moreover such that it would be impossible for debauchery of this kind to be carried on without their approval. The depths of degradation to which these people have sunk in pursuance of their religion is emphasized by the fact that the custom I have described flagrantly defies those elementary principles of modesty with which nature seems to have endowed all human beings and some animals. It is a well known fact, for example, that camels rarely have sexual intercourse in public view, it frequently being found impossible to mate them in captivity unless they are covered with a sheet.

It is scarcely surprising that libertinism and all its consequences, including venereal disease in every form, flourish in a country where the passions are so systematically aroused and have such ample opportunities of gratification. Consider the great number of widows in the prime of womanhood who, being forbidden to remarry, are only too ready to yield to the seducer. Modesty and virtue do not concern them; their only fear is that their misconduct may be found out. In order to prevent such a contingency they invariably resort to abortion, which they practise without the slightest scruple or remorse. There is not a woman among them who is not an adept in such matters. Even little girls of ten or twelve know how to bring about a miscarriage.

Besides the depravities which are common to all castes, there are numerous forms of degeneracy peculiar to the more highly educated Brahmans. Many of them possess abominable books in which are systematically described and taught forms of debauchery so unspeakably low that the Western mind cannot conceive of them. These books also treat in detail of such matters as the art of giving variety to amatory pleasures, the delights of carnal intercourse between human beings and animals. They likewise contain recipes for the concoction of aphrodisiacs and of philters which are claimed to have the property of inspiring unholy love. I am told that even the libertines who employ these potions would be overtaken by nausea if they knew what they contained.

To have intercourse with a courtezan, or, for that matter, with any unmarried woman, is not considered sinful by the Brahmans, for these men, who look upon the violation of any trivial custom as a heinous sin, profess to see no harm in unbridled debauchery or wholesale seduction. It is primarily for the gratification of their desires that dancing-girls and prostitutes are attached to all Hindu temples, and they may often be heard intoning a scandalous line which, freely translated, means "To have intercourse with a prostitute is a virtue which takes away sin."

Priestesses, or "wives of the gods," as they are generally called, are attached to the temples of both Siva and Vishnu, ostensibly to gratify the sexual desires of those deities. They are quite a distinct class from the temple dancing-girls, though equally depraved, being generally the unfortunate victims of the immorality of the priests. The latter, by way of keeping up a reputation for sanctity and in order to conciliate the families whose daughters they have seduced, put the whole blame on Siva or Vishnu, and the poor gods, as is only fair, do the right thing by taking the girls in marriage. The women who are thus consecrated to Vishnu are known as *garuda-basavis* (wives of the *garuda* or eagle, which is the vehicle of Vishnu) and have the image of this bird tatooed on their breasts. The priestesses of Siva are called *linga-basavis,* or women of the *lingam,* and bear this obscene symbol tatooed on the inner side of their thighs. It seems scarcely necessary to add that the "wives of the gods" are the concubines of the priests.

A notch lower in the social scale are the dancing-girls attached to the temples, who are called *deva-dasis,* or "servants of the gods." Unlike the *garuda-basavis* and *linga-basavis,* who are reserved for the use of the priesthood, the *deva-dasis* are required to grant their favors to any one demanding them who has the wherewithal to pay for them. Just as almost every church in America has its choir, so every temple of importance in India has its band of harlots, whose official duties consist in dancing and singing within the temple twice a day and at public religious ceremonies. The dances are graceful but lascivious; the songs are always obscene, usually descriptive of some licentious episode in the lives of their gods. Such time as the *deva-dasis* have to spare between their official duties they devote to the practice of prostitution. Unlike the "wives of the gods," who become such as the result of priestly seduction, the servants of the gods are trained for a licentious career from infancy. In fact, it is by no means unusual for a pregnant woman, in the hope of obtaining a safe delivery, to make a vow that she will devote to the service of the gods the child which she carries in her womb should it turn out to be a girl.

Until very recently these courtezans were almost the only women in India who could dance, sing and read. Hence, respectable women hesitated to acquire any of these accomplishments. Of all Hindu women, moreover, the *deva-dasis* are the most decently dressed, being particularly careful not to expose any portion of the body. That is why those who are familiar with Hindu customs smile when they see half-naked women taking the parts of Indian dancing-girls on the stage or the motion-picture screen. The concealment of their slim and sinuous bodies is not a sign of inherent modesty, however, as Abbé Dubois pithily remarks, but is merely a refinement of seduction. For experience has taught the *deva-dasi* that for a woman wantonly to display her charms has the effect of dampening sensual ardor instead of exciting it, and that the imagination is more easily captivated than the eye.

"But why," it may be asked, "does not the British Government in India suppress these odious practices and customs? Why does a civilized and Christian power tolerate such abominations?"

The answer is simple. The Hindus outnumber the British in India by almost two thousand to one. Yet, notwithstanding their disparity in numbers, the British have worked miracles in India, as any fair-minded man who is really conversant with the facts will attest. They have already abolished numerous pernicious customs, including that of *suttee,* and they are steadily undermining many others. But they have to go about their task with exceeding care, for these practices, as I have pointed out, are so inextricably bound up with the Hindu faith, their roots penetrate so deeply into the Hindu Scriptures and traditions, that any open and systematic attempt on the part of the British to extirpate them would be considered by the Hindus, almost to a man, as an attack on their religion. Conditions are bad enough in India as they are, but they would be made infinitely worse by a religious uprising, and no one knows better than the British rulers of the country that it would not take much meddling in religious matters to precipitate one.

My own opinion—and you can take it for what it is worth—is that the eventual moral salvation of the Hindus will come not from without but from within. While the mass of the Hindu people are sunk in the lowest depths of depravity and superstition, the victims of a tyrannical priesthood which systematically debauches and exploits them for its own ends, the fact should never be lost sight of that to this general rule there are numerous notable exceptions. Thus, in all the great centers of population are to be found high-minded and highly educated Hindu gentlemen who recognize and deplore as much as any foreigner the wretched state of their people. I am far from belittling the remarkable achievements of the British administrators, or the splendid work of the Christian missionaries of all creeds, when I assert that it is to these Hindus of culture and broad vision that their priest-ridden co-religionists must look for amelioration of their tragic condition.

I have sketched this brief outline of Hindu caste and religious customs not from any desire for sensationalism, but because I know of no other way of bringing my readers to a full realization of the appalling conditions which exist among the Hindus. Instead of mincing words and employing euphemisms, I have permitted myself a candor which, no doubt, will scandalize many of my readers. But I would remind them that they read this chapter deliberately, because they wished to. I gave full warning of its nature at the outset in order that no one might plunge into it unaware. If there are some whose sense of decency has been offended, they have only themselves to blame.

CHAPTER IV

THE LAST STAND OF DESPOTISM

WHEN, a few years ago, that distinguished actor Mr. George Arliss appeared in a play entitled "The Green Goddess," I imagine that most of those who saw it felt that the part of the Indian rajah which he played was overdrawn. That the ruler of a native state the size of Staten Island, a sophisticated and cynical Hindu who wore an orange turban with faultlessly cut dinner clothes and spoke with an Oxford accent, should attempt to force a beautiful young English girl into his zenana in the belief that he could get away with it, and that, when retribution appeared in the form of British bombing planes, he should implore the protection of his goddess—not the flesh-and-blood one whom he had kidnapped, but a horrific idol of stone—was altogether too fantastic and far-fetched to be convincing.

As a matter of fact, however, the author of the play, Mr. William Archer, had produced a by no means exaggerated picture of the conditions which obtain in several parts of India to-day. Though the delineation of the rajah was probably not drawn from life, it is safe to say that it was a composite picture of several Indian princes who could be identified by almost any one familiar with the peninsula, and that the action was based on incidents which have occurred in the native states in very recent times. For almost anything can happen in those feudal kingdoms whose rulers enjoy a degree of power, a freedom from interference, which makes them comparable to the barons of the Middle Ages. And among these ruling princes are char-

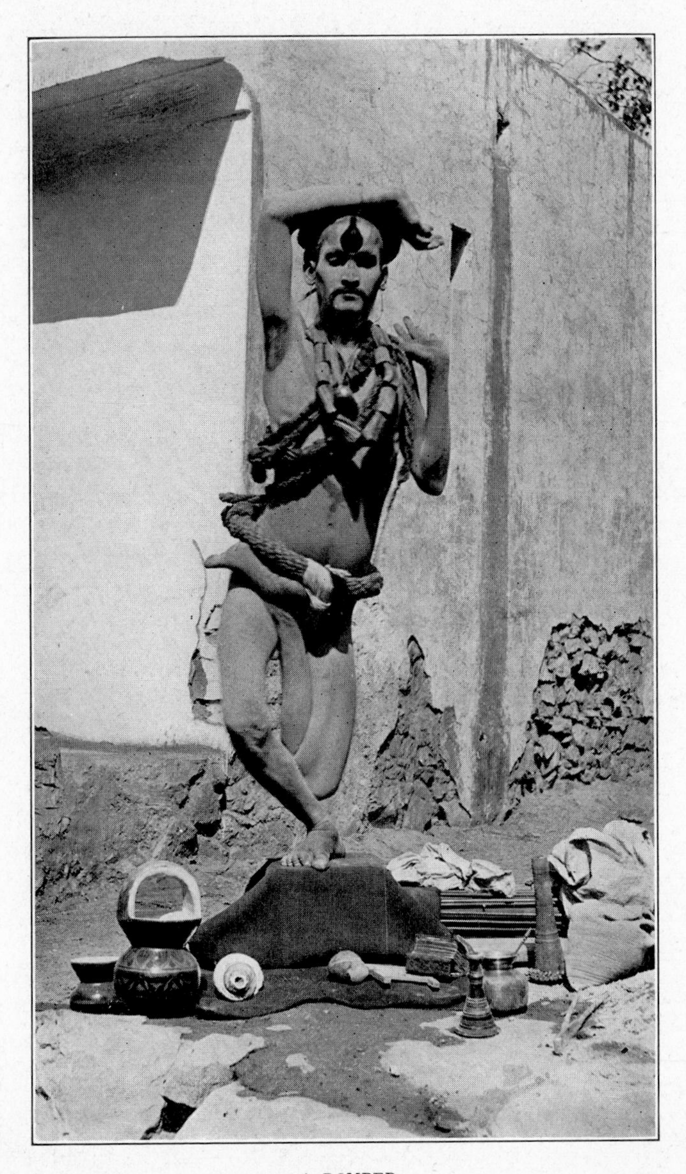

A DOMBER

To the earnings which the men of this caste make by tumbling or slight-of-hand, the women add the sums which they gain by the most shameless immorality, their favors being bestowed on any one who cares to pay for them

NO, THEY ARE NOT MOVING A HOUSE

This is the smartest thing in Indian limousines

acters every whit as theatrical and anomalous as the rajah of Mr. Archer's play. The British residents and political officers at some of the native courts could, were they so minded, relate stories of happenings so bizarre, so incredible to the Western mind, that they would sound like the most improbable fiction.

The conditions which make such happenings possible are due to the fact—which should never be lost sight of in considering the problems, achievements and shortcomings of the British administration—that *about two fifths of the area of the Indian Empire, and nearly one fourth of its population, are not subject to British law.*

It is not generally understood by most Americans, I imagine, that the Indian Empire consists of two great political divisions: British India and Native India.

British rule in India began with the commercial settlements established along the seaboards of the peninsula during the seventeenth and eighteenth centuries by the East India Company in its attempt to secure the Eastern trade. These were gradually augmented by conquest, cession or annexation, the expansion of British territory having steadily continued until very recent times. With the crushing of the mutiny in 1858 British India became a colony, the entire administration being transferred from the East India Company to the Crown. Its relations with the home government, however, are conducted through the India Office, instead of, as is the case with other colonies, through the Colonial Office.

British India, which for administrative purposes is divided into fifteen provinces, is directly under British rule, though, since the setting up of its own legislature in 1921, it has enjoyed a limited measure of autonomy. In fact, its present political status might be described as that of a quasi-dominion within the empire. The Indian legislature, which consists of two chambers, the Council of State and the Legislative Assembly, has power, subject to certain restrictions, to make laws for all persons in British India and for all British subjects within other parts of India, though the governor-general, with the assent of parliament, may enact measures essential for the safety, tranquillity or interests of British India against the wishes of the Council or Assembly. A majority of the members of the two houses are elected by the 3 per cent. of the 247 million inhabitants of British India who have the vote.

Native India, with an area equal to nearly a quarter of that of the continental United States and a population exceeding that of all the countries of South and Central America combined, is not under British rule, nor are its inhabitants British subjects, though it is, directly or indirectly, under British control or protection. Native India consists of about six hundred states, great and small, each ruled by its own prince, or, in a few cases, by councils or ministers. These princes—maharajahs, [1] rajahs, nizams, nawabs, thakurs, sawbwas, sultans—are sovereign rulers, being independent of all external authority save only that of the Paramount Power itself.

The territories comprising Native India range in size from the vast dominions of the Nizam of Hyderabad, with a population exceeding that of New York State and an area equal to that of Italy, to petty principalities like Lawa, in Rajputana, with an area of nineteen square miles, and the Simla hill states, which are no larger than some of our western farms.

The complexity of the political situation is enormously increased by the fact that the Native states do not form a solid block, but are scattered like islands and archipela-

[1] Rajah and maharajah are Hindu titles; nizam and nawab are Mohammedan.

goes all over the peninsula, many of them being enclaves entirely surrounded by British territory. Travancore, for example, is in the extreme southwest, its territory running down to Cape Comorin. The state of Jammu and Kashmir, larger than Idaho, is on India's other fringe, extending northward to the lofty Karakoram ranges, "where three empires meet." Cutch is a great peninsula—only its salt marshes save it from being an island—extending into the Arabian Sea. Bhutan, in certain respects the least advanced of the states, lies along the northeast frontier, its borders for upward of two hundred miles marching with those of Tibet. A still further complication is provided by the religious anomalies existing in certain of the states. Thus, Kashmir, the bulk of whose inhabitants are Moslems, is ruled by a Hindu dynasty, while the Nizam of Hyderabad, the vast majority of whose subjects are Hindus, is himself a Mohammedan.

The institution of many of these states as independent political entities dates back into the dim dawn of history, as do the dynasties which rule them. Others are comparatively recent creations. Mysore has been independent since the third century B.C. The earliest known king of Jodhpur lived in the sixth century of the Christian era. The rulers of Jaisalmer are direct descendants of Krishna. The Maharajah of Jaipur claims descent from Kush, the son of Rama. The history of Baroda state as such began with the break-up of the Mogul Empire. On the other hand, the existence of Lawa as an independent state dates only from 1867, when the Nawab of Tonk, to whom the territory belonged, murdered the local chieftain's uncle and a large number of his adherents, whereupon Lawa was detached from Tonk and placed under the rulership of its own thakurs. It will be seen, therefore, that the Native states are, for the most part, of great antiquity, many of them antedating the beginnings of British power in the peninsula by centuries. As the British boundaries expanded, the states came under the influence of the raj, and treaties were negotiated whereby the princes agreed to acknowledge British suzerainty in return for British guarantees and protection.

The degree of control exercised by the Paramount Power over the Indian states varies considerably, the powers of the princes being regulated by treaty or custom. These range downward from those enjoyed by the Nizam of Hyderabad, who exercises full sovereignty within his dominions, grants titles, has the power of life and death over his subjects, maintains a standing army of 20,000 men, has his own currency and postal system, and is styled "His Exalted Highness," to those of petty chiefs who have the mere right to collect the revenue of a village and are without criminal or civil jurisdiction.

The inhabitants of the Indian states are the subjects of their rulers and are immune from British law. Criminals escaping from British India to a Native state cannot be arrested by the British authorities without the permission of the state's ruler. Save in rare cases, applied to maritime territories, the states have freedom of trade with British India, although they levy their own customs duties.

The variety of the relations which under the terms of the various treaties subsist between the British Government and the rulers of the different states makes it impossible even to summarize them. Broadly speaking, however, the princes appoint their own officials, make and enforce their own laws, levy their own taxes, administer their own finances, and within certain limits maintain their own military forces. In other words, they are masters within their own territories.

But they have no right to make war or peace, to enter

into diplomatic relations with foreign governments or with each other, or to employ Europeans without special permission. The treaties between the princes and the British raj in every case provide that the conduct of the foreign affairs of the Native states shall be delegated to the Supreme Government, which maintains a resident at each of the principal courts, the smaller and less important states being formed into groups, each under the general supervision of a British political officer. These residents and political officers form the sole channel of communication between the Native states and the Government of India and between the Native states themselves. The responsibilities of the political agents vary, of course, according to the importance and progressiveness of the states to which they are accredited. In some instances they are little more than advisers, exercising about the same degree of influence as the American ministers to Haiti and Nicaragua. In others they are invested with a direct share in the administration, and, in the case of a state whose prince is a minor, the agent is the ruler in all save name. All affairs connected with the Native states are conducted by the Government of India through its Foreign and Political Department, which is, in turn, answerable to the viceroy and governor-general, who is the sole representative in India of the Crown.

The nominal sovereignty exercised by the princes does not mean, however, that the Government of India is precluded from stepping in to set right such serious abuses in a native administration as may threaten any part of the country with anarchy or disturbance, nor from assuming temporary charge of a Native state when there is sufficient reason to do so. Nor has the Paramount Power hesitated to interfere when circumstances warranted. In 1875 Maharajah Malhar Rao of Baroda was deposed for "notorious misconduct" and "gross misgovernment," though the charge that he had attempted to poison the British resident, Colonel Phayre, was not proved. Then there is the recent case of the ex-Maharajah of Indore, Tukoji Rao III, who was forced to abdicate in 1926 in favor of his son. The story of his downfall has received wide publicity. He chose as his favorite a beautiful nautch girl, Mumtaz Begum, then cast her off. She escaped from the palace by a ruse and made her way to Bombay, where she became the mistress of a wealthy native merchant. Whereupon Tukoji Rao, caring nothing for the girl herself but infuriated by the affront to his dignity, instigated his agents to murder the merchant. Now, mark you, had the murder been committed in Indore it is unlikely that anything would have been done about it, for a maharajah is theoretically master in his own dominions, particularly when his zenana is concerned. But it was obvious that the Government of India could not permit a prince to engineer an assassination in British territory with impunity, and, in token of its displeasure, Tukoji Rao was ordered to step down from his throne.

Despite the restrictions which make their sovereignty something less than absolute, the native princes do not regard themselves as Britain's vassals but as her allies, and this notwithstanding the fact that some, though not all, of them pay tribute to the Paramount Power. (These contributions, chiefly in lieu of former obligations to supply or maintain troops, range in amount from the million dollars or more paid each year to the raj by the government of Mysore to the thirty-four dollars per annum paid by the state of Rambrai.) Allegiance to the British raj—or alliance, as they prefer to phrase it—has not only immensely increased the security of the princes by insuring them protection against aggression from without and revolution within, but it has magnified their importance and flattered their vanity by focusing upon them the agreeable lime-light of publicity at coronations, durbars and other functions, where many of them have outshone the king-emperor himself. Be it understood that they consider it no more derogatory to their dignity as rulers to acknowledge the supremacy of a throne as ancient and splendid as the British than their ancestors did in acknowledging the suzerainty of the Grand Mogul, or than the rulers of the various German states did when they accepted the political paramountcy of the house of Hohenzollern. And, in point of might and magnificence, George V has proved as satisfactory an overlord as the great Akbar, the Mogul conqueror who made himself emperor of Hindustan in the sixteenth century.

The relative importance of the princes in the eyes of the British raj may be pretty accurately gaged by the salutes to which they are entitled. Thus, the Nizam of Hyderabad, the Gaekwar of Baroda, the maharajahs of Kashmir, Mysore and Gwalior receive twenty-one guns on occasions of ceremony. Chieftains of lesser magnitude receive seventeen, fifteen, thirteen or eleven guns, while there is a long list of nawabs, rajahs, sahibs, sultans, sawbwas and thakurs who are honored by only nine bursts of gun-fire. About four fifths of the five hundred-odd ruling princes, however, receive no artillery salutes at all. But those who are entitled to them rarely forego the honor. For no prima donna was ever more jealous of her prerogatives, more insistent on being assigned the best dressing-room and having her name displayed over the theatre-entrance in electric lights, than these beturbaned royalties are of receiving their full number of guns.

Novelists and dramatists have long been accustomed to depict the Indian states as enveloped in mystery, romance and glamour, as reeking with intrigue, iniquity and lawlessness. They have portrayed the princes as spendthrifts, sensualists and tyrants, with priceless jewels in their turbans and million-dollar strings of pearls about their necks, whose chief interests in life are beautiful houris, tiger shooting and plotting against the British raj. Such pictures are ridiculous and untruthful for, though there is no denying that certain of the princes are bad actors, and that many of them have their moral or political shortcomings, the vast majority are earnest, able, hard-working men, loyal, even if not deeply attached, to the British Government, devoted to the welfare of their subjects, and with a deep sense of their responsibilities.

India is a land of contrasts and contradictions and nowhere are they more noticeable than at the native courts. I have seen princes as magnificently appareled as were their ancestors who clustered about the Peacock Throne, clad in silks and velvets and brocades, loaded with pearls and jewels, and I have spent a morning with a prince who received me in pajamas and nightcap. I have lunched with a maharajah who wore in his ears a pair of black pearls for which he had paid a quarter of a million dollars, and I have dined with another ruler whose sole item of jewelry consisted of a modest seal-ring. In Rajputana I was the guest of a prince who placed at my disposal for sight-seeing purposes an elephant caparisoned in gold and crimson, yet one of his neighboring rulers, whom I visited a few days later, sent me about his dominions in a limousine. There was pointed out to me at a viceregal garden party a maharajah who had recently flogged a valuable pony to death with his own hand because it had "let him down" in a championship polo game, and the same afternoon I had tea with a youthful potentate, also a polo player, who discussed at length, and with great enthusiasm, the work done in his dominions by the Society for the Prevention of Cruelty to Animals. I have held delightful conversations with the aged Begum of Bhopal, who recently abdicated in favor of her son, regarding her labors for child welfare and the amelioration of Indian women, and I have sat at table with a maharajah who is credited with having shot his girl-wife dead because she refused to yield herself to another man in her husband's presence. I am acquainted with a prince who was the greatest cricketer of his time, with another who is ranked among the world's greatest polo players, with a third whose idea of sport is to sit in a red plush box and watch combats between tigers and elephants. I can name at least three princes who have the right to put LL.D. after their names, and another who is prouder of the M.D. he received from an English university, where he completed a course in medicine, than of all his glittering decorations. The Maharajah of Travancore, a Hindu, thought to attain spiritual salvation by constructing a golden cow and then publicly crawling through it; the Nawab of Bhopal, a Moslem, attests his faith by abstaining from all food or drink between sunrise and sunset during the fasting month of Ramadan. In one Native state I was shown prisons which are as up-to-date and as humanely conducted as any to be found in America; in a neighboring state criminals are still confined in unlighted, unsanitary, subterranean dungeons. I know one prince whose pink palace is as large and, in its way, as beautiful as that of Versailles; another whose modest residence would be scorned by many American millionaires, but who has spent millions of rupees on schools and hospitals. And so it goes. There are good and bad among the Indian princes, kind and cruel, progressive and reactionary, just as among other men. But, so far as a visitor like myself could judge, they are characterized on the whole by high standards of intelligence and conduct. It is extremely unjust that the whole of them, nearly six hundred in number, should be judged by the widely advertised follies and iniquities of a few.

The most frequent criticism of the Indian princes is that they are spendthrifts, that they squander on themselves what, if spent at all, should be devoted to the needs of their people. In many cases this criticism is justified; in more it is not. But it is the few spectacular spenders whom we hear about. There can be no denying, however, that the great majority of the princes live in a fashion which would bring the rulers of far larger European states to the verge of bankruptcy—or revolution. India is by no means as rich as most people suppose; the Indian people are poor, so it is all the more astonishing that their princes should have seemingly unlimited cash at their command.

They arrive in London or Paris accompanied by huge entourages of ministers, secretaries and servants, often with women-folk by the score, and take whole floors in the most fashionable hotels. They are lavish spenders in the expensive shops along Bond Street and the Rue de la Paix. At Windsor King George has for a neighbor the Maharajah of Rajpipla—a state but little larger than Rhode Island—with stables of race-horses and polo ponies, garages filled with motor-cars, an army of retainers. Two or three years ago the Rajah of Rutlam, whose territory is only 800 square miles in area, took an Indian polo team to Meadow Brook and himself bore the bulk of the expense. The dethroned Maharajah of Indore maintains an establishment near St. Germain which makes the members of the old French nobility who are his neighbors look like paupers. The Maharajah of Kapurthala, whose collection of emeralds is said to rival that of the late czar of All the Russias, spends the Paris season in a house in the Bois de Boulogne—one of the few private residences actually within those leafy precincts—where he gives fêtes whose beauty and magnificence astonish the French capital. The Aga Khan, the head of all the Mohammedans of India, who is supported by the contributions of the pious, keeps half-a-dozen racing stables in France alone, a shooting-box in Scotland, an apartment in Paris and a château on the Riviera. Another Indian ruler is said to have lost a million francs in a single evening last year on the gaming tables of the International Sporting Club at Monte Carlo.

The splendor in which many of the princes live when at home in India is almost unbelievable. The Maharajah of Patiala has his private race-course, his polo field, kennels containing four hundred dogs of various breeds, huge stables of elephants and horses, and in the royal garage are upward of three hundred motor-cars, including forty-two Rolls-Royces. The twelve-year-old Maharajah of Gwalior lives in a marble palace which would contain a dozen White Houses and then have room to spare, and on ceremonial occasions wears a string of pearls valued at two millions of dollars about his boyish neck. The deposed Maharajah of Indore, on the eve of his departure into exile, issued orders that feasts should be given in every community and sacks of sugar dumped into every well in the kingdom, in order, as he expressed it, that he might "leave a sweet taste in the mouths of his people"! When the young Nawab of Bhopal arrived in Delhi last winter to attend the Chamber of Princes he brought with him, in addition to the members of his family, scores of ministers, secretaries and aides-de-camp, more than a hundred servants, a detachment of household troops, sixty polo ponies and forty motor-cars —all this for a sojourn of only a fortnight. Another prince recently purchased the beautiful club-house of the Gymkhana Club in New Delhi for use as a residence during the few weeks he spends in the capital each year. A quite minor rajah has had built to his order a motor-car for big-game hunting, with steel buffers to protect it from the charge of infuriated animals, a mammoth headlight to dazzle tigers, racks for rifles, a refrigerator for champagne and a first-aid outfit. The ruler of another unimportant state, who invited the viceroy to visit him last winter, is said to have spent $200,000 preparing for the two-day visit—and even then he had to borrow elephants, motor-cars, carriages and uniforms from his neighbors.

Where does the money come from for this sort of thing? No one seems to know. In any event, it was a question to which I received no satisfactory answer. It is true that the incomes of some of the princes are enormous. The revenues of the richest of them all, the Nizam of Hyderabad, total seven and a half crores of rupees, or about twenty-five million dollars, but from these revenues are defrayed all the expenses of running a state the size of Kansas. It is also true that certain of the princes have inherited huge fortunes, that they have fabulous wealth tied up in jewels and plate. Others are heavy holders of foreign securities which yield them handsome returns. It is to be assumed, however, that the majority of them obtain the vast sums which they spend so lavishly by taxing their subjects, though it may be remarked that taxation in the Native states is not as oppressive as might be supposed. The British residents see to that.

Were India a prosperous country, rich in natural resources, there would be less criticism of princely extravagance. But it is not very rich and not at all prosperous, at least according to American standards. Though the popular conception of the wealth of the "gorgeous East" is singularly deep-rooted, the truth is that only a small proportion of the soil can be characterized as fertile. Millions of peasants in India are struggling to live on half an acre. Their dwellings are hovels. Their live stock is constantly underfed. Their own existence is a never-ending battle with starvation, closing, too often, in defeat. Their problem is not to live *human* lives—lives up to the level of their poor standard of comfort—but to live at all and not to die.

I do not wish to be understood as suggesting that extravagance is characteristic of all the Indian princes, for such is not the fact. For every case of wilful extravagance on the part of an Indian ruler there are half-a-dozen where personal expenditure is limited almost to the point of frugality. It frequently happens, however, that a wise and beneficent rule is followed by the reckless administration of a youthful spendthrift, and the ruin of the country is only to be averted by intervention. But the Supreme Government never exercises its right to step in and take control until the internal affairs of a state have become intolerably bad.

The more thoughtful of the native rulers are fully alive to the discontent which is being bred by the squandering of money obtained through taxation, and at a recent session of the Chamber of Princes a resolution was passed advocating separate allowances for the princes instead of permitting them to help themselves from the state exchequer. As the Chamber of Princes is a purely consultative body, without any legislative power whatsoever, and as all discussions in the chamber of the internal affairs of individual states and the actions of individual rulers is absolutely prohibited, this was only a pious gesture. But it was high time that something of the sort was done, for the present haphazard financial system fosters many grave abuses and there is observable a steadily rising tide of popular discontent.

Judging from my own observations, and from my conversations with both British and Indian officials, I have little doubt that the majority of the inhabitants of the Native states prefer to remain under their own princes rather than come under direct British control. This feeling is almost invariably due to personal loyalty to the princes, for their subjects quite generally admit that British administration is more efficient and that the British standard of public morality is higher than the Indian. But the vague unrest—we will call it the awakening of national consciousness for want of a better term—the disposition to question constituted authority, which has swept all Asia in recent years, has not left the Native states untouched. The people are as respectful to their princes as ever, and as loyal, but they are more disposed to stand upon their rights, less willing to accept autocratic decisions blindly. Save, perhaps, in some of the remoter and less progressive states, the people no longer regard their rulers as demigods who can do no wrong.

Though I am convinced that the majority of the Indian princes are genuinely anxious to give their states honest and efficient administrations; though many of them have received European educations either at home or abroad and speak English as fluently as any Briton; though they drive high-powered cars and install radios in their palaces and carry on their correspondence with the aid of typewriters and dictaphones, the veneer of Western civilization is in many cases very thin. In their fear of their gods, their subservience to their priests, their childlike superstitions, they are essentially Easterns.

Consider the case of the Maharajah of Jammu and Kashmir, Sir Hari Singh. Though he sits on the throne of a Mohammedan state, he is an orthodox Hindu. He was educated at Mayo College in Ajmere, the Eton of India; served as page to Lord Curzon when that very superior person was viceroy; went to England with an unlimited letter of credit, a million-dollar string of pearls and a bediamonded turban; and sprang into instant popularity in the British metropolis as a host and a sportsman. He entertained lavishly; was an intimate of the Prince of Wales; was lionized by society, particularly by the ladies.

Suddenly, without explanation, almost overnight, he closed his great establishments and sailed for India. The clubs and drawing-rooms of London were agog with rumors. Shortly these rumors crystallized in print—in front-page newspaper stories. Sir Hari, heir to one of the greatest thrones in India, inheritor of a historic name, had become involved in a peculiarly unsavory scandal with an Englishwoman, a victim of what is known in America as the "badger game." He had been blackmailed by the woman and her husband and their confederate, a former officer in the British army, to the tune of many thousands of pounds—and had paid.

The British Government, fully alive to the danger of outraging public opinion in Kashmir (the majority of the inhabitants of that state, as I have already remarked, are Mohammedans, whereas Sir Hari is a Hindu), fully cognizant of the power exercised by the priesthood, did its utmost to hush the scandal up, to soft-pedal public discussion. Unable to quash the court proceedings, however, officials of the India Office sought to envelop the identity of the chief actor in mystery by having him referred to as "Mr. A." That, of course, served only to whet public curiosity and to bring about further disclosures.

Meanwhile Sir Hari had reached Kashmir. His welcome by the priests and by his subjects was not an effusive one. Mind you, they did not object to what he had done on any moral grounds, but they did object to his having contaminated himself by intercourse with a European woman. Also, there was much talk about the millions of rupees which he had squandered in high living abroad instead of spending on his people at home. He was ordered by the priests to subject himself to the most humiliating penances

—and meekly obeyed. He shaved his head and his mustache, among other things, and spent a ten-day period of purification in the forest. Thoroughly cowed and chastened, this one-time pet of Mayfair drawing-rooms succeeded to the throne, and now all is forgiven if not forgotten.

Then there was the even more recent case of the much-married Maharajah of Indore, who had been dethroned because of his complicity in the Mumtaz Begum episode. Making a tour of the world, he stopped off at Seattle and fell in love with an American girl, Nancy Ann Miller. He already had several wives in Indore, but that circumstance did not prevent him from asking Miss Miller to join his matrimonial establishment, or her from accepting. Nor did she enter into the affair with her eyes closed; no pains were spared to acquaint her with her fiancé's unsavory history. On her arrival at Bombay the American consul, under instructions from the State Department, went out to the steamer and pleaded with her for hours. But she was adamantine.

Then arose an unforseen obstacle to the ex-maharajah's wedding plans. Instigated by his Indian wives, who would have made no objection had the latest bride been an Indian, the priests intervened, declaring that the American girl, being an unbeliever, could not be married to a high-caste Hindu. After weeks of arguments, threats, and persuasions they reluctantly agreed to convert Miss Miller to Hinduism, but their assent was obtained only at a price and by the maharajah's threat that he would become a Mohammedan.

Nothing was left undone to humiliate the detested foreigner. She was purified by ceremonial bathing and then by being smeared with ashes and cow-dung. She walked barefoot around the sacrificial fire, chanting verses from the Matras. She kissed the feet of the high priest and ate

THE CIRCUS IS COMING?

Not at all. Merely a state elephant, frescoed and panoplied, going to the palace to take the maharajah for a ride

A two-bullock-power touring car

A brougham for the women of the zenana

WHEN BETTER BULLOCK-CARTS ARE BUILT, INDIA WILL BUILD THEM

cocoanut from his hand. She poured clarified butter on the knees of a leering idol. Thus she gradually and painfully attained to that high caste of Hinduism, indicated by a painted dot upon the forehead, which enabled her debauched lover to marry her without contaminating himself. No sooner were the wedding festivities over than the couple shook the dust of India from their feet. They now make their home in a château in the outskirts of Paris, far from the smell of *ghee* and incense, from the sound of temple bells. The last time I saw the maharanee, at a tennis tournament, she was looking haggard and worn.

More than one Indian prince has defied his priests and his people by marrying a European woman, but in almost every case that I can recall these mixed marriages have ended in disaster. There was the Maharajah of Kapurthala, for example, who offered his heart, his jewels and a share of his throne to a bewitchingly beautiful Spanish dancing-girl, Anita Delgrado. So they were married, she in the spring of life and he in the autumn, but they did not live happily ever after. For soon the elderly maharajah was yawning and winding his watch while the satin-shod feet of the dainty Anita were impatiently tapping the floor in tune with the dance music. So, having the jewels, she divorced him and married one of his sons by another wife. You can see the handsome couple dancing almost any evening during the season at the Ritz in Paris. They are seemingly quite happy.

Despotism is making its last stand in the Native states of India. They constitute the sole remnants of the world's autocracies. Above the Forbidden City the dragon banner has been replaced by the standard of the Chinese Republic, and a one-time runaway apprentice boy occupies the presidential chair. The Emperor of Japan, a representative of an autocratic dynasty which goes back unbrokenly for five and twenty centuries, has about as much real power as the President of France. The Korean emperors are but historic memories. The Shah of Persia, a dozen years ago a humble trooper in the Cossack horse, is sternly curbed by the Majlis. Turkey, under the dictatorship of its grim soldier-president, seems bent on outwesternizing the West. The Autocrat of All the Russians lies in an unknown grave and the red banner of bolshevism flaunts triumphantly from Moscow to Vladivostok. The Sultan of Morocco is a puppet and the French resident at Rabat pulls the strings.

In the Indian states, and there alone, you may still see what was meant by the age-long despotisms of Asia. There you may still envision those gorgeous and dramatic figures whose simitars maintained the Peacock Throne, with their fabulous wealth and unimaginable splendor; their love of magnificence and pomp, their reckless extravagance, their enervating luxury, their curious customs and deeply rooted superstitions, their palaces ornate, vast and impenetrable, their jealously guarded zenanas, their veiled concubines and sinuous, bejeweled dancing-girls, their belief that women were created for the sensual gratification of men, their contempt for human life, their terrible tortures and awful punishments, their treasure houses filled with gold and jewels, their squadrons of mail-clad horsemen, their hordes of servants and retainers, their fairylike lakes and scented gardens, their priests and idols, their elephants and tigers. The successors of those chieftains, Hindu, Moslem, Sikh and Jain, Punjabi, Bengali, Rajput and Mahratta, still hold autocratic sway in but slightly diminished splendor, still stand fast against the rising tide of democracy, the trustees of a past that elsewhere lives only in poetry.

The Aga Khan, whom I mentioned earlier in this chapter,

while not a ruling prince, for he has no territory, nevertheless exercises more political influence in India than any individual native ruler. This by reason of the fact that he is the spiritual head of the thirty million Mohammedans in India. His sanctity is so great, indeed, in the eyes of his followers, that the water in which he bathes is carefully conserved and sold annually to the representatives of the various Mohammedan sects at a ceremony held once each year at Aga Hall in Bombay. The price paid for this holy water is the Aga Khan's own weight in gold, the scales used for the weighing ceremony being adjusted to the fraction of an ounce troy. As the Aga Khan is a plump little man the price paid for his used bath water is a high one.

It is generally understood that, in recognition of his services in keeping the Moslems of India loyal to Britain, the Aga Khan receives a secret and by no means inconsiderable subsidy from the British raj. His value to the Paramount Power was strikingly evidenced early in 1929, when he presided at the All-Indian Mohammedan conference, held in Delhi. The most momentous question on the agenda was whether the assembled Moslems should indorse the demand, made a few weeks before by the Indian National Congress, a Hindu organization, that India should be granted "dominion status" within a year. The Aga Khan, an eloquent orator and an astute statesman, solved the dilemma by deftly guiding the Mohammedan conference into adopting a resolution which completely ignored the Hindu demands. Whereupon British officialdom heaved a deep sigh of relief, for the virile, warlike Moslems count for far more than the servile, easy-going Hindus, even though the latter vastly outnumber them. If the Aga Khan is worth his weight in gold to his Moslem followers, to the British whom he so steadfastly befriends he should be worth his weight in diamonds.

That the tide of democracy is rising in India, and rising fast, no observing person can doubt. Read the editorials in the vernacular press, which, if printed a few years ago, would have brought their authors to trial on a charge of sedition; listen to the impassioned speeches of Mahatma Gandhi and the other native leaders; hearken to the debates in the Indian legislature; note the altered demeanor of the once-haughty British officials and of the Government of India itself. You may be certain that the princes, no less than the British, see and hear these signs of the approaching storm, for they have their eyes fixed anxiously on the political horizon, their ears to the ground.

The truth of the matter is that the princes are in a most anomalous and perplexing situation. They are torn between a desire to shake off British domination and the knowledge that if the British left that their days as rulers would be numbered. There is no doubt that the majority of the princes secretly detest the British—an assertion to which any Englishman of long experience in India, if he can be persuaded to speak candidly, will testify. But this is not saying that the vast majority of them are not wholly loyal to the British raj, for they are perfectly aware that in the maintenance of British rule lies their own political salvation.

Consider, for a moment, the easy and enviable position of a prince under British protection. He is secure against invasion of his state from without or rebellion within. He need maintain no costly military establishment, for his territories are defended for him. He need engage in no wars, save those in which he joins voluntarily in the cause of the empire, as a great number of the princes did in the World War. His state benefits from the railways and public works built and maintained by the Supreme Government, from its postal and fiscal systems. He can appeal to it for financial assistance, for technical advice, for practical instruction in the multitudinous phases of administration. The princes are well off under British rule and they know it.

They do not want the British to leave; they want them to stay. Their ever-present fear, indeed, is that Britain may desert them; that a constitutional form of government, under one guise or another, may be forced upon them; that they will wake up one morning to find the Nationalists in power, their rulerships swept away, and themselves not much more than peers. Many profess to believe that the first step in this program was taken when the government set up the Chamber of Princes, which might ultimately become an Indian House of Lords—and with about as much power as its counterpart at Westminster.

What threatens the princes is not the constitutional liberty which the peoples of British India are seeking, and which the Simon commission has advocated giving them in gradually increasing doses, but the deepening desire for unity in India as a whole. And this can only be effected at the expense of the princes. When Louis XI achieved some measure of unity in France it was by crushing the great nobles. In England the Tudors so dealt with the feudal barons. The union of Italy under the house of Savoy cost a score of petty sovereigns their thrones. Bismarck welded the German states into an empire and turned their kings, grand dukes and electors into puppets. But more than a third of all India is still ruled by autocratic princes. For the other two thirds, which comprise British India, autonomy within the empire is seemingly not far away. The question is, then: Shall India become one nation from Cape Comorin to the Himalayas, from the Irawadi to the Arabian Sea, or shall it continue part feudal and part free?

No one knows, save a handful of high officials, what

Britain's future policy in regard to India is likely to be, for it is not a topic which is shouted from the housetops. My own guess is that the bureaucrats who run the India Office would prefer to see the Native states maintain something very like their present political status. And this from reasons of imperial safety rather than from sentiment, for the Indian princes, whether they like England or not, are bound to her by ties of self-interest. The British know that so long as the princes remain loyal to the raj, so long can the aspirations of the Nationalists be kept in bounds. And the princes, for their part, know that as long as Britain continues to give them her protection, to enforce their treaty rights, the wave of nationalism which is sweeping over British India will not be permitted to engulf their territories.

In the final analysis the situation resolves itself not into a struggle between British and Indians, as most people suppose, but into a struggle between autocracy, as represented by the princes, and democracy as represented by the Nationalists. The immediate question is, How long can autocracy maintain its present position? Of course, no intelligent person seriously doubts that democracy will be triumphant in the end.

It was in order to find out just where they stand, just what they may expect, that a delegation composed of the most astute and influential Indian princes recently went to London. They went to seek an exact definition of their status within the Indian Empire and to work out a scheme for safeguarding the integrity of the Native states in the event that a further measure of home rule is given to British India as a result of the findings of the Simon commission. The interests of their states are already subordinated to those of British India, the princes declare, and affirm that, should the latter be granted an increased measure of self-government, they and their states would be threatened with political extinction.

Judging from my conversations with the Maharajah of Patiala, who is chancellor of the Chamber of Princes, and several of his fellow-rulers, I obtained the impression that the princes are pretty generally agreed that some form of Indian federation is inevitable. A plan has been worked out which would secure the participation of the princes in all-Indian affairs, but which would leave both Native and British India free to pursue their own lines of development in domestic matters. Whether such a solution would win the approval of the Nationalists in India and their supporters at Westminster is, however, open to grave question. If the Nationalists have their way, and Indian unity is effected, it can only mean that the Native states will become provinces and that the princes must step down from their jeweled thrones into political oblivion. And, from the picturesque and romantic points of view at least, that would be a pity.

CHAPTER V

IN THE SHADOW OF THE BLOODY GODDESS

LONG, long before the first white man set foot in Hindustan, a spot on the Hugli, twoscore miles above its mouth, was consecrated to the worship of the goddess Kali, the Hindu deity of darkness and destruction. Here, at a landing-place on the river-bank known as the Kali Ghat, a religious community arose, gilded temple spires sprang skyward, dark and bloody rites were performed. Hard by this place of mystery and horror, in the closing years of the seventeenth century, an agent of the East India Company—Job Charnock was his rugged name—established a trading-post which, in spite of its unhealthful situation, was destined to become an imperial capital. From the steps leading to the sanctuary of an unclean goddess Calcutta took its name.

Though Calcutta is the second city of the whole British Empire, it has little save its wealth to recommend it. From an architectural point of view it has scarcely a building worthy of a second glance. There is not one really good hotel, not a residence that is remarkable for beauty either of outline or decoration. The native quarter is abominable—a district of narrow, filthy, overcrowded streets, of dilapidated buildings, of dust and refuse and offensive smells. The *bastis,* or hamlets of mud hovels, which form an unsightly fringe, amply justify the reproach that, though Calcutta may be a "city of palaces" in front, it is one of pig-sties in the rear.

Even its position is ill-chosen, for it stands on a dead

flat, low-lying plain, bordered by a pestilential marsh, so that during the greater part of the year it swelters in an atmosphere as close and humid as that of a steam-laundry fatal alike to mental and physical vigor. Yet Calcutta is by no means as unhealthy as might be assumed, and enjoys, moreover, a distinct period of cold weather which is not to be found in the other presidency towns. There are days in winter when the climate is as nearly perfect as climate can be, bright, clear and bracing, without any bitterness of cold. But this pleasant season, all too short, is succeeded by months that are insufferably hot, humid and enervating, when the mercury climbs above the 100 mark, and even under an electric fan one is bathed in perspiration.

Despite the excessive cost of living there, Calcutta is crowded with visitors during the cold weather, which lasts from early December to mid-February, for no city in India can offer so many social attractions or such a varied program of amusements. The Indian Grand National, the greatest sporting event in India, is run at Christmastide on the Maidan. There are polo tournaments between teams representing various of the Native states and the crack cavalry regiments of the Indian army. Cricket matches between All-India and the M.C.C. Glittering state functions at Government House, balls at the Saturday Club, regimental dinners at Firpo's, gymkhanas, fancy-dress parties. The hotels and clubs and boarding-houses are filled to the doors with provincial officials and their families, native princes with their suites, up-country planters, and tourists who have come out from home. This is an aspect of Indian life, however, of which most American visitors see nothing, for the round-the-world tourist steamers seldom drop anchor in the Hugli until the season is over and the hot weather has set in. For, toward the end of February, the season ends abruptly; the visitors depart; the governor and his household hasten to the hills; the clubs and hotels are all but deserted; and for nine months the city is enveloped in an atmosphere of social stagnation.

The fashionable life of Calcutta centers about a vast open space known as the Maidan, its turf scorched by the sun to a tawny brown during the greater part of the year, but a brilliant green during the rains. It is a park, a parade ground and a playing-field in one, for it is intersected by winding drives and dotted with statues of the soldiers and statesmen who enabled England to win and hold her Indian Empire; it provides a setting for military reviews; within its borders are race-courses, polo fields, tennis courts, cricket and football grounds; and a portion of it is occupied by the public gardens.

The Maidan is bounded on one side by the Chowringhee, a thoroughfare lined by smart shops, clubs and restaurants, which forms the front of the fashionable European residential quarter. On the other side, beyond the Eden Gardens, rise the masts and funnels of the shipping in the river. Paralleling the northern boundary of the Maidan is the tree-lined Esplanade, bordered by the spacious grounds of Government House, the residence of the Governor of Bengal, the imposing gateway surmounted, appropriately enough, by a Bengal tiger. At the opposite end, a good mile and a half away, may be descried, rising above the encircling gardens and lagoons, the great white dome of the Victoria Memorial.

To the north of Government House, fronting on or adjacent to Dalhousie Square, lie the European official and commercial quarters, with the colonnaded town hall, the unlovely post-office, the court-house with its slender tower, modeled after the Hotel de Ville at Ypres (one marvels at the incongruity of a Flemish building in an East

Indian setting), and a number of lofty office buildings, the whole dominated by the enormous, many-galleried, red brick pile of the Bengal Secretariat, the seat of the provincial political administration.

But the picturesque landmarks of Calcutta's early and hectic history have almost entirely disappeared before the march of progress. Fort William, begun by Clive after the Battle of Plassey, has been massaged and manicured by landscape architects until it is now scarcely recognizable as a fortification. The "Black Hole" of evil memory, that small and stifling room into which one hundred and forty-six English men, women and children were cast by order of Siraj-ud-Daula, and from which only twenty-three came out alive the next day, is commemorated by a weather-beaten column. One of the few other links with the past is the marble slab in old St. John's, beneath which Job Charnock, the founder of Calcutta, lies buried.

This Charnock must have been a curious and determined character, if the old accounts are to be credited. Some years after he had established his trading-post beside the Kali Ghat he went, accompanied by his usual military escort. to attend the funeral ceremonies of a deceased rajah whom he had known. As was the custom in India until comparatively recent times, the rajah's widow, young and beautiful, was to be burned alive upon her husband's funeral pyre. But the agent of the "John Company" was so smitten with the intended victim's slim and delicate beauty that he forbade the *suttee*. When the priests and mourners protested he ordered his sowars to take the girl from them by force and convey her to his own home. They lived together happily for many years and had several children. But, instead of Charnock converting her to Christianity, she converted him to Hinduism. His conversion could not have been complete, however, for when she died, instead of permitting the body to be burned in accordance with Hindu custom, he gave it Christian burial, though on each anniversary of her death until his own he sacrificed a white cock upon her tomb.

In certain respects Calcutta is as up-to-date as any European city, with pavements, elevatored office buildings, street-cars, taxis (driven recklessly by turbaned pirates), theaters, motion-picture houses and traffic policemen. But imagine, if you please, a municipality with more than a million and a quarter inhabitants which permits herds of cattle to wander along its streets and sidewalks at will. I have seen a spotted heifer poke her head inquisitively into the doorway of the smartest jeweler's shop in the Chowringhee, and I have seen a policeman on duty in Dalhousie Square, which is the Times Square of Calcutta, hold up an avalanche of traffic in order that the leisurely peregrinations of three untended cows might not be interrupted.

Aside from its immense commercial importance—its annual imports and exports have a total value of three quarters of a billion dollars—Calcutta's appeal is mainly a social one, though its prestige in this respect was dealt a staggering blow in 1912, when the seat of government and the viceregal court were transferred for political and climatic reasons to Delhi, the ancient capital of the Mogul emperors.

But if Delhi has become the capital of India, its Washington, Calcutta remains its metropolis, its New York. Of all the cities of the peninsula, it is the most English in atmosphere. Here the homesick exile, if he possesses a sufficiently elastic imagination, can conceive of himself as back in Mayfair or Piccadilly. Here is the Bengal Club, the finest and most exclusive in all Asia. Once within its jealously guarded portals, were it not for the rows of pith topées in the cloak-room, and the turbaned, barefoot servants, the visitor might well imagine himself in one of the clubs along Pall Mall—at least until he looked out of the window. Here is the Saturday Club, where thrice weekly fashionable Calcutta gathers to dine and dance on a superb floor to the syncopated strains of an excellent jazz band. Here, too, is Firpo's, the smartest restaurant and night club in India, where you can get lobsters, if you have the courage to eat them, since they come from the Hugli, upon whose banks the Hindus burn their dead. On Sunday mornings you can motor out to one of the numerous country clubs for breakfast, and wash down your bacon and eggs with cherry brandy. Or you can spend a leisurely afternoon on the river with a visit to the Botanical Gardens, an enchanting wilderness of tropic trees and shrubs and flowers, of leafy avenues and winding lagoons; to Barrackpore, the imposing country seat of the Governor of Bengal; or, still farther up-stream, to the forgotten French colony of Chandernagor, over which the tricolor still floats.

My roving eye was attracted, both in Calcutta and Madras, by the great number of good-looking and extremely chic young women whom I saw in the shops, restaurants, dance clubs and tea-rooms. Though their gowns were usually a shade too flamboyant in color, a trifle too daring; though some of them were a bit overpowdered and overcarmined, with a suggestion of boldness (perhaps defiance would be a better word) about the mouth and eyes, they were, on the whole, as attractive a lot of young girls as I have seen anywhere.

"There's a stunning girl," I remarked on one occasion to an English friend with whom I was dining at Firpo's, indicating a svelte brunette in a geranium-colored gown. "What a lovely figure and complexion! She looks as though she might have some French or Spanish blood in her veins."

"She probably has," he replied dryly, after a brief appraising glance, "but with a dash of the tar-brush thrown in. She is pretty enough, I admit—but she is a Eurasian."

His tone, in which pity, cynicism and contempt were mingled, was that which would be employed by an American in speaking of a pretty octoroon, or by a European in the Philippines of a beautiful mestizo.

When Europeans and Indians intermarry, the children of these unions are Eurasians—or Anglo-Indians, as it is now the fashion to refer to those who have one English parent. Not only the English, therefore, but the Portuguese, the Dutch, the French and the Jews have all contributed to the 130,000 Eurasians in India, and are to be recognized in the names borne by their descendants. Almeida, da Souza, Fonseca, Corneille are all common patronymics among the Eurasians, and the bearers are probably entitled to them, but such names as Claudius or Cornelius suggest that they are assumed and hint at the existence of the bar sinister. Eurasians nearly always call themselves Europeans, and it is often impossible for a stranger in India to detect the difference, though there are certain slight physical peculiarities which betray the admixture of native blood even to the third and fourth generation.

Some Eurasians are engaged in trade, but the vast majority of them find clerical employment in government offices or business houses, or on the railways, and in these capacities often attain to positions of trust, dignity and honor. Poverty is common among them, however, this being due in part, no doubt, to their early marriages and enormous families, but even more to the fact that many of them, deserted by their European fathers, have had to shift for themselves.

The lot of the Eurasians as a whole is a very trying one, yet their plight commands very little sympathy from either European or Indian. They are socially ostracized by the former, and, being neither flesh, fish nor foul, are regarded by the latter with a mixture of contempt and suspicion. No matter how beautiful a Eurasian girl may be—and some of them are very lovely indeed, with lustrous eyes and flawless complexions—or how accomplished or how well mannered, all European doors are closed to her. Of course, she can always find men, eager for the company of any woman who has a pretty face and can speak their own tongue, who will take her to theaters and cinemas, to restaurants and night clubs, for rides in the country or boating on the river. But they never dream of taking her to their clubs to dine and dance or of introducing her to European women. It happens not infrequently, however, that lonely young Englishmen marry Eurasian girls in spite of Society's frowns. That is why nearly all the clubs in India have an unwritten rule which requires a member to hand in his resignation when he marries. If his bride is a European he is automatically restored to membership; but should she be a Eurasian, he never crosses the threshold of the club again. As a result of this rigid observance of the color line many attractive Eurasian girls, often convent-reared and with as light skins as any Englishwoman, rather than take native or half-caste husbands, become the mistresses of Europeans who refuse to jeopardize their careers by marrying them.

Another class deserving of great sympathy is composed of young Englishmen without private means who have come out to India to enter the employ of mercantile concerns. Though Calcutta, Bombay and Madras are among the most expensive cities in the world to live in, these young men are usually miserably paid, yet they are required to dress well, to live in decent quarters and to keep up their end to a certain extent socially. How they manage to exist is a matter of speculation to every one. As they cannot afford to join the clubs which are the centers of European social life and relaxation, and as in the European colony the men outnumber the women two to one, it is not surprising that these homesick youngsters should turn for female companionship to the pretty Eurasians, who are generally only too willing.

Sooner or later every visitor to Calcutta makes an excursion to the quarter known as the Kali Ghat, where, within a temple which is an orgy of carvings, obscenity and horror, the goddess of evil sits enthroned.

You can drive out to the Kali Ghat by motor in twenty minutes, or you can go by river, which is more interesting. With a little license the Hugli may be considered a branch of the Ganges, and here at least is held as sacred as the mother stream. You land at the ghat, or water-stairs, where, particularly in the early morning, thousands of the pious may be seen washing away their sins and cleansing their skins at the same time.

From the river-bank a narrow, evil-smelling lane, lined on either side by shrines of minor deities and stalls in which articles of a religious nature are sold, leads directly to the temple. The lane is crowded with jostling worshipers, priests, temple girls, beggars, *gurus,* holy men. Here are Akacamukhiris and Urdhvatalines, who pose themselves in immovable attitudes, their arms raised to heaven, until the sinews shrink, the joints harden and permanent rigidity sets in. Here are Nagas, Paramahanavas, Avadhutas and others, who in a state of absolute nudity expose themselves to the inclemency of the weather or blister their flesh by sitting within a ring of charcoal fires. Here, too, are fanatics who stretch their emaciated limbs upon beds of sharpened spikes, or clench their fists until the nails pierce flesh and sinew and protrude from the back of their hands. Squatting on the pavement, forming a double line from river-side to temple door, are mendicants suffering from maladies and mutilations so revolting that one's natural sense of pity retreats before the horror of it all. The faces of some are little more than grinning skulls, the features eaten away by black leprosy; others display shocking mutilations; the limbs of still others are twisted by paralysis or mottled with gaping, ulcerous sores; all are caked with filth and acrawl with vermin; all stare at the passer-by with crazy eyes through tangled mats of hair. The stenches are overpowering, the pandemonium appalling. The clamor, frenzied, terrible, beats brazenly against your ear-drums, stupefies your brain, until the mind reels and the world seems to consist of one enormous, overpowering Noise.

This avenue of agonies ends at the gateway to the temple. A flight of steps leads to the pillared portico which surrounds the shrine. The unbeliever may not penetrate the sanctuary itself, but, standing in the portico, he can obtain a view of the dim interior and catch periodical glimses of the idol when, at regular intervals, the great doors which conceal the holy of holies swing back. Shouldered and jostled by the throng of worshipers, we wondered what climax of horror would come next.

We did not have long to wait. Slowly the ponderous doors swung outward, the prostrate pious united in a gasp of awe and adoration, and for a brief moment stood revealed the monstrous effigy of the evil goddess who strikes terror to the hearts of the millions in Bengal. A four-armed woman with out-thrust scarlet tongue and long, disheveled hair, her naked body painted corpse-blue, trampling on the prostrate form of a demon. About her neck a string of skulls, about her loins a bloody girdle. In one hand she grasps a reddened sword; in another a gory human head. A third hand points downward toward hell; the fourth upward toward heaven. The priests chant lugubriously, the worshipers moan in ecstasy, gongs boom and the doors swing shut. We unobtrusively depart. The house of Kali is not a place in which it is wise to linger.

At the back of the temple, in a stone-paved courtyard, a little stream of incredibly foul water trickles through a sort of open drain. This water is sacrosanct, for it has washed Kali's feet. Hindus by the score are stretched prone upon the pavement, lapping up the filthy liquid like thirsty dogs. No, that is not a good simile, for any self-respecting dog would turn away from such water in disgust.

Rounding the corner of the temple we emerge upon a broad stone platform—the place of sacrifice. In the center of the pavement is a great dark smear, as though some one had upset a bucket of crimson paint. From it rises a squat post of stone, worn from long use and ominously stained—the execution stake. In the old days, before the interfering British came, young girls were here beheaded by the priests to appease the dreaded goddess, and rumor has it that only a few years ago a man, fearing the curse of Kali more than the wrath of the raj, sacrificed his nine-year-old son.

But to-day goats alone are offered, for your Hindu, no matter how violent his fanaticism, has a healthy respect for British law. Huddled in a corner was a herd of the terrified animals. Priests in blood-smeared garments dragged them forth, one by one. A noose was deftly slipped about the neck of the bleating victim and tied to the stone stake. The executioner's blade swung upward, shone for an instant in the hot sunlight, descended in a gleaming arc . . .

a muffled crunch, like that made by a butcher's cleaver shearing through bone and gristle, and from the headless carcass a crimson fountain spurted. The heaps of horned heads and hairy bodies mounted steadily. The executioner sweated like a pole-axman in a slaughter-house. The spectators shrieked delightedly. The smell of fresh blood was sickening.

"Come on," I said to my companions. "I've seen enough horrors for one day. Let's go back to Firpo's and have a drink."

"No," demurred our cicerone, the American vice-consul. "We might as well get the horrors over with by seeing the burning-ghats."

"Go ahead," agreed my cousin, though I noticed that he was a little white beneath his tan. "You can't show us anything worse than we have seen already at Madura and here. And it would be a pity to miss anything connected with the religion of these sweet and gentle souls."

The burning-ghats, where the Hindus of Calcutta incinerate their dead, are on the Hugli, a mile or so above the Kali Ghat. You reach them through a pleasant and secluded little garden, where the waters of a fountain plash gently amid the flowers. The crematory consists simply of a broad stone platform built upon the river-bank. Four wood fires were blazing hotly and upon them were four human forms in various stages of decomposition, the limbs contracted into horrid postures. Half-a-dozen sweating natives, naked save for breech-clouts, prodded the bodies with long poles, seeking to break them up. Amid the glowing embers of one pyre a human vertebra was recognizable. A blackened skull broke off and rolled almost to our feet, whereupon an attendant snatched it up and tossed it on the fire again. The place reeked with the mingled odors of wood smoke and scorched flesh.

"It takes fifteen rupees' worth of wood to burn the body of an adult," the official in charge explained politely. "But this one," indicating a slim, white-shrouded form which two of the attendants were bringing in on a litter, "won't cost so much—probably not more than ten rupees. She was young, you see—only about fourteen or fifteen—and quite small."

The men with the poles, having succeeded in reducing one of the bodies to what was in their opinion a satisfactory state of incineration, proceeded to shovel the ashes into the river in order to make space for the erection of another pyre. They formed a thick, black scum upon the waters. Amid the scum bobbed half-charred portions of the deceased's anatomy.

"They float down-stream past the Kali Ghat," the vice-consul remarked, "where thousands of people daily bathe in and drink the water. The scientists assert that running water purifies itself in a mile or so, but I for one refuse to eat lobsters taken from the Hugli."

"Now I *am* going back to town," I declared firmly. "And what is more, I am going to have *two* drinks."

As we emerged from the garden behind the burning-ghat our attention was attracted by a group of natives gathered about some object on the ground. Yielding to my curiosity, I peered over their shoulders. Stretched beside the dusty road, almost in the gutter, was a pretty native girl. She might have been fifteen, perhaps younger. Her face was as pallid as the petals of a gardenia. Her eyes were closed and only an occasional rise and fall of the small bosom showed that she was breathing. Obviously she was at the very gates of death. Yet none of the spectators made a move, lifted a hand to help her. They could not have been more apathetic had they been watching an expiring cat. In India death is so familiar that no one thinks much about it.

"Come away," urged the vice-consul, plucking at my arm. "The girl is dying from cholera."

"Hell's bells!" I exclaimed. "We can't go off and leave her like this. Isn't there something to be done?"

"Nothing," was the answer. "A medical officer has been sent for, though she will probably be dead before he arrives. If we touched her these people would resent it. They would claim that she had been contaminated, and all that sort of thing. It might even provoke a riot. We had better be on our way. We can't help the poor child by staying here."

"Well, all I can say," commented my cousin grimly as we climbed into the waiting car, "is that she chose a convenient place to die in—right at the entrance of the burning-ghats."

We laughed rather constrainedly, but it was noticeable that no one talked much during the drive home.

CHAPTER VI

I MEET A DICTATOR

WHEN, during a luncheon at Government House, I told Sir Stanley Jackson, the Governor of Bengal, that we wished to visit Nepál, he was not encouraging.

"It is one of the most difficult countries on earth to enter," he informed me. "To all intents and purposes it is a forbidden land. The Nepálese are suspicious of foreigners and very rarely grant them permission to cross the mountains into the great valley, though they occasionally permit those who are properly recommended to go into the outlying Terai for tiger shooting."

"It so happens, however," he continued, "that the prime minister of Nepál, Sir Chandra Shumshere Jung, who is the real ruler of the country, has just arrived in Calcutta for medical treatment. He and his staff have taken a house in Theatre Road. I shall be glad to instruct our Political Department to approach him on the subject of your visiting his country, and it might be a good idea to have your own consul-general make a request at the same time. Mind you, I don't hold out much hope of the request being granted, for the prime minister is an independent old gentleman, but we will do everything we can."

Whether he was impressed by the fact that two governments made simultaneous representations on our behalf, or decided that we were politically harmless because we were Americans, I have no means of knowing, but in less than twenty-four hours I received a letter from the prime minister, couched in the most cordial terms, assuring us that we would be welcome in Nepál, and suggesting that I come out to Theatre Road and discuss the details of the journey.

For his brief stay in Calcutta the dictator of Nepál had taken one of the largest residences in the city—a huge mansion of pink stucco standing in the midst of extensive gardens. Large as it was, however, it was incapable of housing all the members of his immense entourage, for whose accommodation a miniature city of tents had been erected in the grounds. Over the temporary palace was flying the flag of Nepál. Gurkha sentries, sturdy little men, very smart and soldierly in their pill-box caps, scarlet tunics and dark blue trousers, paced the lawns or stood motionless as statues before the various entrances. Along the sweeping driveway were parked a score or more of luxurious motor-cars bearing the silver tiger which is the emblem of Nepál. Hurrying to and fro were ministers of state with portfolios under their arms, secretaries, glittering staff officers, messengers and servants in the royal livery. Though I was destined to see enough of it later on, this was my first glimpse of the amazing pomp with which the great overlords of middle Asia surround themselves, and I was impressed accordingly.

After a much shorter wait than would have been the case had I been calling on an American banker, I was received by the prime minister's eldest son, who is a general in the Nepálese army and will eventually succeed his father as head of the Government. It is always difficult to estimate the age of Orientals, but I judged him to be in the early forties, though the black forked beard, cut after the fashion made familiar by Henry of Navarre, caused him to appear somewhat older. He spoke precise but fluent English and possessed that charm of manner characteristic of so many Asiatics of the ruling class. Between his eyes were two small caste-marks, red and white, for the members of the ruling family of Nepál are orthodox Hindus and belong to the highest division of the Brahman caste.

The costume worn by the prince is worthy of description, for I have never seen its like. Perched jauntily on one side of his head was a small round cap of black cloth trimmed with loops and rosettes of soutache braid and with two silken tassels depending from it. A frock coat of light gray cashmere, reminiscent of Primrose and West's minstrels, was thrown open to reveal a khaki-colored vest buttoned with English sovereigns. Jodhpurs of bright yellow nankeen, very baggy above the knees and very tight below, terminated in patent leather shoes with gray suède tops and pearl buttons. The whole extraordinary outfit was completed by *two* neckties, a white silk Ascot, fastened with an immense pigeon's-blood ruby, forming a chaste background for a vivid purple four-in-hand. What a boon it would be for our haberdashers if American men would adopt the custom of wearing two neckties instead of one!

The prince lost no time in getting down to business.

"We shall be very glad indeed to have you and your cousin visit Nepál," he assured me. "We have heard much of the great country from which you come and it is a pleasure to welcome you to our small one. As my father and I shall not return to Khatmandu for some weeks, we cannot, unfortunately, entertain you at the palace, but we have wired the British envoy, Mr. Wilkinson, who is at present on a shooting trip in the Terai, requesting that you may stay at one of the bungalows in the compound of the British legation. The government rest-houses on the road into Nepál will, of course, be at your disposal, and we have already sent forward the necessary instructions to that effect. I am sorry that we cannot at least offer you cooked food—not to do so seems extremely inhospitable—but, to tell the truth, we have no one who knows how to prepare European dishes. Orders have been issued, however, to provide you with vegetables, poultry, eggs, milk and butter, and these can be prepared by your own servants."

"And now," he proceeded, "what about transportation? There are four methods of travel in Nepál—on elephants, on horses, in dandies and afoot. Which do you prefer?"

It was an almost irresistible temptation to choose the elephants, for it would be a distinctly romantic experience to enter the strangest country on earth as Hannibal entered Italy. But recalling the discomforts of a journey which I once made by elephant in Cambodia, I decided on the horses.

"You are both good riders, I hope," the prince remarked. "The ponies with which we shall provide you are well mannered and accustomed to mountain travel, but the trail is extremely steep in places and sometimes uncomfortably narrow. It is, I imagine, like some of the trails in your own Rocky Mountains."

I assured him that both my cousin and I had been raised in the saddle, as it were, but that I could not answer for the horsemanship of our servant, Julius.

"Very well," he said. "We will have a dandy waiting for your bearer at the foot of the Chandragiri Pass, which is the most trying part of the journey."

A dandy, I might explain parenthetically, is a sort of palanquin, peculiar to the Himalayan regions, which is carried on the shoulders of coolies. In shape a cross between a cradle and a coffin, it is too shallow for the occupant to sit upright with any comfort and too short to permit of his lying at full length. Hence, he has to sit with his knees drawn up, resting on the end of his spine. If the coolies are trained to keep in step, the dandy is a tolerably comfortable means of conveyance for short distances, but on long journeys it becomes as excruciatingly painful as any of the instruments of torture employed by the Spanish Inquisition.

"You have chosen a somewhat unfortunate time to visit Nepál," said the prince, "though perhaps, being strangers, you may regard it otherwise, for next week takes place the great annual *mela,* or Hindu pilgrimage. It is expected that at least a hundred thousand pilgrims will cross the passes to worship at the shrines in the holy city of Pashpatti. That means that the trails will be crowded, but we shall detail a military escort to accompany you and you should have no trouble."

Far from the *mela* being objectionable, I hastened to assure him, it would add immensely to the interest and picturesqueness of our journey.

"Before you leave," he said, "I should like to present you to my father, who has expressed a wish to meet you."

He ushered me into an adjoining room, a huge, richly furnished apartment, and a graybearded old gentleman, spare of frame, considerably below medium height, rose from behind a desk to greet me. His simplicity, dignity and kindness reminded me of Mohammed V, the last Sultan of Turkey. I looked at him with interest, for he is one of the most remarkable personalities in middle Asia. Dictator of the mountain kingdom which for half-a-thousand miles forms a buffer between India and Tibet, lord of the Himalayan Marches and keeper of the Northern Gate, he is a valued ally of the British raj. Because he rules his country wisely and with a firm hand—for the youthful king is but a figurehead—because he will have no truck with Russian Bolsheviki or Chinese Communists, because he keeps the wild hill tribes in order, the British officials responsible for the safety of India's northern frontier are able to sleep o' nights. No wonder that the English king has loaded this

Asiatic dictator with decorations and made him an honorary general in the British army.

The prime minister was dressed in the peculiarly cut frock-coat and jodhpur breeches worn by all Nepálese gentlemen save on occasions of ceremony, but, unlike his son, he confined himself to one necktie. His skin was comparatively light for an Asiatic; the regularity and fineness of his features suggested that he was of the purest Aryan blood; his eyes, though piercing, and doubtless stern on occasion, were good-humored; he had the smallest hands and feet I have ever seen on a man. The lips, half-hidden by the grizzled beard and mustache, smiled at me in friendly fashion, but I imagine that under certain circumstances they could be as grim and unyielding as the jaws of a steel trap.

The dictator is not a particularly distinguished figure in mufti, but upon my departure from Nepál he sent me an autographed picture which shows him in the full regalia of his rank—a scarlet coat incrusted with bullion, arabesqued with gold braid, and cluttered with cordons and grand crosses; a helmet-like headdress of pearls fringed with tallow-drop emeralds the size of marbles; and a soaring white aigret held in place by one enormous diamond. When, arrayed in this resplendent outfit, he appeared at Buckingham Palace some years ago, even the blasé English court, accustomed as it is to Oriental splendor, sat up and took notice.

When, from Bombay, I wrote to thank him for the picture and for the many courtesies shown us during our stay in his country, I addressed my letter to—

"His Highness Projjvala Nepál Táràdhisk Maharajah Sir Chandrá Shumshere Jung, Bahádur Ráná, G.C.B. G.C.S.I., G.C.M.G., G.C.V.O., D.C.L., Grand Officer of the Legion of Honor, Thong-Lin-Pimma-Kohang-Wang-

Syan, Honorary General in the British Army, Honorary Colonel of the Fourth Regiment of Gurkhas, Prime Minister of Nepál, Marshal and Supreme Commander-in-Chief of the Forces."

Which, as the wife of a New York mayor remarked to the wife of a European king, "is sure a mouthful." It should be understood, of course, that these are only a few of His Highness' names, titles and honors. They told me in Nepál that it takes a strong man two days and two nights to recite all of them.

After half an hour's conversation, during which we touched on such diverse subjects as bolshevism, base-ball, airplanes, tiger hunting, Ford cars and President Coolidge, the prime minister rose and shook hands with me by way of signifying that the audience was at an end. His son accompained me to my car and wished me a pleasant journey. The rows of attendants between whom we passed salaamed, the staff officers saluted, the guard turned out and presented arms.

"If this is a sample of what Nepál is going to be like," I said to myself, "it promises to be as entertaining as a four-ring circus."

It was with some trepidation that I broke the news to Julius that we were actually going to Nepál, for it is a far, wild country, he was neither robustious nor adventure-loving, and I feared that we might find ourselves without a servant. But, to my surprise, he was distinctly elated at the prospect.

"Khatmandu ver' holy city," he volunteered by way of explaining his enthusiasm. "Hab ver' holy Buddhist temple. When we get there if marster give me leave to go an' say prayer I make much merit. When I go back to Ceylon an' tell priests I been to Khatmandu they all be jealous."

The evening preceding our departure for the north Mr. Willey, the American vice-consul, gave a farewell party for us at the Saturday Club, which is to Calcutta what the Casino is to Newport. He also invited the two pretty American girls whom we had met in Madura. The club has a beautiful ball-room, the gowns worn by the women bore the unmistakable stamp of Paris, and the orchestra would have done credit to any night club in New York. I am not overfond of dancing, but the music was so enticing and the moonlit terrace such a pleasant place to stroll on, that dawn was not far off when we went back to the hotel to pack.

The news that we were going to Nepál had spread, for the English community in Calcutta is not after all a very large one, and a lot of people came up to congratulate us and wish us *bon voyage*.

"You chaps are jolly lucky, you know," said one government official. "I've lived out here for twenty years and I haven't succeeded in getting permission to go into Nepál yet. But you Americans come along, casually tell old Shumshere Jung that you would like to take a look at his country, and he invites you right off the bat. Deuced fortunate, I call it."

Though it is possible to enter eastern Nepál via Darjeeling, this route is rarely used, even by native caravans, for it involves numerous difficulties, the most serious being that of obtaining transportation. According to the itinerary arranged for us by the Nepálese, we were to book tickets to Raxaul, the Indian railhead on the northeast frontier, where an official of the Nepálese Government would meet us and acquaint us with the arrangements made for the journey across the mountains.

Shortly before our departure a *chuprassi* in the red-and-gold livery of the Bengal Secretariat brought me a note from the Political Secretary informing me that we would be met at Raxaul by Colonel Husband of the Indian Medical Corps, who would put us up at the government rest-house, and that during our stay in Khatmandu a bungalow in the compound of the British legation would be at our disposal.

I wish to say at this point that, though the British officials in India have the reputation of being "high hat" toward visitors, such reputation is wholly undeserved, for every one, from the viceroy down, went out of his way to show us hospitality and render us assistance. In the course of my travels I have had much to do with colonial officials in many lands, but not even in the Philippines have I encountered a more courteous, efficient or tactful group of men than those who serve his Britannic Majesty in the Indian Empire.

We were due to leave Calcutta in the evening by the Punjab Mail. Though it is only a couple of miles from the Great Eastern Hotel to the Howrah station, and a taxi should normally make it in ten minutes, we were advised to start from the hotel at least an hour and a half before the train was due to leave in order to allow for delay on the bridge over the Hugli, where there is always a terrific jam of motor-cars, carriages, rickshaws and ox-carts, and for the confusion which invariably prevails in the station itself. Here Julius proved himself really invaluable, for the vast, echoing terminal, crowded with natives going God knows where, was a shrieking bedlam. But he lined up a dozen porters, piled them high with our impedimenta, which had been considerably augmented by the purchase of tinned food and bottled water for the trek into Nepál, and herded the procession to the train.

While my cousin and Julius were superintending the bestowal of the luggage in our compartment, there still being half an hour to spare, I went into the station restaurant to snatch a hasty dinner. Seated at the next table was a singular trio: two Englishmen, planters from their dress, red-faced, loud-voiced, obviously the worse for liquor, and a strikingly beautiful brunette, statuesque, with flashing black eyes, a sullen mouth, and great masses of raven hair—a regular tragedy queen.

They were conversing in undertones when I entered and, judging from the bottles which littered the table, they had been drinking heavily. Soon the effect of the alcohol began to make itself apparent in their raised voices, though I could catch a word only now and then. It was evident, however, that a heated discussion of some sort was in progress. Suddenly the woman pushed back her chair so violently that it crashed upon the floor. Drawing herself to her full height she leveled an accusing finger at her companions, who sat slumped in their seats.

"You dogs! You dirty dogs!" she hissed, dramatic as though she were launching the curse of Rome. "You'd try to cheat me, would you? But you can't get away with it! Before I'm through with you you'll wish that you had never been born!"

Her splendid body shook with passion, her deep voice with scorn.

One of the men, the more sober of the two, made an unsuccessful attempt to placate her.

"Now, Dolores, calm yourself," he implored. "You stand to gain a lot in this affair if you'll only listen to reason. Stick by us and you won't regret it."

The mutinous red mouth curved in a smile of contempt, the black eyes flashed lightning.

"You unspeakable cad! You filthy little louse!" She fairly spat the words at him. "I'd rather be dead than be associated with you any longer. You haven't the backbone of a worm!"

"As for you," she cried, turning upon the other man, "you're always boasting of being a gentleman, but you're nothing but a drunken sot. Forever guzzling whisky instead of keeping your head clear for business!"

The fellow was refilling his glass, but she dashed it to the floor; then swept from the room, crashing the door to behind her.

Five minutes passed, during which the two men conversed furtively, in whispers. By this time my curiosity had become overpowering. Then she burst into the room again, eyes flashing, breasts heaving, spots of color encarmining her cheeks. An infuriated goddess.

"Well," she demanded, towering rigid above the littered table, "what have you decided? Is it to be my way or yours? You can't play with me any longer. One word to . . ."

"Pardon, sahib," came the waiter's deferential voice from over my shoulder, "but Punjab Mail leave in three minutes."

Eager as I was to witness the *dénouement,* there was not a moment to spare if I was to make the train. I dashed madly for the platform. My cousin, who suffers from a complex about missing trains, was leaning anxiously from the door of our compartment.

"Where the devil have you been?" he demanded irritably. "I thought you were going to miss the train."

"Oh," I replied carelessly, swinging myself aboard as the wheels began to turn, "I've been watching an old-fashioned mellerdrammer. But I had to leave before the end of the last act."

I have often speculated as to the identity of the tragedy queen and the nature of her relations with the two villains, and if they eventually got what was coming to them. That is the trouble with this gadding about the world; one is always having to rush out before the curtain falls to catch a train or boat.

Julius aroused us from slumber when it was still dark to warn us that we were approaching Mokameh Ghat, where we were to detrain and cross the Ganges on a ferry. It was distinctly chilly in the dim gray dawn, and in spite of my fleece-lined British warm I shivered. A gang of pirates, their heads wrapped in yards of vivid muslin, invaded the compartment, tossed our belongings helter-skelter through the door and windows, and bore them down the steep mud bank to the waiting steamer. Leaving to Julius the task of adjusting their extortionate demands, we made our way to the frowzy little cabin on the forward deck and ordered breakfast. After half an hour's delay it appeared: coffee which was the color of mud and tasted like it, a couple of dubious-looking eggs, a plate of blackened slabs optimistically called toast, and something alleged to be bacon but which I suspected of being the sole of a discarded shoe.

The Ganges is the holiest river in the world—so holy that those who bathe in it or drink of its waters are automatically cleansed of sin. But I would rather be thirsty and sinful than a victim of typhoid. While as for bathing in it . . . my cousin spied a long dark object floating down the muddy stream and pointed it out to one of our fellow-passengers, a tea planter from up-country.

"There's a fine big piece of timber going to waste," he remarked.

"Timber? Hell!" the planter snorted. "That's a crocodile."

The journey from the north bank of the Ganges to Raxaul was a counterpart of that from Madura to Calcutta, only worse, because the train was an accommodation and stopped on the slightest pretext. The shabby carriage was dingier and drearier than usual in the cold actinic light admitted by the violet window-panes, and the monotonous landscape which slid past did nothing to lessen our boredom. It was impossible to read in the jolting carriage, which had at least one flat wheel in either truck, and we had smoked so incessantly that nicotine was no longer a solace. So we sat and thought, and when the mental strain of thinking became too great we just sat.

At Muzafferpur we had to wait an hour for the train which was to bear us over the next stage of our journey. We arrived there while another of the innumerable festivals with which the Hindu religious calendar is sprinkled was in progress. We knew that something out of the ordinary must be going on by the condition of the natives' garments, which appeared to have been splashed with colored inks. These dyes, which the Hindus throw at each other just as the members of a wedding party at home hurl rice and confetti at the bride and groom, leave huge, unsightly splotches upon the white clothing, so that the wearers look as though they were suffering from hemorrhages, red, purple and green.

For distance, rapidity and accuracy of expectoration the Hindus are in a class by themselves. I once knew an Arizona stage-coach driver who, by virtue of a missing front tooth, could put a neat "U.S.A." in tobacco juice on the barroom ceiling. But your Hindu beats the world when it comes to high, ground and all-around spitting. I don't know whether it is the result of chronic catarrh or ineradicable habit, but he is always at it, everywhere—snuffle-hack-cough-spit . . . snuffle-hack-cough-spit . . . until you abandon hope that his supply of saliva may eventually become exhausted. It is almost like a national anthem. As a result, the sidewalks of Indian cities, the station platforms, the floors of railway carriages are spangled with spittle, usually tinged a bright pink from the universal custom of chewing betel-nut, and through these pools of saliva the barefooted natives stroll unconcernedly, trailing their flowing garments through the slime and spreading contagion everywhere. If the Indian had any knowledge of the Old Testament and any sense of humor the authorities might mitigate the nuisance by posting signs in public places: "Don't spit; remember the Flood!"

"Until I came to India," remarked my cousin, "I always maintained that the filthiest place on earth was the toilet-room in the Stamford railway station, but now I feel as though I should write a letter of apology to the directors of the New York, New Haven & Hartford."

The train jogged slowly northward—*bumpety-bump . . . bumpety-bump . . . bumpety-bump*—across the flat lands of the Gangetic plain. The tiresome landscape flickered past—sandhills dotted with camel-thorn bushes or tamarisk shrub, parched fields, cactus hedges, mud villages, clumps of dejected-looking palms, more fields, mud hovels again—as monotonous and uninteresting as an amateur's motion-picture film.

Suffocating clouds of yellow dust swirled in through the doors and windows, even seeped through the crevices of the floor. Our garments smoked with dust when we moved; on our hands and faces the dust lay in layers a quarter of an inch thick; to get it out of my hair took a whole series of shampooings. The midday sun beat down relentlessly upon the roof of the car, turning the interior into a baking-oven. The dust which caked our countenances was eroded into miniature valleys and ravines and gorges by trickling streams of sweat.

"I wish to God I was back home," my cousin complained bitterly. "One of those crisp, clear winter nights such as we get in Westchester County, with the family sitting around the open fire waiting for dinner to be served and the butler just bringing in a tray of cocktails. Travel is nothing but one damn discomfort after another, anyway. I like a domestic life, children around me, all the comforts of home."

Just then the brakes squealed shrilly and the train jolted to a halt beside the platform of an obscure way station. The door of our compartment—the only first-class compartment on the train—was flung open. In clambered two wholesome looking young Englishwomen, each clasping a small child by the hand. One of the children was about six, I judged, the other perhaps ten. At their heels were three native *ayahs,* each bearing a squalling infant in her arms. To my inexperienced eyes the infants appeared to be of approximately the same age; I could not decide whether they were triplets or twins and a singleton.

After them, tossed in by willing hands outside, came a perfect deluge of luggage—tin steamer-trunks, canvas hold-alls, kit-bags, Gladstone bags, dressing-cases, hat-boxes, bedding-rolls, valises, blankets, pillows, a bundle of umbrellas, a bundle of tennis rackets, two bags of golf clubs, boxes of provisions, a tiffin basket, a case of condensed milk, a sterilizing outfit, a spirit lamp, a wash-bowl in a leather case, a collapsible bath-tub, three folding perambulators, a couple of rhorki chairs, pith helmets in linen sacks, a large tin of biscuits, another of chocolates, a third of toffee, a few bundles of books and magazines, a miscellaneous collection of toys, a laundry hamper, two porcelain receptacles which are more familiar in bedrooms than in railway carriages, *and* a huge clothes-basket filled with diapers.

In less time than it takes to tell about it our neat compartment looked like a maternity ward, day nursery and kindergarten combined. Babies were everywhere: crying babies, teething babies, drooling babies, babies suffering from more or less acute intestinal disorders. Both of the long couches were crowded to capacity and the upper berths were let down to provide space for such impedimenta as there was no room for on the floor. Hanging from the hooks was a whole collection of garments, infantile, juvenile and feminine.

My cousin and I, gallantly surrendering our seats, found a narrow space in which to stand between the basket of diapers and the toilet-room door, but we were driven from even this refuge when the eldest child was taken violently train-sick. One of the *ayahs* lighted the spirit-lamp and started boiling milk on top of my cousin's pigskin dressing-case. Another set her charge on my fawn-colored British warm, but I detected a premonitory expression on the infant's face and rescued the garment just in time.

"Oh, I do hope we are not inconveniencing you," one of the mothers said sweetly. "There really are quite a number of us for one compartment, aren't there? But, you see, it happens to be the only first-class compartment on this wretched train. And I am afraid that our things are taking up quite a bit of room, but we don't like to put them in the luggage van. In traveling it is so much more convenient to have your things with you. *Wilfred, stop trying to break the nice gentleman's cane!* We've been visiting my brother, you see—he has an indigo plantation near Muzafferpur—and now we're taking the children up to the hills for the hot weather. *There, Doris, now you've gone and spilled your milk over the gentleman's overcoat! Aren't you ashamed?* But you won't be bothered with us long. Our station is only seventy-five miles up the line."

"Don't give yourself a moment's thought about us, madam," I assured her. "My cousin was saying only a few minutes ago that he was homesick for a touch of domestic life and loved to be surrounded by children."

"How perfectly sweet of him!" the ladies chorused. "American men are so chivalrous."

My cousin threw me an evil glance.

"You go to hell!" he whispered.

Night had fallen ere we pulled into Raxaul, which was also, as it turned out, the destination of our fellow-passengers. There, I gathered, they would change to another train which would bear them to a hill-station farther to the westward.

When we had disentangled ourselves from the maelstrom of squalling infants, scolding nurses and reproving mothers, we were approached by a middle-aged, soldierly looking man in shooting jacket and breeches. He introduced himself as Colonel Husband of the Indian Medical Corps.

"I say!" he exclaimed, mopping his forehead with a huge bandanna, "I certainly had a fright when I saw you getting out of that carriage. The Political Secretary in Calcutta wired me to expect you by this train and to make you comfortable during your stay in Raxaul. As he said that you were on your way into Nepál I naturally assumed that you would be alone. So, when I saw that caravan of women and children with you, I was at my wit's end what to do, for we have only one spare bedroom at the rest-house, and I knew that we hadn't enough tents to go round. It would have been a very deuce of a mess, wouldn't it?"

We agreed with him fervently.

The rest-house, it seemed, was three quarters of a mile from the station, and, there being no conveyances available, we picked our way down the railway track in the darkness, our steps lighted by servants and police with lanterns. Behind us, watchfully supervised by Julius, straggled a line of coolies with our luggage on their heads.

We found that the rest-house did not belie its name—a long, low bungalow of stone encircled by jalousied verandas. It stood amid trees and flowering shrubs in a spacious compound whose lawns ran down to the bank of the little river which marks the northern limits of British territory. As we entered the gate the statuesque sowar on sentry duty brought his pennoned lance to the perpendicular, crashing the butt upon the ground; a row of house servants in scarlet turbans salaamed a welcome; the rest-house superintendent, a sleek babu, showed us to the airy bedroom which had been prepared against our coming. Coolies filled the shallow tin tubs in the bathroom with hot water and Julius laid out our mess kits. It was almost like being in a country house at home.

After dinner was over and the silent-footed servants had withdrawn, we sat about the table and sipped whiskies and sodas and puffed slender Indian cheroots and listened with absorbed attention to the stories told by our host, who had just completed a long tour of duty as medical officer of the British agency at Srinagar. At first we chatted lightly of life in the Vale, of house-boat days and tiger-shooting and the peccadilloes of the ruling maharajah. But after a time we grew serious and confidential, as white men foregathered in lonely outposts on the fringes of civilization are wont to do, and discussed subjects pertaining to morality and religion with a frankness which would scarcely have been possible in other surroundings. But we were encouraged by our host, who, like all imaginative men who have lived long in the East, had worked out a philosophy of his own.

It had been a hot and tiring day and ere long we caught ourselves yawning, but before turning in we smoked a final cigar upon the lawn. It was a glorious night, the air soft as a woman's breast, though the gentle breeze brought to us a hint of chill from distant snow-peaks. The purple ceiling was sprinkled with a million diamonds and after a time an orange moon rose majestically out of Hindustan.

Across the little river, only a few yards broad, the moonlight shone upon the bayonet of a sentry, and I knew the land he was patrolling for Nepál. Far to the north, barely discernible against the midnight sky, a vague black mass loomed between us and the stars in rugged outline. The outer ranges of the Himalayas. And, hidden behind that mighty barrier, lay the last home of mystery.

CHAPTER VII

LET US JOURNEY TO A LONELY LAND I KNOW

THE morning after our arrival at Raxaul the governor of the Nepálese frontier province, accompanied by his staff, paid us a formal call. He was a genial, moon-faced, stockily built little man clad in a semi-military uniform of khaki. His good-natured countenance was distinctly Mongoloid, but a black pill-box cap was perched incongruously on the side of his head, so that I could not make up my mind which he resembled most—a smiling Buddha or a British Tommy.

He informed us that, in pursuance of telegraphic instructions from his Highness the prime minister, arrangements had been made for us to leave Raxaul by train early the following morning for Amlekgunj, which is the end-of-steel, this narrow-gage line, twenty-four miles in length, being Nepál's only railway. Personally, I believe that the money would have been more wisely expended in building a good road and establishing a transportation system of motor-trucks and buses, as the French have done so successfully in North Africa and Indo-China. But a railway, however short, is, after all, a symbol of progress, and the Nepálese are as proud of their two dozen miles of trackage and tinpot trains as an Amercian boy is of his toy railway set.

The governor further informed us that he had detailed to accompany us a subadar of the Nepálese army —a grade corresponding to that of sergeant-major. The subadar was a fine specimen of the veteran non-commissioned officer, a soldier to his finger-tips. He clicked his heels together and brought his hand up to his lambskin cap, palm outward, in a fashion which showed that he had learned his trade under a British drillmaster; then, as is the Gurkha custom, he thrust the hilt of his *kukri* forward, in token of fealty, for me to touch. He spoke no English and had only a smattering of Hindustani, so that the gossip-loving Julius had some difficulty in conversing with him, but he was faithful, honest, intelligent, and had the faculty of divining our wishes and anticipating them.

Though the great festival at Pashpatti was still a week away, we were told that upward of fifty thousand pilgrims had already passed through Raxaul on their way into Nepál and that twice as many more were to come. Consequently the train, which consisted of a long string of flat- and box-cars, was jammed with the pious; but a private carriage, very clean and comfortable, with large arm-chairs, had been attached for our convenience. Because of the exceptionally heavy load it had been necessary to employ two locomotives, one in front and the other behind—miniature affairs which wheezed and panted as though suffering from chronic asthma.

Though on the level stretches we estimated that the train sometimes attained a speed of fully seven miles an hour, it took us a long half-day to make the twenty-four-mile journey to Amlekgunj, owing to the time wasted at way stations and to the difficulty experienced by the two asthmatic locomotives in negotiating the steeper grades. One of these was so steep that the little engines found the load too much for them, whereupon the male pilgrims to the number of several hundred good-naturedly piled out and lent a helping hand, and, when the train got under way, scrambled aboard again.

It should be understood, of course, that only those pilgrims who are comparatively well-to-do can afford to travel by train. Tens of thousands made the long journey to Pashpatti and return on foot, some of them, those from southern India and the borders of Burma, spending months on the road. Many of the pious are so destitute, indeed, that they do not even possess blankets in which to wrap themselves at night, and for food depend upon what they can beg along the way. As no attempt is made by the Nepálese authorities to enforce sanitary regulations, the wells along the route, none too safe under any conditions, are polluted by the hordes of pilgrims, who leave diseases of all kinds behind them.

For the first hour or so we traversed a fairly well populated and more or less cultivated region, the railway embankment being bordered by bright green paddy-fields and other fields yellow with grain, while here and there were small vegetable gardens and patches of the large white poppies from which is produced opium. Naked peasants laboriously tilled the parched earth with the most primitive of plows, mere iron-shod beams of wood, hauled by snowy oxen. Now and again we saw elephants at work clearing the brush and moving heavy timbers, the huge beasts being to the agriculturists of Nepál what tractors are to American farmers. Farther on we entered a grazing country, where herds of humped-backed cattle, white, gray and roan, cropped the withered vegetation. Occasional groves of majestic banyan-trees provided the only relief to the expanse of dust-deep, sun-scorched plain.

Paralleling the railway was a road of sorts, scarcely more than a deeply rutted track, along which plodded strings of bullock carts, the spokes of their unshod eight-foot wheels set at right angles, cumbersome and creaking. Along the road pressed also an endless stream of pilgrims, their scanty belongings on their backs, caked with dust and sweat, parched from thirst, stumbling from fatigue, but spurred on by religious fervor.

The villages at which we halted were for the most part miserable affairs, mere clusters of hovels with walls of sun-baked mud and thatched roofs, though occasionally we saw a more pretentious building, with the gaudily frescoed plaster walls and carved wooden balconies characteristic of Indian architecture. Every village had its tank or pool, and in nearly every case cows or buffaloes were standing knee-deep in the water which the villagers used for drinking, cooking and bathing. But the Nepálese, like the Indians, are apparently immune from zymotic diseases, and this is fortunate, for a question of mere sanitation cannot be permitted to interfere with the comfort of cattle, which, being sacred animals, are never disturbed. Moreover, the cows provide the butter which, clarified into the substance know as *ghee,* is offered to the idols, not to mention the dung, which, molded into bricks and dried in the sun, is the universal fuel of middle Asia.

Modesty is a quality not possessed by the Hindus. I doubt, indeed, if the majority of them know the meaning of the word. Whenever the train stopped at a village scores of the pilgrims would drop off, make a dash for the near-by pool, divest themselves of their scanty clothing, perform their ablutions in full view of their fellow-passengers, rinse their mouths in the water made holy (and filthy) by the presence of the sacred cattle, don their cotton garments, rewind their turbans, and scramble aboard just as the whistle blew. The cars provided for the pious being destitute of toilet facilities, both men and women unblushingly attended to the demands of nature along the right-of-way.

We had not been long across the frontier before we observed a striking change in the appearance of the people.

The slim, delicately formed Indians, with their chocolate-colored skins and regular features, began to give way to short, rugged, stockily built folk with the flat noses, slanting eyes and yellow skins which denote Mongol extraction. Mingled with these Mongolian types, however, and like them natives of the country, were men of slimmer build and greater stature, their features unmistakably Aryan, their skins brown instead of yellow.

The inhabitants of Nepál represent so many different tribes and races that any attempt to classify them satisfactorily is almost out of the question. The most important are the Gurkhas, Newars, Hurungs, Magars, Limbus, Kiratis, Lepchas and Bhotias. As a result of this ethnic mélange at least half-a-dozen distinct languages are commonly employed within the kingdom's borders, these ranging from Sanskrit, the most ancient of the Indo-European tongues, to the gibberish spoken by the jungle dwellers. The English ethnologist, Brian Hodgson, who spent many years in Nepál, once asked the authorities if they could arrange for him to talk with one of these savage aborigines in order that he might make a comparative study of the man's speech. The authorities promptly assented and a few days later a naked, wild-haired denizen of the jungle was delivered at the scientist's house—in a cage.

It is enough to say that an overwhelming proportion of the 5,600,000 inhabitants of Nepál belong to one or the other of the two principal races, the Gurkhas and the Newars, who represent respectively the victors and the vanquished, the rulers and the ruled. Their original physical characteristics have been so greatly modified by intermarriage, however, that it is often impossible to determine to which race an individual belongs.

The origin of the Newars, who were the first inhabitants of Nepál, has long been a matter for argument and speculation, some authorities maintaining that they came into the country during the eleventh century in the train of a Carnatic king, while others insist with equal vehemence that they are not of Aryan but of Mongol stock, having migrated from Tibet into Nepál before written history began. The latter hypothesis is supported by their cast of features, their language, their character and their customs, all of which point unmistakably to Mongolian extraction. In any event, the Newars constitute the largest section of Nepál's population; they form the artistic elements of the country, being remarkably ingenious and skilful as carpenters, masons, metal-workers, sculptors and painters; and they have left their imprint on every building of importance in the land. The amazing temples, the magnificently decorated shrines, the grotesque but beautifully executed statues, the astounding wealth of color and carving which one sees everywhere in the great valley—these are all due to the Newars.

The Gurkhas are a Rajput race, originally from Udaipur in Rajputana. Driven from their own country in the fourteenth century by the Moslem invaders, they took refuge amid the inaccessible hills on the western confines of Nepál. A highly warlike people, they were bent on extending their territories to the eastward, but no important advance was made until 1742, when an ambitious and aggressive ruler, Prithi Narain, came to the throne. He lost no time in embarking on a campaign of conquest, but it took him five and twenty years to achieve his aim, the eighteenth century being well into its latter half before he entered Khatmandu and imposed Gurkha rule upon the Newar inhabitants of the great valley. He thus laid the foundation of the Gurkha dynasty, which has lasted to the present day.

The Gurkhas, born soldiers who love fighting for fighting's sake, constitute the dominant element of the state. They are probably the finest fighting material in all Asia, barring not even the Japanese. Several regiments of them went to France with the Indian expeditionary forces, and the Germans still speak with awe of the terrible little brown men who, undaunted by machine-gun fire and storms of shrapnel, charged irresistibly across the fields of Flanders, swinging their dreaded *kukris* and roaring their strange, barbaric battle-cries.

That Nepál has benefited enormously by the Gurkha conquest it would be idle to deny. Its Gurkha rulers are energetic and progressive; they have built up a military organization which for sheer efficiency has few equals anywhere; and they have given the country a sound, stable and sympathetic administration. The aptitude for fighting displayed by these hardy little mountaineers, plus their spirit of enterprise, explains the astounding successes of Jenghiz Kahn, Tamerlane and the other central Asian conquerors of six or seven centuries ago.

Sandwiched between two great empires, it would be surprising if Nepál had not had its vicissitudes. In 1790 the Gurkhas, athirst for further territory, invaded Tibet, but were defeated by the Chinese and retired within their own borders. A commercial treaty between India and Nepál was signed in 1792 and a British resident sent to Khatmandu, but he was recalled two years later. In 1815 frontier aggressions by the Gurkhas compelled the Government of India to despatch a punitive expedition against Nepál. The hillmen were at first successful, but as the result of a decisive victory gained by General Ochterlony they sued for peace in 1816, the treaty of Saugali, by which they lost their richest districts of Kumaon and Garhwal, being signed the following year. Since then the relations of the British with the inhabitants of the mountain kingdom have been uniformly friendly.

When the Indian Mutiny broke out, and the revolting Sepoys swept the peninsula with fire and sword, Jung Bahadur, the then prime minister of Nepál and one of the most remarkable men central Asia has produced, promptly despatched four thousand troops to the aid of the beleaguered British and shortly thereafter followed himself with a much larger contingent. As a reward for this service Great Britain restored to Nepál the greater portion of the Terai. In 1854 hostilities broke out a second time between Nepál and Tibet, the former this time being successful. In 1856 a treaty was concluded between the two governments whereby the Tibetans bound themselves to pay the sum of ten thousand rupees annually in order to encourage trade relations with their late enemies and agreed to receive a Nepálese envoy at Lhasa.

In 1923 a fresh treaty was signed between Great Britain and Nepál, the former acknowledging the latter's independence, internal and external. Though in spite of this certain English writers insist on referring to Nepál as a British protectorate, or even as one of the Indian states, it is nothing of the sort, being as free to pursue its own policies, to administer its own affairs, whether domestic or foreign, as, say, Belgium. A British envoy resides at Khatmandu, where he is treated as an honored prisoner, not being permitted to go beyond a certain prescribed area without the permission of the Nepálese authorities, and Nepál maintains a diplomatic representative at Delhi.

For upward of a hundred years the Government of Nepál has steadfastly followed a policy of "absolute but friendly isolation." Though the hermit kingdom convincingly proved its friendship for Great Britain during the World War by supplying the latter with men and money, it has kept its gates closed to Europeans. This policy has resulted in a complete absence of disputes between Nepál and her powerful neighbor; at the same time no exploration of the country has been possible. The greater part of Nepál is, in fact, as much an unexplored wilderness as many parts of Africa, it not even being known with certainty which is the best route to Khatmandu.

The sovereign of Nepál, or Maharajadhiraja, as he is called, is but a dignified figure-head, whose position can best be likened to that of the Emperor of Japan during the shogunate. The present king, his Majesty Maharajadhiraja Tribhubana Bir Bikram Jung Bahadur Shah Bahadur Shum Shere Jung Deva, was born in 1906 and ascended the throne on the death of his father in 1911. The prince royal and heir apparent is still a child, having been born in 1920, when his father was only fourteen. The youthful king never leaves his country, seldom appears in public, and in the active administration of the state takes little or no part.

Such things as a constitution, suffrage and legislative assemblies are unknown in Nepál, which is a military oligarchy. The real ruler of the country is the prime minister and supreme commander-in-chief, the holder of this exalted office having enjoyed a complete monopoly of power since 1867, when it was permanently delegated by King Surendra Bikram Shah under pressure of the nobles. The office of prime minister is hereditary in the same family, special rules determining the succession. All the sons of the prime minister have the rank of princes and hold commissions as generals in the Nepálese army, which is in consequence a family affair.

This thumb-nail sketch of Nepál's history and government being concluded, we will now resume our journey into the forbidden land.

After a time the villages grew less frequent, all but disappeared, the cultivated tracts ran out in scrub and forest, and the train toiled slowly upward along a narrow right-of-way chopped from the virgin jungle. Now we were entering the finest big-game preserve in all Asia, perhaps in all the world, the haunt of the elephant and the rhinoceros, of the leopard and the tiger. It had been comfortably cool in the open country below, where a mild breeze was stirring, but here, hemmed in by solid walls of vegetation, the heat was terrific, the only current of air being the artificial one created by the motion of the train. This, though it produced a fictitious coolness, was by no means an unmitigated comfort, for it brought to our nostrils the stench of the unwashed pilgrims in the cars ahead.

At Amlekgunj—"the Place of Freedom"—which is the present northern terminus of the Nepálese railway system, and, owing to the forbidding nature of the country, will probably remain the terminus for a good many years to come, attempts were being made to create a modern town. The jungle was being systematically cleared away by gangs of coolies and elephants; a substantial stone station had been erected; and streets, instead of being left to their own devices, as is customary in Asia, were being staked out and graded according to a well-conceived plan.

The orders issued by the prime minister had been obeyed to the letter—and woe to the man who fails to obey the orders of the overlord of Nepál!—and at Amlekgunj the transportation for the next stage of the journey was awaiting us: a small motor-car for ourselves and a Ford for the servants and the luggage.

On the advice of the prime minister, who had warned us that the wells along the route into Nepál, none too safe at any time, were certain to be polluted by the pilgrim horde, we had brought with us from Calcutta an ample supply of bottled water. This I insisted seeing stowed in the Ford myself, for I had a vivid recollection of an experience in the Arabian desert some years before, when the camel bearing our entire supply of drinking water had lain down and rolled, so that throughout the remainder of the journey we had to assuage our thirst at the filthy water-holes.

It is about twenty-five miles from the railhead at Amlekgunj to Bhimpedi, where the motor-road ends and the trail begins, the highway, if it can be dignified by such a name, following for a part of the distance the stony watercourse of a stream known as the Bichaliola Naddi. Considering the frequency with which it is washed out by mountain freshets, the road was in astonishingly good condition when we went over it, this being due to the enormous number of soldiers who were engaged in filling, grading and bridge-building. So numerous were these sturdy little men in their uniforms of a poisonous cobalt blue that I assumed that the entire Nepálese army must be concentrated in this region. It developed, however, that these troops, to the number of ten thousand, formed the personal escort of the prime minister. They had accompanied him from the capital to the frontier and were now awaiting his return from India. As his Highness expected to remain in Calcutta for some weeks, he had given orders that during his absence the troops of the escort should be employed in improving the roads instead of idling in camp. A very sensible arrangement, and one which might be imitated to advantage by some of the overmilitarized Balkan states.

A few miles out of Amlekgunj we were halted by a man astride a beautiful white pony. Though a native, he was in European dress, shooting-jacket, breeches and quilted topée, and was followed by a mounted orderly. I noticed that the subadar and our native drivers treated him with profound deference.

"They telephoned me from Birgunge that you had started," he said, addressing us in perfect English. "You will find ponies and coolies awaiting you at Bhimpedi, and the superintendent of the rest-house at Sisagarhi has been notified that you will arrive there this evening and spend the night. I am sorry that I cannot be in Khatmandu while you are there, as I should like to show you around, but my duties keep me in the Terai."

He saluted courteously, put spurs to his horse, and cantered off.

"Who is he?" I asked the subadar, who had stood rigidly at attention while the rider was speaking.

"That," was the awed reply, "is his Excellency the chief of the Electrical Department. He is a royal prince, a general in the army and a cousin of the king's."

"We're certainly making a hit socially," my cousin remarked dryly. "A prime minister to give us a send-off in Calcutta. A governor to meet us at Raxaul. Now a royal prince. I expect that when we reach Khatmandu the king himself will be awaiting us on the palace doorstep."

We were now traversing the region known as the Terai, that broad belt of forest and jungle, of rugged hills and tumbling streams, of rock-walled ravines and leafy glens, which forms Nepál's first line of defense along her southern borders. Owing to the extreme difficulty of obtaining permission to enter even this outlying district, big game is probably more numerous in the Terai than anywhere else in Asia. Its forests are roamed by huge herds of wild elephants; the two-horned Asiatic rhino goes crashing through its jungles; the gaur, ferocious and treacherous, is a constant source of danger to the hunter; the tiger, yearly becoming scarcer in India, is still plentiful here.

It is a region of savagery and romance, the Nepálese Terai, the name conjuring up from the past the shades of Gautama Buddha, the founder of Buddhism, who was born, spent much of his life and died in this region; of Nana Sahib, the arch-fiend of the Indian Mutiny, who here sought refuge from British vengeance; and of Jung Bahadur, that great warrior and mighty hunter, who in these jungles found recreation killing tigers with a spear.

The Terai enjoys an unenviable reputation because of the prevalence, from March to November, of a deadly form of malarial fever known locally as the *awal,* it being considered little short of madness for Europeans to travel in this pestilential region save during the cooler months of the year. This broad zone of malaria-haunted jungle provides Nepál, indeed, with almost as strong a line of defense as her mighty barrier of mountains, for a European army which entered it would almost certainly be decimated by disease.

There is something peculiarly sinister and ominous about the jungle of the Terai. You have the uneasy feeling that danger in one form or another lurks around every turn. The road plunges abruptly into a gloomy defile. The rocky walls close in. The sky is shut out by forest giants whose branches interlace in a green ceiling overhead. The gentle breeze which generally prevails in the open country is succeeded by breathless, stifling heat. Over everything a strange, oppressive silence broods. Suddenly, aroused by the labored panting of our cars, the forest awakes. Unfamiliar birds of gorgeous plumage flash amid the treetops. A big gray ape chatters at us maliciously from his perch on an overhanging rock. A leopard, camouflaged almost to invisibility by his spotted hide, steals on stealthy feet across the road. There is a sudden crash of underbrush behind the jungle wall—an elephant or a tiger perhaps.

The humidity is now terrific. The jungle steams and the rocks radiate heat. The atmosphere is as stifling as that of an orchid-house. The metalwork of the car, and such portions of the leather seat-cushions as are exposed to the sun, become too hot to touch. The coolies who stagger along the road, bent almost double under appalling burdens, gasp for breath and leave dark pools of perspiration in the yellow dust when they halt to rest.

Fortunately for them, however, there are stone drinking-fountains at intervals of a few miles, supplied with water brought down by pipes from the mountains. These are due to the humanity of a princess of the royal house of Nepál, who, sickened by the terrible suffering which she witnessed while traveling by this route, gave orders that fountains be constructed and maintained at her expense.

Bhimpedi, a small and unlovely town with straggling bazaars, dilapidated mud houses, a shabby temple or so, and the usual tank, marks the end of the motor-road and the beginning of the trail over the Sisagarhi Pass. It lies in a broad, platter-shaped valley, stony and treeless, adown which meanders a shallow stream. To the north, half a mile beyond the river, a range known as the Churia Ghati—the first and lowest of the mountain chains which we must cross in order to gain the valley of Nepál—rises abruptly from the plain. Though its height is approximately that of the Presidential range in New Hampshire, it is scarcely more than a ridge in comparison with the stupendous Himalayan heights beyond.

Through my glasses I could descry the trail which we were to take mounting skyward in a series of zigzags which looked like white saber-scars on the face of a frowning giant. A mere shelf blasted from the sheer rock, it appeared perilously steep and narrow, though it proved to be a pleasure promenade compared with what we were to encounter farther on. Perched on a commanding crag near the summit, 2225 feet above the valley floor and more than twice that height above the level of the sea, I could make out the ramparts of the hill-fort which guards the entrance to the pass, and, still higher up, the white walls of the dâk-bungalow where we were to spend the night.

We rattled across the hot and glaring plain, dropped into and climbed out of the boulder-strewn river-bed, and drew up before a cluster of thatched huts in the shadow of the mountain. At first glance I thought that we had stumbled on a traveling circus, for assembled at the foot of the trail were elephants, ponies, donkeys, palanquins, men naked save for loin-cloths, other men in mince-pie hats surmounted by silver tigers, soldiers in bright blue uniforms. The scene was as full of life and color as a show at the New York Hippodrome. The subadar pointed to the aggregation of men and animals, then to ourselves, showing his white teeth in a broad grin. "For the sahibs," he announced proudly. Then I realized that it was not a circus after all, but our safari, our caravan.

Let me see if I can recall the composition of the outfit. To begin with, there were three Tibetan ponies. Two of them, superb white stallions, bore English saddles with safety stirrup-irons. The stirrups and bits were burnished, the russet leather gleamed like polished mahogany, linen slip-covers shielded the saddles from dust and sun. The third pony, not so fine an animal, was evidently intended for Julius. A drove of diminutive donkeys, scarcely larger than the burros of our Southwest, pack-saddles girded on their backs, stood with hanging heads and drooping ears, after the dejected fashion of their kind. Then the elephants, half-a-dozen of them, swinging their trunks restlessly and swaying their huge bodies in what appeared to be an elephantine attempt at the black-bottom. Instead of the glittering howdahs which we had seen on the temple elephants at Madura, each beast bore what appeared to be a mattress—pad is, I believe, the proper term—held in place by two enormous belly-bands. Hard by, surrounded by their bearers, were two of the coffin-shaped palanquins known as dandies which I have described elsewhere. Drawn up beside the road, standing rigidly at attention, was a detachment of Gurkha infantrymen, very smart and businesslike in khaki tunics, shorts and puttees, the broad brims of their felt campaign hats looped up at one side after the fashion of the Australian horse. Beyond were a number of soldierly looking men in somber uniforms of dark gray linen who were distinguished by a most singular form of headdress, resembling a turban which had been run over by a steam-roller, crested with the silver tiger which is the emblem of Nepál. I judged them to be a sort of military police, something after the order of the East African *askari*. Sprawling about on the sun-baked earth were a score or more of baggage coolies, pack-baskets similar to those used by Canadian guides strapped to their backs and held in place by a band encircling the forehead. And, finally, a miscellaneous collection of syces, cooks, servants and hangers-on. In command of the outfit was a grizzled old shikari, lean and agile as a panther, his skin tanned by sun and wind to the color of a much-smoked meerschaum.

The shikari advanced, saluted gravely and spoke a few words in Gurkha to the subadar, who put them into labored Hindustani for the benefit of Julius, who in turn translated them into English of a sort for us.

"He want to know," explained our Singhalese factotum, "whether marsters wish to ride on elephants or on ponies or in dandies. He not know which you like best, so bring 'em all."

"We'll take the ponies," I decided, after a consultation with my cousin. "I don't much fancy the idea of riding up that trail clinging to an elephant's back. It doesn't appeal to me at all. Besides, if we use the ponies we won't have so far to fall."

"I not ride on elephant either," announced Julius. "When I in Mysore on tiger hunt two-three years ago with 'nother marster, I fall off elephant an' break shoulder. I take dandy."

"You will not," I said brutally. "I'm not going to have four coolies hauling your lazy carcass up that mountain in a box on a day as hot as this. You can either take the other pony or walk."

"My insides not feel ver' happy on horse," complained our Admirable Crichton. "Too much jounce. Too much belly-ache. Mebbe I walk."

"You remind me of the colored soldier," I commented, "who refused to join the cavalry because he said he wasn't going to be bothered with a horse when the retreat began."

Until the caravan began to load up I had not realized how much impedimenta was required for a journey into Nepál. Our own duffel, supplemented by the food, water, bedding and other necessities, made an impressive total, but so many coolies and animals had been provided that there wasn't enough luggage to go around. When all was in readiness our ponies were brought up and we swung into the saddle. One of the mahouts dexterously mounted his elephant by shinnying up its tail, hand over hand. We put ourselves at the head of the procession and, guided by the shikari, it moved off toward the mountains. What a pity, I thought, that all this transient glory should be wasted on a few unappreciative natives, that we could not be seen by the folks at home.

Though the trail from Bhimpedi to the summit of the Sisagarhi Pass is a comparatively safe and easy one, it is not wholly devoid of thrills. It is nowhere much over a yard in width, frequently attains a grade in one-in-three, and progresses tortuously upward by an interminable series of acute angles and hairpin turns. In places it was so narrow that, by leaning from my saddle, I could expectorate into a quarter of a mile of emptiness. Now I understood why our saddles were provided with stirrups which would break open if the ponies lost their footing. But the really hair-raising parts of the trip, which nearly gave me a permanent pompadour, were to come later on.

I would not have believed that it was possible for elephants to traverse such a trail had I not seen them do it. It was fascinating to watch them. When one of the huge beasts came to a point where the trail doubled around a projecting shoulder of the cliff he would halt, reach around the corner with his trunk—from the other side it looked as though an immense snake was squirming up the face of the rock—and, after assuring himself that the way was clear, would cautiously advance one ponderous foot and then another, heaving his hind-end around only after his forefeet were securely planted.

Almost as amazing as the agility of the elephants was the endurance displayed by the coolies. Though bent under heavy burdens, they had no difficulty in keeping pace with the ponies. But our own coolies were lightly laden compared with some we passed. In Kenya Colony and in Tanganyika Territory, where the safaris move for the most part over comparatively level ground, the British authorities rigidly limit each porter's load to fifty pounds, but here, in the most mountainous region on earth, the coolies commonly carry twice and even thrice that weight and seemingly think nothing of it.

At one spot where the trail broadened we halted in order to rest our ponies. While we were waiting for the sturdy little animals to get their wind we heard the silvery tinkle of a bell, the coolies behind us pressed themselves close against the face of the cliff, and a slim and sinewy native, naked save for a bit of cloth about his loins, his perspiring skin gleaming like burnished bronze, passed us at a brisk trot, taking the long, steep grade with as little effort as though he were running on the plain. He carried in his hand a short length of bamboo, from one end of which hung the little bell whose warning we had heard; over his shoulder was slung a leathern pouch. He was the mail-runner, so the subadar informed us, on his way to Khatmandu. For every letter which enters or leaves Nepál is carried by runner. There is no other way. Fifty miles and even more a day these Himalayan postmen cover, never slackening speed, pausing only momentarily to drink and not at all for food or rest. The tinkle of the little bells gives warning of their approach, and every one, high or low, must clear the way under pain of heavy punishment.

> From aloe to rose-oak, from rose-oak to fir;
> From level to upland, from upland to crest;
> From rice-field to rock-ridge, from rock-ridge to spur,
> Fly the soft-sandaled feet, strains the brawny brown chest.
> From rail to ravine—to the peak from the vale—
> Up, up through the night goes the Overland Mail.

Upon rounding a shoulder of the mountain, half-way to the summit, my attention was attracted by a slim steel cable, a mere cobweb at that distance, which was festooned from peak to peak. I knew that it was not a telegraph wire—it was much too large for that—yet I could not guess its purpose. I was enlightened very shortly, however, for presently a sort of platform swung from a trolley came sliding down the cable and a few moments later another one appeared, going up. It was the government-owned ropeway, fourteen miles in length, by means of which articles not exceeding half a hundredweight are transported from Bhimpedi to the valley of Nepál.

The sun was just disappearing behind the snow-peaks of the western Himalayas in a burst of gold and crimson splendor when our tired ponies breasted the final pitch and the lichened ramparts of the little hill-fort of Sisagarhi rose to view. A Gurkha sentry challenged sharply, the subadar replied, the guardian presented arms with a clatter, and we rode on, past the gates of the stronghold, to the dâk-bungalow which nestled against the mountain slope.

The rest-house was a long, low structure of stone, its enormously thick walls covered with freshly whitewashed plaster. Before it was a stone terrace and below this a stretch of greensward which had been cropped so closely by a herd of mountain goats that it looked as though it had been cut with manicure scissors. At one end were the quarters for the servants, who, having spied us when we were still far down the trail, had the cooking fires alight. They brought brass basins and quaint ewers filled with hot water; we doffed our dusty garments and scrubbed ourselves until we glowed.

From one of the chop-boxes Julius, who came stumbling in an hour behind us, weary and footsore, produced a bottle of Scotch and another of soda water. From tin cups we drank to those we had left behind us, to the success of the expedition and to our own good health, so that by the time dinner was ready our fatigue had entirely disappeared. Chickens and eggs and milk and butter had been brought in, just as the prime minister had promised, and Messrs.

Armour, Heinz and Campbell provided the rest. Under other conditions we would have thought it a pretty indifferent sort of meal, I suppose, but up there, on the roof of the world, our appetites whetted by the long ride and the tonic of the clear, brisk air, the food tasted better than any I have ever had in the Ritz.

There was only one room in the rest-house—a long, low-ceilinged chamber with smoke-blackened rafters and a fireplace which took logs the size of a man. The floor was of stone, destitute of rugs or carpet, and the furniture consisted of a rude table, a couple of camp chairs and two canvas army cots. The subadar, solicitous for our comfort, produced from somewhere a pair of greasy-looking pillows, but, as I don't care for the scent of hair-oils, pomades and tonics, particularly the brands patronized by the Nepálese, I used my rolled-up overcoat instead. A prison cell would have seemed overfurnished compared with that room, but despite its barrenness it was really quite cozy and homelike when the logs had been set going and we sprawled before the leaping flames with a bottle of Scotch between us and the smoke rising in gray spirals from our pipes.

My cousin, who has not ridden in recent years as much as I have, was dog-tired and turned in early, but I was in no mood for sleep. Our surroundings were so strange and fascinating that I must savor them to the full. So, wrapping myself in my British warm, for the nights in those altitudes are distinctly chilly, I went outside and perched myself upon a parapet overlooking the valley.

Dimly outlined against the starry sky, a sentinel, feet apart, rifle grounded, stood motionless on a bastion of the fort, a silhouette cut from black paper. Far, far below twinkled a few pin-points of flame which I knew for the lights of Bhimpedi. Farther to the south, though I could not see them for the darkness, stretched the malarial jungles of the Terai and, beyond them again, the plains of Hindustan.

Squatting about their camp-fires were the soldiers of the escort and the coolies, their figures black and grotesque against the leaping flames. From the straggling hamlet which clung precariously to the mountainside a few yards below the rest-house came the wail of a native pipe and the chatter of pilgrims' voices speaking strange, outlandish tongues. An elephant trumpeted hoarsely. A pony whinnied. A night bird emitted one long clear call. The wind moaned eerily through the branches of the tall, bare trees. From somewhere in the forest, a wayside shrine perhaps, a strong gong groaned and a drum boomed far.

Behind the fort the trail which we were to follow on the morrow, its stone-strewn surface transformed into a silver stairway by the magic of the moon, wound upward to the summit of the pass. I was impatient to be on our way, to learn what mysteries awaited us beyond that dark divide.

There's a whisper on the night wind, there's a star agleam to guide us,
And the Wild is calling, calling, let us go.

CHAPTER VIII

WITH THE PILGRIMS TO PASHPATTI

I HAVE an incurable aversion to early rising, but the subadar had warned us that the next stage of our journey was a long and arduous one, and that we must start at daybreak if we were to make the Chandragiri Pass by nightfall. It was still dark, therefore, when we turned out upon the cold stone floor; we breakfasted cheerlessly, by the light of a lantern, in the chill grayness which precedes the dawn; and ere the sun had pushed its rim above the distant forests of the Terai we were on our way, the picturesque cortège of horses, donkeys, elephants, soldiers, syces and coolies stringing itself out for a quarter of a mile behind.

Shortly after leaving the rest-house the character of the road abruptly changed. What had been a smooth, if steep and narrow, path became for men and beasts a trail of torture. From the summit of the Sisagarhi Pass a track inconceivably rough and steep, obstructed at frequent intervals by huge boulders and fallen trees, strewn with loose stones which our feet sent clattering in miniature avalanches, dropped precipitously in a succession of twists and turns, at first through dense jungle, then between the frowning walls of a gloomy defile, to debouch into a long and narrow mountain valley through which tumbled a glacial river in a succession of cascades and cataracts.

At several points we were compelled to dismount, not only out of pity for our ponies but from regard for our own necks, for the pitches were so steep, the footing so insecure, that it would have been impossible to have kept our saddles. Even when relieved of our weight it seemed as though the ponies, nimble and sure-footed as they were, must break their legs or be carried over the edge of the cliff by masses of sliding rubble. Compared with that ride down the northern slope of the Sisagarhi, the widely advertised descent into the Grand Canyon by the Bright Angel Trail is tedious and tame.

Here, I thought, is where the elephants fade out of the picture. A circus-trained animal might conceivably descend the Eiffel Tower but not the Sisagarhi. Yet here they came, tail to trunk, slowly, majestically, in stately procession, advancing with infinite caution. The huge beasts displayed a sure-footedness and agility which I had never dreamed that they possessed. They surmounted or detoured boulders the size of grand pianos, they slipped on lichen-coated rocks and tobagganed amid showers of flying rubble, they pivoted their great carcasses on spots no larger than the top of a barrel, but on they came, alternately coaxed and prodded by their mahouts, as inexorably as fate. I have never witnessed a stranger or more impressive scene than when the slate-gray monsters, lurching like so many battle-tanks, emerged from the jungle and began their perilous descent between the towering walls of rock. So it must have been, I imagine, when the great conquerors—Alexander, Jenghiz Khan, Tamerlane, Akbar—seated atop their war elephants, came riding down from the passes to the Asian plain.

Now we were engulfed in the onsweeping tide of pilgrims. All through the night, while we were asleep, they had poured over the pass in an endless river of humanity, picking their way with the aid of lanterns and torches, so that, seen from below, the mountain slopes were festooned with strings of dancing lights. Down the rocky declivities they streamed, across the valley floor, through the swirling river, up the long, steep slopes on the farther side, to disappear at last beyond the distant sky-line. Conspicuous in their white or gaily colored garments, we could follow them with our glasses for miles.

There were thousands, tens of thousands of them; it seemed as though they would never cease. Men, women, children, even babies in arms. The sick, the lame, the blind. Townsmen and countrymen. Priests and pundits. Monks and mendicants. The wealthy and the destitute. The holy and the unholy. A few, comparatively rich, traveled in litters borne by crews of sweating coolies; some were on horseback or astride of donkeys; but the vast majority were afoot. I have witnessed many spectacles which were both piteous and thrilling—the retreat from Mons, the exodus of the civilian population from bombarded Antwerp, the migration of the Bedouin, the flight from the great eruption of Vesuvius, the hadj to Mecca—but I have never seen, and never expect to see, anything so moving, so impressive and withal so pitiful as this mighty Hindu pilgrimage to Pashpatti.

One might say, as my cousin did, that it was merely an example of wasted effort and squandered energy, that these folk might better have stayed at home, in their shops, at their work-benches, on their little farms; but the inescapable fact remained that it constituted a sublime example of religious faith. They were not flying from a ruthless enemy, remember, nor escaping from a convulsion of nature, nor were they lured by a thirst for gold or land. At the cost of enormous sacrifices and appalling hardships these people—not far from a quarter of a million in all—the vast majority of them desperately poor, had left their homes in distant India, their families, their occupations, and, with not enough to eat and not enough to wear, sleeping at night on the bare ground, shivering beneath their scanty cotton garments in the chill winds from the great snows, exposed to many forms of danger and every form of disease, were struggling over this Himalayan *via dolorosa,* not in the hope of any material advantage but in order to gain salvation. It was at once an avenue of agony which they were following and a road of religion, a highway to happiness and a path of pain. They believe in a creed which I detest, but to their unshakable faith in that creed I raise my hat in respect and admiration.

The pilgrimage unrolled before our eyes an amazing panorama of Hinduism, for it included representatives of every caste and from every corner of the Hindu world. Here were Rajputs, Punjabis, Bengalis, Madrassis and Tamils; men from the mountain valleys of Kashmir, the teak-forests of Burma, the palm-fringed coasts of Malabar and Coromandel, the distant archipelagoes of the Andamans and the Nicobars. Here were followers of Brahma, Vishnu, Rama, Krishna, Siva, Indra, Vigneshwara and the countless other deities of the Hindu pantheon. Here were worshipers of bulls, cows, monkeys, snakes, birds, fishes, and of those inconceivably obscene symbols known to votaries of Siva as the *lingam* and the *namam.* Here too were folk who in the practice of their religion perform rites so hideous, so bestial, so unspeakably lewd, that the mind staggers at thought of such depravity and foulness.

The most curious and loathsome of the innumerable types of devotees who straggled past us were the so-called holy men, who are really professional beggars, religious mendicants, parasites who solicit alms in the precincts of the temples or attach themselves to pilgrimages such as this. These *melas* are, indeed, the only occasions when the holy men travel in such large numbers, though they seldom wander about quite alone. Their manner when demanding alms is nearly always insolent and audacious, and often threatening. They generally pursue their begging to an accompaniment of dancing and singing; the more indecent their ballads, the more freely they are interlarded with obscenities, the better they are calculated to attract offerings. In many respects they resemble the mendicant friars of the Dark Ages who roamed the highways of Europe and followed the Crusades.

Though at night the common run of pilgrims stretch themselves on the bare ground, the holy men find food and lodgings in the villages along the route, each householder taking in one or more of them, so that they travel without cost to themselves. If the host of one of these parasites happens to have a young daughter—and by that I mean a girl over six or seven years of age—the self-imposed guest demands her for the night, and invariably obtains her, for no devout Hindu would bring down upon his head the curses of a holy man for the sake of preserving his daughter's virginity. Far from objecting, he would feel flattered. It is safe to say, indeed, that the only virgins left in the country-side after the pilgrimage had passed were babies.

Half or wholly naked—for many of them wore nothing save half a gourd held in place by a cord about the loins—their bodies smeared with ashes and cow-dung, their faces streaked and dotted with scarlet, white and ocher, their matted beards straggling over hirsute chests, their long hair dyed orange or vermilion and twisted into topknots wound with strings of charms and beads, these holy men were as grotesque and horrible as the creatures of a disordered brain. Some of them had leopard skins slung over their shoulders in lieu of blankets; many wore about their necks or on their legs strings of little bells whose tinkle gave warning of their approach. Each one carried a brass begging-bowl, a bronze gong and a conch horn, the paraphernalia of their trade being completed by an iron rod at either end of which hung a little brazier containing the live coals for burning the incense which they use in making sacrifices. Daubed with paint and offal, caked with dust and sweat, crawling with vermin, smelling to high heaven, they were filthy and hideous beyond the imagination of decent men. In fact, the filthier one of these fellows is, the greater his sanctity in popular opinion. Judged by zymotic standards, most of them deserved canonization.

Likewise there were holy women, not quite so naked as the men, but, were such a thing possible, even more repulsive and disgusting. To witness the self-degradation of a man is repellent; to see a woman degrade herself is revolting. Both men and women, needless to say, are as devoid of any moral sense as the animals which they worship and like which they live. They cohabit with each other or with any one else, shamelessly, anywhere, whenever the opportunity offers. And, as a result of this promiscuity, wherever they go they leave a trail of venereal diseases behind them.

Perhaps half a notch above the holy men in personal cleanliness and morals, but below them in popular estimation, were the jugglers, conjurers, snake-charmers and miscellaneous mountebanks who had joined the pilgrimage for purposes of gain, just as those of the same ilk flock to county fairs at home. Some of these charlatans drive a thriving trade with a credulous public in love-philters, potions and charms. From them can be obtained weird concoctions which are guaranteed to enable the purchaser to seduce another man's wife or to cause the death of the lady's husband.

Others are acrobats or conjurers, some of whom perform feats of agility and legerdemain which would have taxed the ingenuity of the late Mr. Harry Houdini to reproduce. Most of these conjuring exhibitions are extremely crude, readily seen through by the discerning, but some are really amazing, the more so because of the meagerness of the performer's apparatus and because he gives his performances in the open, unaided by lights, curtains or mechanical devices. I have seen the mango trick performed by an Indian conjurer clad only in a loin-cloth, his paraphernalia consisting only of a flower-pot and a sheet, with a skill which defied detection. On the other hand, I have never seen a boy climb a rope which had been tossed into the air and disappear, though I have met one or two persons who claimed to have seen it.

The best known of the conjurer castes is that of the Dombers. To the earnings which the men make by tumbling or sleight-of-hand the women add the sums which they gain by the most shameless immorality, their favors, if favors they can be called, being bestowed on any one who cares to pay for them.

Some of the Hindu jugglers specialize in snake-charming, usually employing cobras, the most poisonous of all serpents. In spite of their care and skill in handling these deadly reptiles, it sometimes happens that they are bitten, and this would almost certainly cost them their lives did they not take the precaution to excite their snakes every morning, causing them to bite several times through a thick piece of cloth, thereby expending the venom which re-forms daily in their fangs.

A curious feature of the pilgrimage was provided by the fanatics who, whether to gain silver or salvation, or perhaps with an eye out for both, indulge in various revolting forms of self-torture and mutilation. One man, doubtless a member of the same sect as the fanatic I saw at the Kali Ghat in Calcutta, had held his right arm above his head so long that the member had become withered and useless. The body of another was gridironed with the scars which he had inflicted on himself with red-hot irons. A third carried on his shoulders a couch of sharpened spikes on which he was wont to stretch himself at intervals, one hand held out to the passing pilgrims for alms. His body was so toughened, I imagine, that the spikes caused him only a minimum of pain. There were still others who had thrust long skewers through their lips, cheeks, arms or chests, so that little streams of blood cut crimson furrows in the dust which caked their bodies. One wild-eyed, wild-haired creature bore a brazier of glowing coals, on which he would dance from time to time with his bare feet. Still another votary, who had evidently taken a vow to make the pilgrimage caterpillar fashion, would stretch himself on the ground, rise again, advance a couple of paces, and repeat the asinine performance. When I saw him he was making his singular progress through a village street, but I suspect that he was not so meticulous when he was out in the country, where no one was watching. I certainly should have enjoyed seeing him employ that form of locomotion coming down from the Sisagarhi Pass. He could have made excellent time by putting his toes in his mouth and rolling down the mountainside like a hoop-snake!

Many of the pilgrims were apparently persons of means who had undertaken the pilgrimage, no doubt, in fulfilment of vows made to their gods, and traveled luxuriously in dandies or curtained litters. Only a few rode horses, but a number were astride of mules or asses. And I also saw a number of weak or aged women, a score at least, borne in baskets strapped to the backs of coolies. Into these receptacles they were wedged like huge rag dolls, bent almost double, their feet hanging out behind and their heads lolling on the porter's shoulder. When it is remembered that it takes a coolie thus burdened in the neighborhood of a week to make the journey over the mountains you will have a better idea of the excruciating discomfort involved in this form of travel.

The strength and endurance of the Nepálese coolies, as I have observed elsewhere, are astounding. A load of one hundred and fifty pounds is not uncommon, and the coolie who carries it will do his twelve to fifteen miles a day, depending upon the nature of the trail, for the equivalent of eight cents per diem. The women are apparently as sturdy and tireless as the men. I saw a woman coolie carrying on her back a teakwood chest the size of a large wardrobe trunk—one of those wardrobe trunks which would cause two burly American expressmen to complain bitterly if they were asked to carry it up a single flight of stairs. Yet this stocky little brown woman was carrying her enormous burden up a flight of steps a mile high, puffing unconcernedly at a huge calabash pipe and bearing in her arms a suckling baby.

The scenes along the trail were often heartrending. Lying at intervals beside the track were those who had fallen from sheer exhaustion. Indeed, scores if not hundreds of the aged and infirm die on every pilgrimage. At sight of the elephants a young woman went into violent hysterics, evidently as a result of the terrific physical and nervous strain. An aged blind man groped along, clinging to the belt of his companion, who could see. A paralytic crawled by upon all fours, like some huge species of beetle. (I wondered how many months he had been upon the road.) A white-haired pilgrim was rubbing the limbs of his equally aged wife, who had collapsed from fatigue and could go no farther. Stretched on the steps of a wayside shrine was the corpse of a man, his wife and children gathered about it in silent misery. A little farther on a woman was giving birth to a baby in a field, with no medical attendance, without so much as a blanket to lie on.

But, undeterred by these individual tragedies, the mighty river of humanity rolled on, rolled on.

So dense became the throng as we pushed down the winding valley that our police and syces had literally to make a path for us by force, shouting *"Hai! Hai! Hai!"* shoving the pilgrims aside, and at times even laying about them with their whips. Yet the pilgrims, who, as my cousin aptly remarked, looked and acted like a flock of Highland black-faced sheep, took this rude treatment submissively, neither by word nor sign betraying any resentment. Barring the holy men, who either glowered maliciously or turned their backs at sight of my camera, I did not once observe a hostile glance cast in our direction or hear an unfriendly word.

The vast majority of the pilgrims, as I have already remarked, were wretchedly poor. Without blankets, clad in the thin cotton garments of the lowlands, they stretched themselves at night on the bare mountain slopes, aching in every bone and muscle, their feet numb with pain, chilled by the piercing wind, clinging shiveringly to each other in a pathetic attempt to achieve at least fictitious warmth. Though, upon their arrival at Pashpatti, they are fed at the expense of the king, and though most of them find shelter of a sort in the temples and monasteries, they must carry the bulk of the food required for the journey with them, for the mountains which they traverse are unproductive and the miserable villages are few and far between.

The garments worn by the pilgrims were of all the colors in the spectrum, so that the moving column looked like a rainbow stretched athwart the mountainside. The majority wore white, which, incidentally, is a sign of mourning in Nepál, but there were poisonous pinks, screaming scarlets, bilious blues and violent purples. Some of the combinations, however, were enchanting—tobacco-brown and corn-yellow, indigo and pale blue, light green and lavender, claret and cerise—the effects thus produced rivaling the most ravishing creations of Poiret and Paquin.

All save the very poorest of the women were littered with cheap jewelry. So bedecked were their persons with nose-rings, ear-rings, necklaces, bangles, bracelets, girdles and anklets that when they moved they clashed and clattered like a gun-team. Their costumes, though usually of the cheapest materials, were graceful and alluring: full muslin skirts gathered at the waist, and short, semi-transparent jackets, sometimes elaborately embroidered in gold or silver thread. As the two garments failed to meet, a narrow strip of bronze-brown torso was revealed between.

I had heard so much about the beauty of Indian women that in an assemblage as vast as this I had confidently expected to find any number of lovely creatures—slim, supple damsels with smooth brown skins and languorous, provocative eyes, like the houri described in those familiar verses which begin, "Pale hands I loved beside the Shalimar, where art thou now?" But I was woefully disappointed. Many of them were slender and graceful enough, due, no doubt, to their practice of bearing burdens on their heads, and most of them were brown as a cigar, but I saw only one whose hands I would have been tempted to hold, whether in the perfumed darkness beside the Shalimar or anywhere else. Her hands happened to be clean because when I came upon her, as I rounded an abrupt turn in the trail, she was in the midst of taking a bath. She could hardly have been more than seventeen—a lovely creature, with delicately formed features, slim, rounded limbs, firm, pointed breasts, and a skin of lustrous gold-brown satin shot with rose. She had slipped off her *sari,* unloosed her wealth of blue-black hair so that it cascaded over her shoulders, and was standing, entirely nude, in the attitude of "September Morn," beneath a little waterfall. She made a charming picture, a young goddess of the hills, and I called to the subadar to bring my camera. But she divined my intention, even if she did not understand the words, and, ere I could focus the instrument, she had deftly wound herself into her *sari* again. I tried to cajole her into posing, for she was coquettish rather than alarmed, but she shrugged her lovely shoulders mischievously, flashed me a dazzling smile and fled. Had I had young Richard Halliburton's flair for adventure and facility for getting out of scrapes, I should have followed her—and probably would have received a knife-thrust in the back from one of her gentlemen friends for my pains.

The scenery in the valley which lies on the northern side of the Churia Ghati range is enchantingly beautiful and in places approaches the sublime. A river—I believe that it is called the Panoni, but I am not certain—roaring down from the great heights has cut its way through the rock in a series of precipice-walled canyons and leafy glens. At one point it drops from sight completely into a subterranean cavern and does not reappear until a mile or so farther on. It swirls along tumultuously, here hurtling over lofty ledges in waterfalls which look like the tails of tall white horses; then pausing for a moment, as though for breath, in deep, clear pools, before resuming its headlong course. One moment its waters flow silently, like dark green glass, through defiles as narrow as a mill-race; the next they are churned into foam and spray by the teeth of unseen rocks.

In one deep pool we saw some natives fishing with huge nets, which they cast with amazing dexterity and drew in with considerable success. Being myself a fisherman, I halted to watch them. It is not generally known, perhaps, that in these Himalayan streams is found one of the great game-fishes of the world—the mahseer. Black bass, brook trout, salmon, maskalonge, tuna, tarpon—I have caught them all and all are very well in their way, but for sheer sport and unmatchable thrill give me a mahseer on a light rod. I asked Julius to ask the subadar to ask the fishermen if they ever caught mahseer in this particular river. One of the men nodded affirmatively and held his arms at full stretch by way of illustrating the fish's size.

"On what kind of tackle does he catch them?" I inquired. "Does he use live bait or a fly or a spoon?"

With some difficulty the import of my question was made clear to the Nepálese Zane Grey.

"He say," interpreted Julius, "he use dynamite."

Particularly colorful were the scenes at the fords, where thousands of pilgrims were bathing in the chilly waters. The men, stark naked, shone like bronze statues in the brilliant sunshine. The women, a degree more modest, entered the river draped in their thin *saris,* which, once wet, clung to them tenaciously, revealing every line and contour of their lithe forms. The banks were covered with acres of garments drying in the sun. Animals—horses, donkeys, bullocks, buffaloes, elephants—a perfect menagerie of them, were being watered in the same pools where the pilgrims were drinking and bathing, befouling the water with their offal and stirring up the mud with their hoofs.

According to the calendar, it was mid-February, but it might have been late spring in this isolated, mountain-girt valley if one were to judge by the vegetation, for the fruit trees were bursting into bloom and the whole Vale was a sea of blossomed snow. Apples, pears, cherries, peaches, apricots, almonds, oranges, bananas and melons all thrive in Nepál, and, while they do not attain the size of our American fruits, they are nearly equal to them in flavor. At roadside stalls and in the bazaars of the hamlets through which we passed, sweet potatoes, popcorn and peanuts were being sold in great quantities to the pilgrims, the sight of these familiar products lending to the strange scene a touch of home.

Marku, a small town beside the river, which is here spanned by an iron bridge, was choked with pilgrims—*constipé,* as the French would put it—and the local merchants were driving a roaring trade. Hundreds of the weary devotees were sprawling in the dust of the single street or squatting on their heels in the scanty shade afforded by a few discouraged looking trees. The terrace of a little temple, its three dagobas surmounted by gilded finials, was carpeted with recumbent forms. A snake-charmer was doing his hackneyed stuff before a tumbledown caravanserai. Leaning from a decrepit balcony, pantomiming suggestively for the benefit of the passersby below, were three or four hard-faced women with staring patches of carmine on their cheeks and kohl-blackened eyes. Evidently the local *filles de joie.* From within came the twang of stringed instruments and the monotonous *tumpa-tumpa-tump* of tom-toms.

At Marku we left the river and the valley behind us, the trail climbing by a short but extremely steep ascent to a broad and breeze-swept table-land, its gently rolling surface broken by a series of low hills as round and brown as the breasts of a Hindu woman. The terrain was almost destitute of trees, but the sides of the road were gay with clumps of scented pink mimosa and there were patches of wild begonias in many colors. Dotting the slopes were a few houses, distinctly Tibetan in architecture, with curiously shaped tiled roofs and pinkish-orange walls. It was easy riding upon the plateau, and, exhilarated by the cool breeze from the great peaks beyond, we spurred our ponies to a gallop, for the first time leaving the coolies and pack-animals far in the rear.

While crossing this table-land we encountered a picturesque little cortège. It evidently had no connection with the pilgrimage, for it was going in the opposite direction. It may have been a wedding procession—and then, again, it may not. First came a dozen musicians assiduously engaged in extracting tortured sounds from various weird instruments—cymbals, flutes, conch-horns, drums. After them straggled a group of men armed with spears and swords and carrying long bamboo poles from which flaunted banners of many colors. Then an enormously stout man bearing aloft a huge saffron-colored umbrella. And, finally, a curtained dooly borne by a score of coolies. As I reined my pony aside to let the litter pass, the curtains parted a few inches and I caught a fleeting glimpse of a pair of ravishing eyes and a bewitching little face with lips like ripe cherries. I know that the lips smiled at me provocatively and I think—though of this I am not certain—that a slim white hand furtively beckoned me to follow. I am not beyond the romance-loving age, thank heaven, and I confess that I should have liked to have seen more of the lady of the litter, to have learned who she was and whither she was going. But my cousin was waiting impatiently ahead and the escort was coming up behind, so I resolutely turned my back on romance and trotted on. Perhaps it was as well that I did so, for a few moments later a big, black-bearded fellow, evidently a local chieftain, mounted on a fine white pony and followed by two retainers with rifles across their saddle-bows, came pounding down the road in pursuit of the palanquin.

Some miles after leaving Marku we overtook two motor-cars of a well-known American make which were being transported to Khatmandu for the use of the royal family. The wheels had been removed, each being carried by a coolie. The chassis were slung from long bamboo poles, two hundred coolies, divided into four relays, being assigned to each machine. This chanced to be a level stretch —one of the few such on the entire journey—and the coolies were moving at a brisk, swinging walk, doing perhaps three miles an hour. In the mountains, however, where the going is inconceivably difficult, they sometimes cover little more than that distance in an entire day. What puzzled me was how, on the narrow, precipice-bordered trails, they succeeded in getting a motor-car with a 140-inch wheelbase around corners so sharp that even a pony has difficulty in negotiating them. But give a native of these regions a length or so of stout bamboo, a sufficient force of coolies, and time to think out the problem, and he will undertake to move anything. The electrical power-house erected by the Government at Khatmandu provides a striking illustration of the extraordinary skill of the Nepálese in this form of transportation, every piece of ironwork and machinery, including the huge dynamos, having been brought in by coolies. There is no other way.

Now we descended again, this time by easy gradients, into the smiling Vale of Chitlung, or, as it is sometimes called, Little Nepál, a lovely, fertile valley hemmed in by forest-mantled mountains. At Chitlung we halted in order to give the baggage coolies time to rest, for here commences the most trying portion of the entire journey, the terrible climb to the saddle of the Chandragiri Pass, more than eight thousand feet above the level of the sea, which marks the summit of the last of the series of great natural ramparts protecting Nepál on the south.

Compared with the task that now confronted us, all that had gone before was but a pleasant promenade. I could scarcely bring myself to believe that this slender path which so giddily zigzagged skyward, now skirting the brink of yawning chasms, often no more than a succession of footholds chopped from the rock, formed the principal, and, indeed, the only practicable route from India into Nepál. It was like scrambling up the roof of a Gothic church, for in many places the trail attains a gradient of forty-five degrees and occasionally even more. In order to make the steeper acclivities possible for anything save goats, thousands of rude steps have been hewn from the almost perpendicular mountainside, one of these series forming what amounted to a giant staircase, more than two miles long.

Here, of course, riding was utterly out of the question, but we hung to the stirrup-leathers and let the ponies haul us along. Even so, we were compelled to pause at frequent intervals for breath, for, coming from the low-lying Indian plain, it seemed as though our lungs would burst in that rarefied air a mile and a half above sea-level.

Yet we, healthy and in the pink of condition, had no cause to complain, for keeping pace with us up that awful trail were the pilgrims, men and women, young and old, thousands upon thousands of them, many staggering under heavy loads. A man with empty eye-sockets groped a slow way upward, his faltering footsteps guided by his little son. A cripple, both legs amputated at the knees, made astonishing progress on his clumsy crutches. A woman, a baby at her breast and dragging a small child by the hand, dropped athwart the trail in a dead faint. A dozen coolies, bearing a dooly swung from a bamboo pole, breasted the acclivity, here so steep that the feet of the men in front were on a level with the heads of those in the rear. A squat brown porter, not five feet tall, panted by, his breath coming in great sobs, on his back a basket containing a woman.

Now the ascent became so appalling that even our police and syces, inured to fatigue as they were, halted every few yards, gasping for breath. Yet the trail, which we could see for miles ahead, was so crowded with pilgrims that in places they jostled each other. And behind and below us were other thousands, the endless stream stretching down the mountain, across the Chitlung Vale, up the slopes on the other side, until it was lost to sight beyond the distant table-land. It was an example of physical fortitude and religious devotion of which I never expect to see the like.

The last few miles were a veritable nightmare. Though a chill wind drove down upon us, we were soaked to the skin with perspiration. My eyes were blinded with sweat. Every bone and muscle held an intolerable ache. The calves of my legs swelled until it seemed as though they must burst my field-boots. My shoes felt as though they were soled with lead, like those worn by a diver; I could scarcely place one foot before the other. My lungs labored like a blacksmith's bellows; a trip-hammer had replaced my heart.

Our progress was inconceivably slow and arduous. We would climb a hundred feet and halt to rest and then climb a hundred more and rest again. The stench from the sweating bodies of the pilgrims was overpowering. It hung in odoriferous clouds above the trail as it did in European towns during the war after the armies had marched through them. The air was filled with gasps, groans, cries, imprecations, the crack of whips, the creak of leather, the jingle of metal, the panting of overtaxed lungs, and the ceaseless *shuffle-shuffle-shuffle* of tired and dragging feet. For these poor folk it was a way of agony, yet despite their spent bodies and tortured limbs, they pressed doggedly upward and ever upward, many with the rapt expressions of sleep-walkers, for before them, somewhere beyond that purple rim which seemed tantalizingly to grow no nearer, lay the holy city whose attainment spelled spiritual salvation.

You who read these pages while seated in a comfortable arm-chair, you whose idea of physical fatigue is to play thirty-six holes of golf or to do a long day's shopping, you who complain when your breakfast is late in being served, or when you have to stand because the subway trains are crowded—how can I hope to convey to you any adequate conception of the fatigue and misery, the heartbreak and horror, of this pilgrimage to Pashpatti? You can't conceive of it, because you have not seen it, because your mental horizons are too circumscribed, because your upholstered, *à la carte,* easy-going lives afford no basis for comparison. Oh, hell! What's the use?

At long, long last we breasted the final pitch and staggered out, on legs so weary that they could scarcely bear our weight, into the rock-walled defile which forms the saddle of the pass. The narrow space was so thickly strewn with prostrate, panting pilgrims that it was with difficulty that we avoided stepping on them. But what a panorama rewarded our eager eyes! What an introduction to that mysterious land which it had cost us so much toil to reach! Our weariness was swept away by the sublimity of the scene as a draft of fresh air clears a musty room. I shall remember that moment as long as memory lasts.

The pine-clad southern slopes of the range had had an almost alpine character, but, by one of those abrupt transitions peculiar to Nepál, the northern slope was clothed with a tangle of tropic vegetation, rank-growing and vivid green —lofty sal- and sisu-trees, and others whose names I did not know, spreading banyans, stately palms, fragrant acacias, flowering mimosas, rattans, huge bamboos, giant tree-ferns, the whole festooned with lianas, intertwined and bound together with creepers, hung with orchids and parasitic growths of every kind. Below this wide green zone of vegetation, three thousand feet down, lay the broad valley floor, flat as the top of a table, checkered with the brown squares of plowed lands and the green ones of sprouting grain. And away to the eastward, glittering in the sun, rose three congeries of gilded roofs and pinnacles which I knew for the templed cities of Khatmandu, Patan and Bhatgaon.

The opposite side of the valley was hidden by a curtain of fleecy clouds, but these parted even while we looked, as the stage curtains are drawn aside in a theater, to disclose the sublimest scene that this world has to offer. Stretching along the horizon from east to west as far as the eye could see rose, range upon snowy range, the main chain of the Himalayas, the wilderness of snow-bonneted peaks scintillating in the rays of the sun like uncut diamonds. Almost opposite us was Dayabung, and behind it, looming over its shoulder, was the still mightier Gosainthan, while, far away to the eastward, Kinchinjunga, Kubra and Singalelah marked the frontier of Sikkim. And in the middle distance—a hundred and fifty miles away as the airplane flies but seemingly not a tenth of that distance—one small peak showed solitary and clear against the cloudless sky. Wrapped in robes of snowy ermine, majestic, imperial, aloof, Everest, the monarch of all mountains, reared itself twenty-nine thousand feet into the Asian blue.

As we stood staring, speechless, overcome by awe, we were joined by the soldiers of the escort, the syces and the coolies. At sight of the broad and smiling valley which lay outspread at our feet, and the stupendous barrier of snow peaks beyond, they with one accord dropped weapons and burdens on the ground, flung their hands above their heads in a spontaneous gesture of adoration, and cried, as a man might cry aloud the name of his loved one, "NEPÁL! NEPÁL! NEPÁL!"

CHAPTER IX

THE FORBIDDEN COUNTRY

To OBTAIN a single fleeting glimpse of Everest is a rare and precious privilege, as will be attested by every one who for that purpose has journeyed to Darjeeling, the only point in India from which the peak is visible; to see it for several days running is little short of a miraculous dispensation. For the great mountain is like a beautiful but haughty lady who, save on infrequent occasions, persists in hiding her bewitching countenance behind a veil of mist and clouds. She deigned to smile on us, however—perhaps because she knew that we did not seek her conquest but had come only to stand at a respectful distance and admire—and on three days in succession drew aside her veil to dazzle us with her surpassing loveliness. An ice-empress, wrapped in ermine and diademed with diamonds, she is as alluring as she is aloof. No wonder that men by the score have laid down their lives in vain attempts to win her.

Before we descend the slopes of Chandragiri, perhaps it would be as well for me to tell you something of the mysterious and forbidden country which lies outspread at our feet like a map in bas-relief. Nepál is in shape a rough parallelogram, five hundred and fifty miles in length and about a fourth of that in average breadth, wedged between India and Tibet, with the British-protected state of Sikkim snuggling up against its eastern border. Though the area of the kingdom is scarcely greater than that of Florida, there may be found within its borders every variation of physiography and climate, from the eternal snows of the Himalayas to the eternal summer which prevails on the plains of the Terai.

Nepál is in reality a maelstrom of mountains. Stretching along the country's northern frontier in a stupendous wall is the main range of the Himalayas, bastioned on the west by Dhawalagiri and on the east by Kinchinjunga, with any number of tremendous peaks, including Everest, in between. South of these, falling away in tiers, like the seats in a stadium, are numerous secondary ranges, varying from sixteen thousand feet in height to a mere six thousand. These are intersected at intervals by lateral ranges, the country being thus gridironed into a vast number of detached valleys and isolated glens. Protecting Nepál on the south are the two ranges which we crossed by the Sisagarhi and Chandragiri passes, the southernmost of these barriers, the Churia Ghati, dropping down into the forests, jungles and rice-fields of the Terai, which in turn merges into the plains of Hindustan.

Almost in the center of this chaos of corrugation, like a single splendid emerald set in deeply wrought platinum, is a small green oval, perhaps thirty miles long by twenty wide—the valley of Nepál. Overshadowed by the mighty peaks which rise from its very edge, it clings to the world's white eaves.

This, the one flat and fertile spot in the whole of the tossed and tumbled configuration, is the very heart and soul of the country. Here are the capital and all the larger towns, together with shrines and temples without number. Here, hemmed in on all sides by the wildest and most inaccessible regions of the Himalayas, are concentrated the life and activity of the state. So perfect, indeed, is the continuity of the mountain wall around this verdant vale that, were it possible to block the one pass through which the Baghmatti River flows to the plains, the waters, unable to escape, would convert the valley once more into a lake, which it was in prehistoric times.

In a country possessing such an amazing range of altitudes the flora and fauna are, of course, extremely varied, the transitions from the torrid to the temperate and from the temperate to the frigid zone being in places—as at the summit of the Chandragiri Pass, for example—positively startling in their abruptness. These zones are not always sharply defined, however, the climate and vegetation being affected by local conditions. Consequently, tropical animals and plants are often found in the interior, while species ordinarily characteristic of the great heights find their way down the spurs into the lowlands.

By far the greater part of the sixty thousand square miles of Nepálese territory has never been trodden by a white man. Unexplored, unmapped, virtually unknown, it is literally the last home of mystery. The nature of the country which lies to the west, the north, the east of the Vale, what manner of people dwell in its hidden valleys, are matters for conjecture, for no European can speak of them from first-hand knowledge. The adjoining country of Tibet, traditionally regarded as the final great secret of geography, has had its Hedins, its Savage Landors, its Younghusbands, and the literature on the subject fills many bookshelves. But the bibliography of Nepál consists of less than a score of volumes, and nearly all of these accounts are largely circumstantial. A British punitive expedition penetrated Tibet within recent years; British trade commissioners and missionaries are now established within its borders. But more than a century has passed since a foreign military force violated the soil of Nepál; no missionaries are permitted within the country; and the British representative at Khatmandu is a virtual prisoner in his own legation.

The abysmal lack of knowledge in regard to the hinterland of Nepál is due in some measure to the savage and inhospitable nature of the terrain itself, but even more to the distrustful attitude of the government, which professes to see in every explorer, scientist, prospector, sportsman, and missionary who seeks admittance a potential threat to the country's cherished independence. And the liberty-loving mountaineers are prepared to resist penetration, pacific or otherwise, by every means in their power, peacefully if they can, forcibly if they must, for they have no intention of permitting their country to be absorbed, under the guise of a protectorate or a sphere of influence, by that empire on which the sun never sets.

Owing to this deep-seated fear that they may harbor designs against the nation's independence, and because they are not wanted anyway, Europeans are very rarely permitted to enter the valley of Nepál on any pretext whatsoever. It is safe to say, indeed, that the Americans who have succeeded in penetrating as far as the capital could be numbered on the fingers of a single hand. When we were in Nepál the total European population consisted of but seven persons: the British envoy, his niece, an English electrical engineer in the Nepálese service, his wife and two small children, and an English trained nurse employed by the royal family. A tiny island of white men in a sea of brown ones, and the white man's world very far away.

The policy of the successive rulers of Nepál has always been shaped toward one end—the preservation of the country's splendid isolation. Encircled by the impregnable ramparts of the Himalayas, and still further guarded on the south by the malarial jungles of the Terai; peopled by a race of warriors who would rather fight than eat;

the only practicable ingress from the south through defiles so narrow and lofty that they could be, and have been, held against overwhelming odds by a handful of riflemen; with an admirably trained and well-equipped field army which numbers not far from fifty thousand men and a reserve which includes every able-bodied man in the kingdom, Nepál would prove a hard nut to crack.

It is not surprising, therefore, that this Himalayan kingdom can lay claim to being the one independent state in Asia which has remained virtually immune from European influences. By this I do not mean to imply that the Nepálese authorities have frowned on modern improvements, or have ignored the object-lessons provided by Western civilization. The Government is, on the contrary, distinctly progressive, its excellent electric light and water systems, the large and up-to-date power-house, the fine modern hospital in Khatmandu, the railway to Amlekgunj, the ropeway over the mountains, and the few but well-engineered roads which it has built, proving that it is eager to do as much for the welfare of its people as restricted resources and the limitations imposed by nature will permit.

But the manners and customs of the people, their religions, arts and industries, their mode of life and in a large measure their form of government, are to all intents and purposes the same as they were a thousand years ago. As aloof as the great peaks which surround her, unaffected by any foreign influences, undisturbed by the political transitions and social upheavals which have taken place in the outside world, Nepál, an island amid a sea of mountains, provides a striking illustration of what India was like before Islam set its indelible mark on almost every aspect of Indian life. Here, as Mr. Percy Brown has truthfully remarked, may be seen an ideal picture of the Middle Ages—the Middle Ages of the East.

It began raining soon after we commenced the descent of the Chandragiri Pass, and long ere we reached the valley floor what had started in as a mountain drizzle became a tropical downpour. And let me assure you that when it rains in the Himalayas it *rains*. The heavens open, as though a celestial dam had given way, and the waters descend in a deluge. When dry, the trail down the northern slope, though steep and narrow, is tolerably safe if negotiated with caution, but in wet weather it becomes as slippery and as dangerous as a glacier. Being impatient to reach our destination, I spurred my mount to a trot—and almost paid for my recklessness with my life. Rounding a hairpin turn, where the yard-wide trail was bordered on one side by a perpendicular wall of rock and on the other by an equally sheer precipice, we struck a small patch of soft and rain-soaked soil, treacherous as Virginia red clay. The feet of my pony suddenly shot out from under him and I thought for one horrid instant that we would both disappear into the yawning abyss. But, as the little animal fell, the safety stirrups opened automatically, leaving my feet free, and I hurled myself from the saddle. The pony's off hind leg was actually over the edge of the precipice, but with the agility of a cat he managed to scramble on to firm ground, where he stood trembling. I freely confess that I was trembling too.

It was lucky for us that the rain began no sooner, for an hour or so of that terrific downpour would have washed out the trail and left us marooned upon the mountainside. Even so it was not an enjoyable experience, for huge boulders, loosened by the rain, hurtled across our path, and the veil of fog which enveloped everything was in places so dense that we could not see the trail a dozen yards ahead. The rain, diverted by my topée to my British warm, ran down into the tops of my boots, so that after a little time my feet were immersed in miniature lakes. The saddles were wet and clammy; our fingers so numb that they could scarcely hold the reins. But the police and syces, their heads and shoulders muffled in blankets, plodded along stoically. They were used to it.

When we at length drew rein at Thankot, a cluster of squalid huts at the foot of the trail, we were dispirited and irritable; gone was the elation with which we had first viewed this valley of Nepál. But things began to take on a tinge of cheerfulness when we found awaiting us a big American car with a chauffeur in the livery of the royal household at the wheel. The prime minister had overlooked no detail. I might mention, in passing, that there are nearly a dozen cars in Nepál, all made in the United States, all belonging to members of the royal or ruling families, and all brought over the mountains by coolies at the cost of enormous labor and patience. For the use of these few cars the government has constructed a passably good road, seven miles long, from Thankot to Khatmandu, and other roads radiate from the capital to Patan, Bhatgaon and Pashpatti.

In our eagerness to reach the valley and find shelter from the rain we had paid no heed to Julius and the coolies, who, we assumed, were close behind, but upon arriving at Thankot they were not in sight. We waited an hour, shivering in our wet garments, but they did not put in an appearance. This was serious, because they had our dry clothes, our food supply, and, most important of all, our entire stock of whisky. We were greatly irritated. To make matters worse, darkness was not far off and the rain was coming down harder than ever. There seemed nothing for it but to let Julius, who was accompanied by the subadar, shift for himself and ourselves keep on to Khatmandu.

The road from Thankot to the capital is fairly good

when dry, but in wet weather it is a holy terror. Furthermore, our Nepálese chauffeur betrayed an abysmal ignorance of the rudiments of driving a motor-car. He might have been efficient enough behind a team of bullocks, but at the wheel of a car he was a distinct wash-out. Because of his top-knot his cap would not stay in place, and he was constantly taking both hands off the wheel to adjust it. It was a very smart cap, with a colored cockade, and of it he was inordinately proud.

Despite the fact that the road was narrow, highly crowned and perilously slippery, he insisted on giving us a demonstration of what his car was capable of in the way of speed. He started off at a clip which fairly took my breath away, the wheels first skirting the edge of one ditch and then skidding to the edge of the other.

"Slow up, you God-damn fool!" my cousin shouted. "Do you want to wreck us?"

The Nepálese, who understood no word of any language save his own, evidently thought that we were complimenting him, for he answered by stepping on the gas all the harder. The needle of the speedometer showed that we were doing close to seventy miles an hour.

"I wish now," I called to my cousin, "that I had followed the advice of my friends and taken out some accident insurance. It doesn't look to me as though we are going to see the last inning."

At that instant my half-joking prediction came within an ace of being fulfilled. Taking the brow of a hill at such terrific speed that all four wheels seemed to leave the ground, we went hurtling down the slope on the other side like a runaway train. A slow-witted peasant chose this inauspicious moment to drive a herd of humpbacked native cattle into the middle of the road. Now cattle are sacred animals in Nepál, and the man who kills one is subject to the death penalty, or at any rate to imprisonment for life, to say nothing of his soul being condemned to eternal perdition. I don't know whether our driver feared most for his soul or his life, but in order to avoid plowing into the mass of sacred beasts he jammed on foot- and hand-brakes simultaneously. What might have been expected happened. The car, abruptly checked in its mad career, swerved, lurched perilously, and, missing the edge of a six-foot embankment by a hair's breadth, skidded completely around, so that we found ourselves looking up the hill which we had just descended.

"Listen, my friend," I said to the now thoroughly frightened chauffeur, tapping him on the shoulder with my heavy riding-crop, "you'll either drive slowly from now on or I'll paste you over the head with this and take the wheel myself. I haven't come all the way to Nepál to be killed in a motor smash."

He didn't understand my words, but he grasped my meaning, and, though he glowered at me balefully, he reduced his speed to the pace of a funeral procession.

As we were entering the outskirts of Khatmandu a chuprassi, who was evidently on the lookout for us, stepped from a sentry-box beside the entrance to a walled compound and held up his hand. When the car came to a halt he salaamed and proffered me a scented blue envelop bearing my name in a chirography that was unmistakably feminine.

"I didn't know you had any lady friends up here," remarked my cousin.

"I didn't either," I replied, "but it's hard to escape 'em. It's hell having such a fatal attraction for the women."

The note proved to be from Mrs. Roy Kilburne, the wife of an English electrical engineer in the employ of the Nepálese Government and one of the three European women in the kingdom. She and her husband, it seemed, were expecting us, having been notified by telephone of our coming by the prince whom we had met near Amlekgunj. They couldn't put us up, unfortunately, Mrs. Kilburne wrote, because they had no spare bedroom, so arrangements had been made for us to occupy one of the bungalows in the compound of the British legation. We were to take all our meals with them, however, she continued; in short, to regard their home as a sort of filling-station. She and her husband would drive over to the legation that evening to see that we were comfortably settled and to bring us back to their house for dinner. That is my idea of full-length hospitality, for we were, after all, utter strangers and they were taking us on faith.

The British legation, a rambling structure in the early Victorian style of architecture, stands amid trees and gardens in an enormous walled compound on the city's outskirts. Scattered about the fifty acres of grounds, besides the residency itself, are several guest houses, offices, servants' quarters, and barracks for the guard of Indian sowars.

The bungalow assigned to us was a two-story affair encircled by verandas below and above. It was doubtless a very delightful place in warm weather, but now it was damp, chilly and cheerless. To add to our discomfort, we were caked with mud, soaked to the skin, and had had nothing to eat since early morning. And heaven alone knew what had become of Julius, the subadar and the baggage coolies. At five o'clock they had not shown up. At six o'clock they were still missing. By seven o'clock we were becoming alarmed.

At half-past seven the Kilburnes drove up in a Ford to take us home to dinner. He was a clean-cut, fine-looking young fellow, with that air of efficiency characteristic of men in the engineering profession. He had the cordiality of manner often found in Englishmen who have lived long abroad but comparatively seldom in those who have spent their lives at home. Mrs. Kilburne was a perfect peach—slim and svelte, with a flawless complexion, a bewitching smile and a real sense of humor. Her smart tweed sports suit bore the unmistakable stamp of Savile Row and her trim tan brogues could only have been turned out by a bootmaker who knew his business. They were as genuinely glad to see us as though we had been old, old friends.

When I told Kilburne that Julius and the coolies were missing he immediately got busy.

"There's a police post a little way down the road," he said. "I'll run down there in the car and ask the officer in charge to send out a searching party. The trail is very slippery owing to the heavy rain and it is possible that they have met with an accident or been held up by a wash-out."

He returned in half an hour to inform us that the police had just received word from their patrols that a dark-skinned man who looked as though he was a foreigner, accompanied by a Nepálese non-com, both much the worse for wear, had been reported entering the lower side of the town. Hard on the heels of these encouraging tidings the lost ones appeared. The subadar, though covered with mud and plainly tired, was as soldierly and alert as ever, but Julius, the usually immaculate, was a picture of dejection. He looked like something that the cat had brought in. His pith topée had been reduced by the rain to a mass of pulp, the brim drooping about his face like a decomposing mushroom. The green lining had run and emerald rivulets coursed down his mud-bespattered countenance and dripped from his chin on to his pale blue sweater. His trousers, once of spruce white duck but now brown to the knees with mire, had shrunk until they clung to his legs like tights. He was shivering from cold, hunger and exhaustion.

"Where have you been?" I demanded, though not overharshly, for this bedraggled object would have aroused any one's pity. "We have been waiting for you for hours. We thought you were lost or had fallen over a precipice."

"When we start down from top of pass," Julius explained, "my pony he want to turn round an' go other way. He ver' obstinate beast. Not a good place to have controversy with quadruped. Too slippery, too steep, too far to fall without stopping. So I get off an' walk. When it get dark I lose my way an' almost step off mountain. Subadar he catch me, pull me back. I much frightened. Then we walk ver' slow. Six-eight hours. Rain all the time. I not think much of this Nepál country. Like Ceylon better."

"Take off your wet clothes," I told him, "and get into bed. Then take a couple of shots of whisky and some quinine. You'll be as chipper as ever in the morning."

And he was.

"Now we had better go over to the house and have some dinner," Kilburne suggested. "If we keep the cook waiting much longer he'll walk out on us."

"Do you dress for dinner?" I asked.

"Well, generally," he admitted. "It gets pretty lonely up here, you see, particularly in the evenings, and a stiff shirt-front helps to bolster up a drooping spirit. It's good for one's morale to dress for dinner, even if you are alone. But don't bother to dress to-night; come just as you are."

The Kilburnes occupied a very attractive stone bungalow which had been built for them by the Government. I gathered that the Government was generous in its dealings with its only European employee, for Mrs. Kilburne told me that when she had her first baby the king had sent all the way to Calcutta for a trained nurse, and when her second baby was born the prime minister had presented her with a Jersey cow so that the children might have pure milk.

The house had large rooms, and, it being a raw night, logs crackled cheerily in the open fireplaces. There were some fine old pieces of mahogany, evidently brought out from England; a grand piano which, like nearly everything else, had been carried over the passes on the backs of coolies; on the walls, lending warmth and color to the rooms, were numerous sporting scenes, painted by Mr. Kilburne's father, several Tibetan *thankas,* some curious native weapons and an autographed photograph of the prime minister in a silver frame. The dinner was as faultlessly cooked and served as though we had been in Mayfair instead of in a Himalayan valley.

Over the coffee and cigars we told our hosts about the new plays in the London theaters, the latest song-hits at the London music-halls, what the men were wearing in Piccadilly and the women in the Rue de la Paix, all the inconsequential gossip which they are eager to hear who have been long away from home. The Kilburnes had been in the East for five years, I think they told me, but hoped to return to England on leave in two years more. Mrs. Kilburne was already marking off the remaining weeks of their exile on a calendar. They spoke longingly of an old, ivy-covered house in Devonshire—at least, I think it was in Devonshire—with sweeping lawns and stately elms and clumps of rhododendrons by the gate. I gathered that they planned to refurbish it and live there again some day, when they had made their pile.

It has often seemed to me that the pioneers and empire-builders receive rather more than their portion of honors and fame. The wives who follow their husbands into the far places, who share their exile cheerfully, courageously, without complaint, are, to my way of thinking no less deserving of stars and crosses and strings of letters after their names. Consider the dreariness of their lives. They are often stationed in posts far removed from other Europeans. Their children, before they reach their 'teens, are sent home to school. Then, while the men are occupied in building dams or bridges, in drilling troops or administering justice among savage tribes, the women, with no incentive save devotion, sit patiently in their stifling bungalows and wait for the long, weary days to end.

"How on earth do you manage to pass the evenings?" I inquired. "Is there a movie to go to?"

"No," replied Kilburne, "the Government does not permit cinemas—for religious reasons, I suppose, or perhaps because it fears they might put new ideas into the heads of the people, make them discontented."

"No dances, I suppose?"

"Hardly," laughed pretty Mrs. Kilburne. "There are only two other white women in all Nepál—the envoy's niece and an orthopædic nurse who cares for one of the princesses."

"Bridge, then?"

"Whom can we play with? Neither the envoy nor his niece cares for cards, and the nurse is occupied at the palace."

"Have you a phonograph?"

"Not yet," replied our hostess, "but we hope to get one."

That led me to tell them of the latest records, and I even ventured to repeat as much as I could recall of the dialogue between the Two Black Crows. It wasn't much of a performance, and would have fallen flat at home, but this homesick young couple thought it was the funniest thing they had ever heard and laughed until the tears came.

HOLY, HOLY, HOLY

Crazy eyes staring through tangled hair dyed vermilion, a matted beard meeting a hirsute chest, a naked body smeared with cow-dung and a-crawl with vermin, the holy man squatted beside the trail in an odor of sanctity and filth

KHATMANDU

But it might be the Tower of Babel, so diverse and bewildering are the architectural styles, the races, the religions, the costumes, the colors, the tongues

"Do you have any difficulty getting things to read?" I asked. "Books, newspapers, magazines?"

"The Bombay and Calcutta newspapers reach us quite regularly when the trail is not washed out by rains," replied Kilburne. "They are brought in by runner and are sometimes only a week or ten days old. The English magazines are usually two or three months old when we get them, but that doesn't matter so much.

"The life here really isn't so bad," he continued, "though of course it grows pretty lonely at times, particularly during the winters, when we are sometimes cut off from the outside world for weeks at a time. But some of the best shooting in the world, far better than any in India, is to be had in the Terai; there are ovis poli on the high mountains, and mahseer in many of the streams. Then there is plenty of riding, and the native ponies are very nice little animals too, though, curiously enough, the Nepálese have never taken to polo."

"But," put in our hostess, "you have forgotten to tell them about our golf-course. We are tremendously proud of it. It was built by the Government and has eighteen holes. I play there with some of the princes nearly every afternoon. They are the only Nepálese who are permitted to use it. You see, it is a very exclusive affair indeed."

"Do all the princes wear two neckties apiece," I inquired, "like the prime minister's son whom I met in Calcutta?"

"Well," she replied evasively, for the wife of a government official has to be diplomatic, "their costumes would certainly create a sensation on a golf-course at home."

As I looked at this young couple, cheerful and apparently contented in spite of their exile, I mentally contrasted their monotonous existence with the lives of those who live in rural districts in America and loudly bewail their isolation. I thought of farmers I know who have radios and phonographs, motor-cars and concrete roads to run them on, who can obtain books from public libraries for the asking, who find the daily paper in their letter-boxes each morning, who can motor into a near-by town for the movies or to the city for the theater and shopping, whose houses are equipped with oil heaters and electric cooking-stoves and washing-machines, whose children are educated at good schools, and who, when they become lonely, can always call up their neighbors on the telephone.

When we had lighted fresh cigars, and the turbaned, silent-footed servants had cleared the coffee things away, Kilburne placed on the table a radio set, evidently home-made.

"Suppose we listen in on the outside world," he said casually. "We have a good deal of difficulty in getting Calcutta or Bombay—the intervening mountain ranges have something to do with it, no doubt—but I have plenty of power from the electric station and can nearly always tune in on Moscow or Petrograd, and sometimes we pick up some of the western European stations."

He threw over a switch, manipulated a couple of ebonized dials, and an instant later, with scarcely any preliminary static or buzzing, we heard, loud and clear, a guttural voice speaking in German. A brief pause. Then the same voice, this time speaking in our own tongue, though with a strong Teutonic inflection:

"*Diss ist Eindhoven, Holland, broadcasting,*" announced the unseen speaker. "*Blease stand py a momend. . . Ve vill now to a concerd lisden py der Scheveningen Casino jazz band.*"

Followed a sudden burst of music, a cacophony of string and reed and brass, of fiddles, flutes, saxophones and drums, which set our feet a-tapping. It was as distinct and almost as loud as though the musicians were in the next room. Yet they were half the world away. And we, their listeners, were in the heart of Asia, under the very shadow of Mount Everest. It gave me one of the greatest thrills I have ever known.

"Yes, science has certainly accomplished some remarkable things," I hear you say complacently.

Science? Not at all. Magic! Sheer magic!

CHAPTER X

ON THE EAVES OF THE WORLD

WERE a man to be set down by an airplane in Khatmandu, he might guess for days where he was and guess unsuccessfully.

The encircling snow-peaks, rising range upon range into the blue, would suggest the Alps, though the mightiest of the Alpine peaks are insignificant in comparison. He would find something vaguely reminiscent of Addis Ababa in the setting of the city, nestling amid groves on a valley floor hemmed in by mountains. The vast Maidan, or parade ground, possibly the largest in the world, would inevitably recall Tehran. The fantastic Hindu temples and shrines with their wealth of carving and coloring, the enormous white dagobas of the Buddhist sanctuaries, the gilded roofs and pinnacles gleaming in the sun, the innumerable idols in brass or stone, all these would remind him of Mandalay, Benares, Bangkok, Pnom-Penh. But the many-storied pagodas, with their tiled roofs and upturned eaves, would divert his thoughts to Canton or Peking. The labyrinth of dim alleys and twisted lanes, lined by hole-in-the-wall shops, their fronts open to reveal the gaudy Eastern merchandise within, might well cause him to conclude that he was in the bazaars of some Moorish or Tunisian town. The white palaces, hidden behind mysterious walls, could hardly fail to bring to mind the villas of the Turkish pashas beside the Bosphorus. In the tall and slender tower erected by Bhim Sen there would be a hint of those stately minarets which flank the great madresseh at Samarkand. The old, old houses, with their overhanging second stories, their weathered wooden balconies and latticed windows, would hold memories of Cairo, Fez, Stamboul. And the inscrutable features of the blood-splashed god in the Durbar Square, where the great sacrifices take place, would seem to bear a dim relationship to those other stone images, deities of ancient Egypt, which stare unseeingly across the Theban plain.

But the people themselves—the Gurkha soldiers in their round black caps and bright blue uniforms; the Newars in tight-waisted jackets and skin-tight breeches; the beturbaned Indians with caste-marks of white, ocher or vermilion painted between their eyes; the filthy Tibetans, clad in fur hats, long quilted coats and high boots of red leather; the wild-haired Bhotias and the shaven-headed Brahmans; the Buddhist lamas in woolen robes and pointed hoods of dirty orange; the Hindu holy men, their naked bodies calcimined with ashes and cow-dung; the Sikh sowars of the legation guard, gigantic warriors with black beards braided and tied up under their chins; the Nepálese women, in balloon skirts and zouave jackets of many colors, jingling with jewelry—all these, plus the pandemonium of outlandish tongues, Sanskrit, Newar, Parbatiya, Tibetan, Hindustani, Chinese, could only lead the bewildered stranger to assume that he had stumbled on the Tower of Babel.

I am in something of a quandary when it comes to drawing a word-picture of Khatmandu, because it is unique, no other city in the world affording any adequate basis for comparison. This is due in part to the numerous races represented in the population; to the extraordinary mixture of religions, Buddhist topes standing alongside Hindu temples and Tantric shrines; and to the fact that the architecture is a combination of Chinese and Indian.

The vivid imaginations of the natives enable them to see in the general ground-plan of Khatmandu a resemblance to a gigantic sword—the sword of Manju Sri, a warrior-saint who in the dim dawn of history came out of the mountains of the north and is venerated by the Newars as the founder of their country. In those distant days, so they will tell you, the present valley of Nepál was a lake. And in this case, at least, the geologists corroborate tradition. After looking the ground over, Manju Sri, who must also have been something of a drainage engineer, decided that the waters of the lake could be drawn off by cleaving a passage through the mountain barrier. Dynamite, steam shovels and hydraulic drills being still in the womb of time, he solved the problem by the simple expedient of gashing the obstruction with a mighty blow of his sword, whereupon the released waters poured southward through the cleft thus made, draining the lake-bed dry. Should your Occidental skepticism lead you to question the veracity of the story, the Nepálese will dissipate your doubts by showing you the narrow defile between the Phulchoah and Champadevi hills through which the Baghmatti River makes its way to the plains of Hindustan. It is still called the *Kot-bar,* or "sword-cut," of Manju Sri.

For upward of a thousand years the present capital of Nepál was known as Manju Pattan, after the legendary hero who drained its site. Toward the close of the sixteenth century, however, it received its present name, in allusion, so tradition says, to an ancient building which still stands near the Durbar Square, being now used as a hostel for pilgrims. I can offer no plausible explanation of why the Nepálese substituted the name of a ramshackle frame structure—for in Newar *kath* means "wood" and *mandu* "house" or "temple"—for that of the city's saintly founder. But it is their city, after all, and they are at liberty to call it what they please.[1]

Stretched along the city's southern flank, forming the edge of the sword-blade, as it were, is the Maidan, an enormous drill plain, fully a mile long by a quarter of a mile in width, and as level as a floor. It is spacious enough to permit the maneuvering of a small army, and troops to the number of ten thousand may be seen there at drill every morning. From the center of the Maidan rises a solitary and venerable tree, beneath which the king stands when he reviews the army, and overlooking it is a huge edifice of stone, the military hospital, surmounted by a fine figure of a Gurkha infantryman in field kit marching forth to war.

One morning, passing the Maidan, we stopped the car to watch the troops at drill, whereupon the general in command courteously invited us to inspect them. Drawn up in motionless ranks of cobalt blue was a full brigade of infantry, with their colors and field music, and in their rear a regiment of artillery armed with small brass field pieces, though I believe that the Nepálese army now possesses a considerable number of modern field guns. In drill and discipline the Gurkhas are superior to any troops in Asia, unless it be the Sikhs and Japanese, and in physique they vastly surpass the latter. So essentially are the Gurkhas a warrior race that great numbers of them have taken service in the Indian army, which has twenty complete battalions of these mountain fighters.

Ranged along one side of the Maidan, each the center of a miniature plaza, are bronze equestrian statues of former

[1] The name of the capital of Nepál is spelled variously, Katmandu, Khatmandu and Kathmandu, the last being the form used by the Nepálese Government. Khatmandu, however, most nearly approximates the local pronunciation of the name.

rulers of Nepál, including the famous Jung Bahadur. They are the work of European sculptors, full of fire and action, and would do credit to any capital, let alone an obscure Asiatic one, being infinitely superior to the effigies of Teutonic heroes which line the Sieges Allée in Berlin.

In the center of a spacious square hard by stands a slender stone tower, two hundred feet in height, which resembles a Turkish minaret. It is the tallest and most striking structure in Khatmandu, visible from all parts of the valley, but it is totally without historical or architectural significance, having been erected by a wealthy Gurkha general to gratify a whim, whence it is known as Bhim Sen's Folly. It is related that Jung Bahadur once jumped his horse from the top of the tower on a wager, but the top may not then have been as far above the ground as it is to-day, for in that great sportsman's time the tower was in the course of construction. And skeptics seek to still further rob the tale of its glamour by asserting that straw was strewn to a great depth at the foot of the tower in order to break the fall of horse and rider. But some one is always trying to take the pleasure out of life, as witness the assertion of the historians that George Washington never chopped down the cherry-tree.

In the very heart of Khatmandu, the focus of the city's official, commercial and religious life, is a large, irregularly shaped open space known as the Durbar Square, from the great Durbar Hall which overshadows it. The remaining sides of this square are occupied by temples, shrines and pagodas, covered with a bewilderment of carving, gleaming with gold leaf, their eaves hung with myriads of little bells which tinkle musically in the gentlest breeze. All of the structures are raised well above the ground on plinths and are reached by flights of steps whose stones have been worn deep by the feet of countless generations of the pious.

Ranging at will about the square are humpbacked sacred cattle, and set here and there are huge bowl-shaped drums, as high as a man, with heads of tightly stretched leather. When they are beaten by the priests during religious festivals or as a call to sacrifice, they sound like thunder in the hills, their reverberations being audible from one end of the valley to the other.

Set on a low brick plinth at one end of the square is a most singular statue—a nude figure in highly polished black stone, resting on one knee, its hands pressed together in supplication. From the neck hangs a sort of breast-plate or amulet; on the head is a lofty bonnet or crown resembling those worn by the Babylonian kings; affixed to either shoulder are stone appendages which may or may not represent wings. I was unable to learn the name of the deity which the figure presumably represents, or anything about it, but it gives every indication of great antiquity. Though undoubtedly of Hindu or Hindu-Buddhist origin, the treatment and general effect are strikingly Egyptian. I saw nothing else in Nepál which even remotely resembled it.

At the other end of the square stands an image of quite another order—just such an idol as we pictured in our childhood's imagination. It might be the god of fear, and very probably is, for it is inconceivably hideous and terrifying. A six-armed horror, twenty feet in height, with goggling eyes and a cruel, leering mouth, clad in a sort of kilt which reveals a protruding belly, it is a phantasm which could only be envisioned by a lunatic or a man suffering from delirium tremens. It is smeared with some vermilion substance to resemble blood, festooned with blood-dappled blossoms, and flanked on either side by grinning, grotesque monsters, half-lion and half-dragon. Even in the hot sunlight, with all its garishness revealed, it is enough to send the cold chills coursing up and down one's spine. You feel that it typifies the very essence of evil.

Before this unclean god take place the great sacrifices, hundreds and sometimes thousands of buffaloes being slaughtered in a single day to appease the ferocious spirit which it represents. For, just as the Hindus regard the cow as a sacred animal and consider it sacrilege to kill one, a crime which in Nepál is punishable by death, so it is held meritorious to slaughter a buffalo, which is looked on as the symbol of the world's wickedness.

Set in the uneven pavement before the idol is a stone sacrificial post to which the victim is tethered. The executioner, a brawny ruffian, naked to the waist, approaches, swinging a *kora,* a weapon with a wide, curved and enormously heavy blade. At sight of him the animal instinctively recoils, thereby extending its neck, whereupon the swordsman, with one powerful sweep of his razor-bladed weapon, severs the head from the body. In half an hour, so expertly does the executioner perform his grisly task, the whole square is awash with blood, headless carcasses are strewn everywhere, the stench is nauseating. And through it all the great drums speak in tones of thunder, bronze gongs groan, the priests raise their voices in a shrill, barbaric chant, and the pious prostrate themselves upon the bloodied stones in fear and supplication.

The weekly sacrifices on the altar of the Red God in the Durbar Square pale into insignificance, however, beside the holocaust with which the Gurkhas celebrate the great annual festival known as the Kali Puja. The Kali Puja, which lasts for a period of ten days, commemorates the victory of the bloodthirsty Kali, the goddess of destruction, over the demon Mahishasur, who is usually represented in the form of a buffalo, wherefore that beast is regarded as accursed. It reaches its climax in the ceremony of the blessing of the colors, when the army propitiates the goddess by the sacrifice of thousands of buffaloes, every officer being expected to furnish one or more animals, according to his rank. This curious and sanguinary rite is the Nepálese equivalent to the trooping of the colors as performed each June by the regiments of the household brigade on the Horse Guards' Parade in London.

Though the Kali Puja is celebrated with great pomp and ceremony at every divisional and regimental headquarters in the kingdom, the principal ceremony is held in the courtyard of the Kot, a building, or rather a congeries of buildings, occupied by the offices of the high command. In other words, the Nepálese War Office. The Kot is a peculiarly fitting place for the enactment of this wholesale slaughter, for in September, 1846, it was the scene of one of the bloodiest episodes in Nepálese history. The moving spirit in the affair was a young and ambitious colonel, Jung Bahadur, who had in the preceding year effected the murder of his uncle, Matabar Singh, the prime minister of Nepál. Instigated by the queen, with whom he was carrying on an *affaire de cœur,* Jung determined to rid himself at a single blow of all who stood in his path to power. This design he executed by what is known as the massacre of the Kot. It is a horrifying story of unarmed men being hunted from room to room and killed like rats, of others herded helplessly in the open courtyard and picked off by riflemen posted on the balconies, while the ranee, leaning from an upper window, whooped the assassins on with cries of "Kill! Kill! Kill!" By this massacre Jung Bahadur made himself undisputed master of Nepál. His enemies disposed of, he proceeded to fill with his friends the posts left vacant, and, by way of making a clean sweep, banished his royal coadjutor and paramour. The latter was distinctly an act of gross ingratitude, but I suppose that the poor man was nervous o' nights with a lady of such a vengeful disposition lying beside him.

For the celebration of the festival in question the great courtyard of the Kot is massed with detachments of officers and men representing all the regiments in the army, each with its stand of colors. When buffaloes to the number of some thousands have been beheaded, and the pavement of the Kot has become a crimson lake, the prime minister, who is likewise commander-in-chief, followed by a priest bearing a basin of fresh blood, approaches in turn each regimental standard. Dipping both hands into the basin of gore, he clasps the silken folds, leaving on either side of the standard the imprint of a bloody hand. Guns boom, priests chant, massed bands play the national anthem, and the hot Asian sun beats down on a scene of slaughter which would have delighted the heart of Nero.

Of the bewildering collection of religious edifices fronting on the Durbar Square, the most noteworthy is the Temple of Taleju, which is a sort of chapel royal, devoted solely to the use of royalty, the goddess Taleju being the patron-saint of the ruling house of Nepál. Here Prithi Narain, the Gurkha conqueror of Khatmandu, offered a human sacrifice in celebration of his victory, whereupon, according to tradition, the goddess visited him in a dream to express her displeasure. As a result of this heavenly rebuke, the practice of sacrificing human beings went out of fashion in Nepál then and there.

A few paces away is the huge and not unimpressive Durbar Hall, Indian in architecture but Chinese in adornment, where the king and the prime minister hold their durbars or audiences. Apparently built without a plan, probably by a succession of architects, it is a confusing labyrinth of apartments, offices, corridors, passageways and courtyards. These courts, of which there are half-a-hundred or more, each with a name, communicate with each other by narrow doorways, so that, in the unlikely event of the Kot massacre being repeated, the occupants may offer a determined resistance, holding each courtyard in turn. Even after the endless succession of heavy doors were battered down, their enemies would have difficulty in finding them in that bewildering maze of masonry.

Squeezed in amid the richly decorated temples and public buildings, like seedy intruders, are numbers of ancient houses, some of them dating back to far before the conquest. For the most part ramshackle structures, with tiled roofs and tipsy-looking balconies which threaten to tumble down at any moment upon the passer-by, they are nevertheless delightfully picturesque, their façades incrusted with wood carvings whose crude colors have been mellowed by age and weather. They would drive an artist to distraction, these old, ornament-laden dwellings; overwhelmed by the wealth of detail, the vivid colors, the flickering sunlight, the mysterious shadows, he would be at a loss which to paint first.

The bazaars of Khatmandu do not differ materially from those of other Eastern towns—the same confusion of narrow, winding, unevenly paved streets fringed by little stalls in which the merchants sit cross-legged amid their piled-up wares, the same dim and clamorous thoroughfares where weavers, saddlers, armorers, potters, metal-workers, jewelers, ply their respective trades. The bazaars are but a screen, however, for scenes yet more picturesque. Follow the alleys which meander through them in all directions like the veins in a leaf, and, framed by carved and vine-clad gateways, you will catch fascinating vignettes of sun-bathed courtyards, of enchanting little pagodas with upturned, bell-hung eaves, of hideous idols garlanded with flowers and splotched with *ghee* and vermilion, of legendary creatures made from brass or stone, of massive, iron-bound doors opening on to God knows what mysteries beyond.

The suburbs of Khatmandu are for the most part dull and uninteresting, the residences of the numerous princes and the members of the aristocracy which are scattered along the broad and well-kept thoroughfares radiating from the city being hidden behind high walls. Those of them which I saw were of white stucco, many in a pseudo-Moorish style of architecture, and were surrounded by extensive gardens.

On the southern outskirts of the city, near the confluence of the Baghmatti and Vishnumatti rivers, is the palace of the king, an enormous pile of masonry, plastered and whitewashed, containing hundreds of rooms. Over it flies the royal standard of Nepál—for the king leaves his capital rarely, his country never—and sentries in scarlet tunics pace to and fro before the lofty gates.

The most interesting feature of an otherwise rather commonplace palace is the imposing state staircase, which is lined on either side by mechanical devices, all of American make—cash registers, automatic scales, roulette and other gambling machines, nickel-in-the-slot contrivances for the dispensation of chocolate, chewing-gum, peanuts and the like. These are not placed there for utilitarian purposes, you understand, though I have no doubt that the ennuied young monarch enlivens a tedious existence by operating them on occasion. Such things being rare and costly in Nepál, they are employed purely for decorative purposes, just as the stairways of European palaces are lined with statues or potted plants. Ridiculous, you say? Well, I am not so certain about that. It all depends upon the point of view. We value orchids, for example, as much for their rarity as for their beauty, whereas a native of the tropics, where they are to be had for the picking, never gives them a second glance. Oriental rulers, moreover, have an inherent fondness for mechanical things. The Sultan of Kotei, in Dutch Borneo, once showed me his most cherished possession—a gilded bird which would sing when wound up. And the most conspicuous object in the treasure-room of the shah's palace in Tehran is a fine copy in marble of the Venus de Milo—with a large gilt clock set in her stomach!

Despite the extraordinary skill of the Newars in carving and metal-working, there is astonishingly little of artistic merit to be purchased in the bazaars of Khatmandu. But when the Kilburnes learned that we wished to purchase some souvenirs of Nepál they told their head chuprassi to send for certain merchants who dealt in such things, so that, returning from a drive one afternoon, we found the long veranda of the bungalow transformed into a museum. There were gilded idols, evidently the loot of temples, embroidered altar-pieces, ivory carvings, jade ornaments, beautifully damascened weapons, caskets of gold and silver, some of them studded with semi-precious stones, and some magnificent examples of the massive native jewelry, made of beaten gold and incrusted with diamonds, emeralds, rubies and turquoises. Though, owing to the fact that tourists are unknown in Nepál, the market for such articles must be extremely limited, the prices were in all cases high and in some cases exorbitant. I looked covetously on a superb pair of ear-rings, set with gems, each the size of a bread-and-butter plate, but when the owner demanded the equivalent of three thousand dollars for them I lost interest. And, unlike most Orientals, there is no bargaining with Nepálese merchants.

By far the best things we bought were obtained from

the Tibetan envoy to Nepál, a young Chinese with Chesterfieldian manners and a European education, who is known locally as the "China ambassador." Rich Tibetans, making the long pilgrimage from Lhasa to the venerated Buddhist shrines in Nepál, bring to the envoy numerous gifts, usually native works of art, and by the surreptitious sale of these he is enabled to augment his salary materially. At the request of the Kilburnes he sent his secretary over to the bungalow with a selection of Tibetan *objets d'art* which would have made the Metropolitan Museum envious. Among them were some magnificent examples of ancient *thankas*. These are paintings of a religious nature, usually several feet square, mounted on banner-like strips of rich brocade for use on the walls of the temples. The one I purchased was entitled "The Wheel of Life." It depicts a leering creature, half-human and half-demon, holding in his talons a sphere on which are scores of exquisitely executed little scenes, from the brush of a master miniaturist, symbolizing everything that happens to members of the human race from the moment they enter the world until they pass out of it again. I did not scrutinize the *thanka* very closely when I bought it, but subsequent examination revealed features so appallingly obscene that, in order to hang it in my home, I shall have to adopt the expedient employed by the directors of the Grand Salon in Paris some years ago, when they were compelled for decency's sake to hang a green curtain before a certain prize-winning but scandalous picture. My *thanka* was likewise provided with a curtain, a gay affair of Chinese silk, but I suspect that it was intended to preserve the colors of the picture rather than the morals of the beholders.

The mélange of religious beliefs in Nepál produces endless confusion in the mind of the visitor. The national

HIS DIRTINESS SITS FOR HIS PICTURE

The Lama Superior, the highest Buddhist authority in Nepál, looked like a cross between a doge of Venice and an old and dissolute Buddha. If sanctity were gaged by filth, he deserved to be canonized

THE INDIA OF OUR CHILDHOOD'S IMAGINATION

A bewilderment of palaces, temples, gateways, spires and carvings jumbled together under a hot blue sky

religion of the Newars, who are the original inhabitants of the country, is Buddhism, and has been since the cult was introduced into Nepál five and twenty centuries ago. Indeed, it may be said to have originated there, for the Buddha was born in the Terai. The Gurkha conquerors, however, brought with them their own religion, a very early form of Hinduism, in certain respects not far removed from nature worship. As time went on, the Newars became dissatisfied with their simple, rugged faith and began to adopt, one by one, the mystic rites and elaborate ceremonies of the new-comers. As a result, their religion has become so mixed and veneered with Hinduism that it would not be recognized by the Buddha himself. Entirely abandoning the monastic institutions of Buddhism, the Newars have in great measure adopted the Hindu rules of caste, though even these sit but lightly on them. They burn their dead, eat the flesh of buffaloes, sheep, goats and fowls, and consume enormous quantities of spirits.

This commingling of the two religions has produced many similar anomalies. Thus, there will sometimes be seen almost side by side in the same temple, be it Buddhist or Hindu, a figure of the Great Teacher, calm, dignified, reposeful, and a multi-headed, multi-armed monstrosity, adrip with blood and fat, symbolizing all that is restless and terrible in a faith that rules by fear.

But interwoven with these is a third and darker form of worship, a mysterious and obscure belief, hints of which are to be found everywhere, though the actual ritual is fortunately veiled from the eyes of all save the initiated. Peering furtively from under the broad eaves of the temples in the form of obscene wood-carvings, leering in lurid colors from the walls of the shrines, suggested in a thousand lewd but subtle forms, unobtrusive yet ubiquitous, Tantrism holds its unhallowed sway, hundreds of thousands of Nepálese practising in secret its unspeakably revolting rites.[2]

The Tantric creed has been described as "a diseased excrescence borrowed from the Hindus and based upon the worst parts of Sivaism." Though the members of the unholy sect comprise a large proportion of the inhabitants of Nepál, they never admit their fellowship in it, and its details are so jealously guarded that of them but little is known, which is fortunate so far as public morals are concerned. It is sufficient to say that the Tantrikas, as the adherents of the faith are known, worship the female energy of the god Siva, and in pursuance of the teachings contained in their sacred works, the Tantras, practise not merely indiscriminate adultery, but every form of incest and sodomy. Indeed, the abominations taught by the Tantrist creed and sedulously practised by its devotees would have made the most brazen Sodomites feel as unsophisticated as Little Rollo.

The Tantric scriptures, known as the Tantras, consist of a series of dialogues between Siva and his bride in one of her many forms, but generally as Urma or Paravati. The Tantrikas consider them a fifth Veda, maintaining that they possess as great antiquity and greater authority than the four holy books recognized by the commonalty of Hindus. So great, indeed, is the efficacy of the Tantras that those who follow them implicitly are promised absolution for even the most atrocious and unnatural sins.

In these dialogues the goddess ingenuously questions the god as to the approved method of performing certain acts and rites, and the incantations to be used in connection with them. These he explains at length and in revolting detail, though even he must have felt some sense of shame, for he solemnly warns his bride that they involve a great mystery and must on no account be divulged to the profane.

[2] See "Picturesque Nepál," by Percy Brown.

I have seen translations of portions of the Tantrist scriptures, which, it must be understood, are followed not only by a large section of the population of Nepál but also by great numbers of Indian Hindus. Though I am fairly hard-boiled, I confess that I recoiled in disgust and horror at the bare contemplation of their teachings. They bespeak such utterly unbelievable degradation and bestiality, they frankly encourage such unspeakable relations between fathers and daughters, sons and mothers, brothers and sisters, between members of the same sexes, even between humans and beasts, that they should be read, if they must be read at all, in a latrine and then promptly consigned to the cesspool in which they presumably originated.

There are said to be 2733 temples and shrines in the valley of Nepál, and, judging from the enormous number of dagobas, pagodas and gilded finials which dot the landscape, from the representations of gods and goddesses which one encounters at every turn, this is not an exaggeration. Though certain of the Hindu temples, particularly those in Patan and Bhatgaon, are magnificent structures, possessing an amazing wealth of adornment, by far the most imposing religious edifices in the valley are the Buddhist temples of Shambu-Nath and Bodh-Nath, both situated near Khatmandu. The former, set on the summit of an isolated hill in a very picturesque and commanding position, is the richer and more popular of the two, but Bodh-Nath, rising from an open plain, is the largest and perhaps the oldest temple in Nepál, being the most venerated shrine in the Buddhist world outside of Lhasa.

Immense throngs of Tibetan pilgrims visit this ancient tope each year, the terrible journey over the main range of the Himalayas from Lhasa to Khatmandu taking fifty days. Squat men with yellow skins, slanting eyes and flat noses, in fur caps, red quilted coats and high red boots, long-haired, greasy and verminous, sometimes accompanied by their women-folk and children, usually followed by shaggy and ferocious dogs, they pour down from the northern passes by the tens of thousands, drums, gongs and conch-horns sounding, to pitch their black tents on the plain beside the stupa, to say their prayers and make their simple offerings, to circumambulate the sacred spot, often on their bellies, twirling their prayer-wheels and chanting the interminable *Om mani padme hum* [3] which is the shibboleth of their faith.

Despite the contrast in their situations, one on a plain, the other on the summit of a sugar-loaf hill, Bodh-Nath and Shambu-Nath bear a striking resemblance to each other architecturally, for each consists of a huge onion-shaped dagoba of solid concrete. Set on the dagoba is a square plinth, known as a *toran,* from which rises a gilded finial, that of Bodh-Nath resembling a step-pyramid, the one at Shambu-Nath suggesting a stack of golden plates which diminish in size as they ascend. Surmounting the spire is something that resembles a huge crown, elaborately ornamented and glittering with gold-leaf. Each temple is further characterized by a most singular and striking feature, for painted high up on each face of the *toran* are great pairs of inscrutable, brooding eyes which lend to the extraordinary structures a weirdly human appearance, for the eyes are so cunningly painted that they seem to be alive. They gaze serenely over the valley, north, east, south and west, just as they have done for upward of a thousand years, watching the farmer in the field, the artisan at his bench, the traveler on the road, like the all-seeing Eye of God, which is, I suppose, what they symbolize.

We drove out one sunny winter afternoon to Bodh-Nath, where we were met by the Tibetan ambassador, who was

[3] "Oh, the jewel in the heart of the lotus. Amen."

a friend of the Kilburnes. He was a slender, smiling Chinese—a native of Canton, I imagine—who had been educated in Calcutta, spoke English with astonishing fluency and was blessed with a highly developed sense of humor. He represented a curious combination of Eastern breeding and Western training, and this was symbolized, as it were, by his dress, for he wore a mandarin's cap with a button denoting one of the higher grades, and a long coat of mulberry brocade, but beneath the hem of the garment showed a pair of bright yellow sports shoes, obviously American made, green golf stockings and tasseled garters.

The ambassador, it appeared, had arranged for us an audience with the Lama Superior, the supreme Buddhist authority in Nepál, who resides in a monastic residence of his own, a sort of archiepiscopal palace, in the vicinity of the temple. This prelate is delegated by the Dalai Lama at Lhasa to watch over the spiritual interests of the multitudes of Tibetan pilgrims who annually visit the Buddhist shrines in Nepál, and is also charged with general supervision of the two great temples of that faith at Bodh-Nath and Shambu-Nath. In point of holiness he is inferior only to the Dalai Lama himself and is venerated accordingly.

I had expected, though I scarcely know why, to meet a benign and impressive personage, something after the order of a Roman cardinal, but the figure which sat cross-legged on a divan in the dim, low-ceilinged room of the *vihar* was the personification of ignorance and filth. A pair of slanting, shifty eyes peered suspiciously from a sodden, yellow face; the few black hairs of a drooping mustache failed to mask the sensual mouth and pendulous lower lip. The nails of the hand which he extended limply held ebony crescents of dirt; and though the odor he exuded may have been that of sanctity, it was more suggestive of the need for soap, hot water and a scrubbing-brush. But he was holy, very holy, as emphasized by the reverence paid him by his priests and attendants, who were constantly kneeling to kiss his grimy hands and even the toes of his red slippers. The ambassador, who, like most Chinese Nationalists, was not overly religious, regarded him with an amused condescension which he took scant pains to conceal.

When the Lama Superior caught sight of my camera he insisted that I take his picture. I explained that this was impossible because there was not sufficient light in the *vihar* for a successful exposure.

"Very well, then," said his Holiness, when my reply had been translated, "I will have the picture taken in a tent."

In that case, I ventured to suggest, it might be well to have an altar of sorts set up so as to provide an appropriate setting. To this the lama assented eagerly and proceeded to issue the necessary orders. Priests and servants hastened to do his bidding, and in little more time than it takes to tell about it an altar had been improvised in a tent, an enormous affair of black goats'-hair, in the temple courtyard; the walls had been hung with brocades and *thankas;* enough bells, conch-horns, drums, lamps, candlesticks and other religious paraphernalia scattered about to fill a room in a museum; and a low throne lugged in for his Dirtiness to sit on.

While these preparations were in progress the lama, aided by half-a-dozen attendants, proceeded to array himself in his sacerdotal robes—a voluminous, curiously cut overgarment of reddish orange and a pointed hood of the same color, with lappets coming down over the ears, which resembled the caps worn by the doges of Venice.

All being in readiness, the lama, looking like an old and very dissolute Buddha, waddled out to the tent and seated himself cross-legged on the throne; the clergy, ranging themselves about him in a semicircle, assumed expressions of appropriate sanctity. Resting the camera on the knee of a large gilt god, I set the shutter for a time-exposure. When it was over, the lama said something to the ambassador.

"What does he want now?" I asked.

"His Holiness wants the picture," was the answer.

"But the film has to be developed first," I explained, "and printed."

"Yes, I've told him that," said the envoy, "but he doesn't understand. He insists that you have the picture hidden in the black box and he wants it now. He thinks you are holding it out on him."

"Tell him," I said, giving the amused ambassador a surreptitious wink, "that taking the picture of so holy a person involves much magic. It is in the black box, it is true, but before it may be seen by human eyes it must be treated with sacred herbs and incantations said over it."

My reply seemed to satisfy the lama, for it was within the range of his intellect. That the herbs and incantations used by Mr. Eastman's magic-workers were efficacious is proved by the accompanying illustration.

The other great Buddhist temple, Shambu-Nath, is perched, as I have already remarked, on the summit of a solitary sugar-loaf hill which rises abruptly from the plain a few miles north of Khatmandu. To climb the hill was in itself something of a pilgrimage, for it involved the toilsome ascent of more than six hundred stone steps, flanked by countless Buddhas. When I reached the top, panting and perspiring, I felt that I had achieved some measure of merit myself.

The summit of the hill consists of a level space of perhaps two acres, so crowded with shrines, altars, dagobas and images that there is barely room for them all. From their midst rises the immense hemispherical bulk of Shambu-Nath itself, its four pairs of painted eyes staring down from the *toran*. Encircling the base of the temple, which must measure not far from an eighth of a mile in circumference, was a magnificent grill of wrought-iron surmounted by revolving bronze prayer-wheels, hundreds and hundreds of them. Scores of pilgrims were engaged in their devotions, circumambulating the dagoba on their feet, on their knees, on their bellies, or on all three in alternation, reaching up every few paces to twirl the prayer-wheels and chanting in endless iteration the litany of their religion.

Two or three miles to the east of Khatmandu, where a wooded mountain spur comes down to meet the plain, are the water-gardens of Balaji. Built in a series of terraces are stone-rimmed, bamboo-shaded pools in which enormously fat carp glide about lethargically. The upper pools feed the ones below and the waters of the lowest overflow through a great number of dragon-headed spouts (vaguely suggestive of the gargoyles which peer from beneath the eaves of Notre Dame) into a stone channel running along the foot of the buttressed retaining wall, so that in one's ears is always the pleasant sound of running water.

A cool and tranquil spot, like the Shalimar at Srinagar, in which to spend an afternoon in *dolce far niente,* feeding the gluttonous fish or watching nude brown maidens disporting themselves in the peacock-tinted waters. But Balaji, like nearly everything else in Nepál, has its hint of horror, which is here found in a small tank, overhung by trees, near a temple lewd with Tantric carvings. At first glance the visitor recoils, for floating in the pool is what appears to be the body of a dead man, the corpse-gray face, framed by a hood of serpents, rising a few inches above the surface. No, it cannot be a dead man, you decide upon a second glance, for the breast is gently heaving. Then you realize that it is not a man at all, but a stone figure reclining at full length upon a bed of snakes, with all but the face submerged. The skill with which the features are sculptured, and the rippling of the water over the body, give the impression that the figure is alive and breathing.

The figure represents the god Narain, one of the many forms assumed by Vishnu. According to Nepálese mythology, this deity was present when the Great Ones churned the ocean into foam in order to obtain from it the water of eternal life, and inhaled the poisonous fumes which arose from the depths during the operation. To allay his torturing thirst he sought pure water on the slopes of Gosainthan, the sacred mountain, twenty-six thousand feet in height, whose snowy peak on clear days may be descried away to the northward. A Hindu Moses, he smote the face of the mountain with his trident, whereupon three crystal-clear streams accommodatingly gushed from the rock. Their waters, collecting in a depression below, formed a pool, in which the parched and weary god lay down to rest and cool himself.

This pool, set high upon the mountainside and attainable only at the cost of enormous exertion, has long been a famous place of pilgrimage, the pious asserting that in its depths may be discerned the figure of Narain sleeping upon his bed of snakes. As no white man has ever set eyes upon this sacred lake, you will have to take the Hindus' word for it. For some obscure reason tradition has decreed that if the king should ever visit the lake and look upon the features of the sleeping god he would fall dead upon the spot. Doubtless only a superstition of the ignorant, the successive rulers of Nepál have argued; but why take the chance of being stricken by divine wrath, particularly as it is a hard trip to the lake anyway? So they built the pool at

Balaji, with its carved figure of Narain, and there Maharajadhiraja Tribhubana Bir Bikram Jung Bahadur Shah Bahadur Shum Shere Jung Deva may worship to his heart's content without fear of tragic consequences.

Julius was missing when we returned from Balaji to our temporary home in the legation compound. This was annoying, because it was already late and we wished to bathe and dress for dinner. Half an hour later he came limping in, dust-covered, weary and apologetic.

"Where have you been this time?" I demanded.

"I make little pilgrimage to Shambu-Nath, marster," he explained. "Ver' holy Buddhist temple on top of high hill. Climb steps, turn prayer-wheels, say prayers, make offerings, give two rupees to head priest. Make much merit. Now I ver' holy. My friends make hell of hullabaloo when I get back to Ceylon."

"You look pretty well tuckered out," I remarked, "but no doubt you feel a lot better spiritually."

"Yes, could do with small drink of spirits, marster," he agreed eagerly. "Religion good for soul but ver' tiring for rest of me."

CHAPTER XI

THE GOLDEN CITIES OF THE VALE

THE most astonishing thing about Bhatgaon is that such a city could exist at all and the outside world remain in virtual ignorance of it. Even the scientific and motion-picture expeditions which scour the earth in quest of the interesting, the beautiful, the strange, have overlooked it altogether. Many standard works of reference fail to mention it at all; others contain but the barest reference to it. Barring the electric lights which a progressive central government has recently installed, and, I believe, a single telephone wire, it has remained unchanged for centuries. The description written by Colonel Kirkpatrick, one of the earliest European explorers of Nepál, is as true to-day as when it was written upward of a hundred years ago.

Effectually isolated from the outer world by natural and political barriers, one almost as insurmountable as the other, this city of temples and palaces, the one-time capital of the Newar kings, rears its pinnacles and pagodas above the valley floor, mysterious, alluring, golden. No one knows when its first stones were laid, but there is reason to believe that it was already hoary with antiquity when the present site of London was peopled by painted savages and Paris had yet to be founded on the meadows beside the Seine. Certainly there was a community here when Gautama Buddha passed this way five hundred years before the beginning of the Christian era.

Bhatgaon lies eight miles to the east of Khatmandu,

across a fertile, smiling plain. The approach to it, as to most Oriental cities, leads through mean and narrow streets, past squalid dwellings whose rickety wooden balconies almost meet above the narrow thoroughfares, with here and there a sculptured gateway, a bit of carving, a gilded shrine, an exquisitely wrought grill, to hint at what waits ahead. Then you abruptly round a corner and find yourself in the great Durbar Square. . . . You halt agasp, your eyes dazzled, your senses reeling. For you are looking on a scene which has not its like in all the world. It is too fantastic to be real. You feel tempted to pinch yourself to make certain that you are not dreaming.

But how can I hope to depict it for you? Here superlatives fail miserably; utterly inadequate are all the words between the covers of the dictionary; one searches in vain for comparisons. The confusion of architectural forms is bewildering. Only a kaleidoscope could show such a variety of design, such a wealth and brilliancy of colors. Theatrical, yes, yet utterly beyond the ability of a Reinhardt, a Belasco or a De Mille to envision. But, mind you, there is about it no single hint of garishness. The structures are too massive, the sculpturings too admirably executed, the materials too rare and costly, the general effect far too glorious in color, too imposing in line, to admit of such a criticism.

The golden temples of Siam, the pagodas of the summer palace in Peking, the sculpture-crowded terraces of Boroboedor, the grotesque structures which line the bank of the Ganges at Benares, Samarkand's wealth of colors, the carvings at Angkor, the torii of the Shinto sanctuaries in Japan—Bhatgaon holds vague suggestions of them all without actually resembling any of them. I who have seen all, or nearly all, the famous cities and buildings of the world, give you my word that were there nothing else in Nepál save the Durbar Square of Bhatgaon it would still be amply worth making a journey half-way round the globe to see. I do not expect to be believed, of course—that would be expecting too much of human credulity and of the human imagination—but it is at least a satisfaction to know that those few white men who have seen this hidden city will admit that I am not exaggerating.

You will picture in your mind's eye, if you please, an enormous, stone-flagged open space, too irregular in form to be called a square, full of white light and deep purple shadows beneath the Asian sun. You will conceive of this space as not merely crowded, but literally jammed, with palaces, temples, pagodas, towers, monasteries, shrines, altars, spires, columns, standards, plinths; with figures of gods, men, beasts and monsters in brass, bronze and stone. They are arranged according to no preconceived scheme, but have sprung up through the ages, like trees in a forest, wherever there was space for them.

Think of the buildings as incrusted from ground to eaves with solid masses of the most intricate and delicately executed carvings, always beautiful, usually bizarre, frequently obscene. Next imagine the confusion of roofs and pinnacles as covered with plates of gilded bronze, so blinding in the hot sunlight that the eye can scarcely dwell upon them. Images of gods and goddesses, of kings and saints and heroes, of devils and demons, of elephants, lions, bulls, birds, rats, bats, lizards, serpents and legendary creatures, in some cases of enormous size, are introduced into the mural carvings, guard the entrances to the temples, or are scattered about promiscuously, apparently with no set plan. Serene-faced, contemplative Buddhas rub shoulders with the horrific deities of the Hindu pantheon, while here and there, never conspicuous but omnipresent, leer unclean Tantric gods. Every doorway, every window, every balcony, every terrace, almost every foot of wall space even, is cluttered with carvings in gilded metal or painted wood, many of them as exquisitely wrought as the finest goldsmith's work.

Now envision the great, rambling square as swarming with priests, monks, holy men, mendicants, pilgrims, soldiers, merchants, farmers, artisans, coolies and women, with Gurkhas, Newars, Bhotias, Tibetans and Indians, some almost naked, some wrapped in skins, others in garments of every tint in the spectrum. And finally, if by this time your powers of imagination have not been exhausted, picture at the end of the vista formed by this lane of golden buildings a distant mountain, its peak gleaming in the sunlight as though powdered with crushed diamonds, soaring nearly six miles into a vault of cloudless blue. Imagine all that, if you can, and you will still have but a feeble and imperfect conception of Bhatgaon, the strangest city in the world.

One could devote an entire volume to the place, a large volume at that, and still dwell only on the high points, so overwhelming is the mass of material, so astounding the wealth of detail. The truth is that it defies description. The best I can do is to touch superficially on a few of the city's more extraordinary features, supplementing my account with the accompanying photographs and leaving the rest to my readers' imaginations.

From the standpoints of the architect and the artist, Bhatgaon is a cave of Aladdin. It is a jumble of architectural fantasies, a vast storehouse of the treasures of Newar art. In the Durbar Square alone are enough carvings and statues to fill a score of great museums to overflowing. For here, in this forgotten valley, artist-priests and master-craftsmen have been at work unceasingly for generations beyond reckoning. Here the architectures of two great religions meet and mingle. Here have been concentrated the artistic energies of a nation. Here is to be found a living fragment of India as it must have been in those glowing, glorious, far-off days before the Moslem came.

Perhaps the most outstanding feature in a scene of which every component clamors for attention is a square column, forty feet in height, which is the focal point for the buildings scattered about or abutting on the square. The capital of the column consists of an immense lotus, the symbol of purity and divine birth, and twining itself around the petals is a snake, the emblem of eternal life. The lotus, in turn, supports a square, dragon-guarded throne, on which sits cross-legged, with clasped hands, under a gilt umbrella, a golden statue of Rajah Bhupatindra Mall, mightiest of the rulers of Bhatgaon, under whom the city achieved its greatest glory. There he has sat for upward of two hundred years, gazing serenely out across the golden roofs of the city which he did so much to beautify.

Close by, set on a ten-foot plinth of glazed red brick, is an arch, or, rather, a belfry, which is a cross between the gateway to a Chinese pagoda and the torii of one of the Shinto temples at Nikko in Japan. Slung from a beam beneath the broad eaves of the belfry's gaily tiled roof is an enormous bronze bell, covered with bas-reliefs, whose sonorous tones can be heard on still days throughout the length and breadth of the Vale.

The statue of Bhupatindra Mall looks directly down upon the architectural triumph of his reign, the magnificent Durbar Hall, with an entrance which for elaborateness of detail and beauty of treatment has no rival in all Asia. The door itself, like the doorway in which it is set, is of copper gilt, chased and chiseled into a riot of design, the whole forming a patch of concentrated lucency in the hot sunlight. Carved in bold relief on the door-posts and lintel are the figures of a whole series of minor gods, one above the other. From the trefoil tympanum above the door a scowling deity spreads its many arms like some huge and horrible variety of spider. A molding of serpents and lizards, inextricably intertwined against a background of delicately wrought foliage, frames a work which in conception and execution is worthy of Benvenuto Cellini. Of surpassing beauty under any conditions, the best time to see the Golden Gate is in the late afternoon, when the full force of the westering sun bursts upon it like a bomb.

A few paces from the Durbar Square is another and smaller plaza, the Taumari Tol. Here, rearing itself fantastically above a series of five terraces, is the Nyatpola Deval, a five-storied pagoda sometimes referred to as the Temple of the Terribles. The broad eaves and upturned corners of its serried roofs; the little bells which hang from them and tinkle musically in every breeze; the elaborately carved, vividly colored columns, rafters and antefixes, all show an unmistakably Chinese influence. The temple takes its name from the five pairs of grotesques, or "Terribles," which flank the flight of steps leading to the shrine. On the lowest terrace crouch the turbaned effigies of two wrestlers in the service of the king, who, tradition asserts, had the strength of ten ordinary men. Next come two elephants. Then two ferocious looking lions. Above them, two dragons. And, on the topmost terrace, two demons, Singhini and Vyaghini, reputed to be the most powerful of all. The temple, probably built toward the end of the seventeenth century, was originally intended as a shrine for some secret Tantric divinity. Perhaps the god was of so lewd a character that even the Newars balked at it, for the shrine is now unoccupied.

Opposite the Temple of the Terribles is a sanctuary of a wholly different architectural style and much more richly adorned. It is dedicated to Bhavani, the obscene goddess worshiped by the Sakti sect of Hindus. In this sect, as in most others, there is a right-hand and decent path, and a left-hand and indecent mode of worship, the latter, to which most of its Nepálese votaries belong, being characterized by periodical debauches of unspeakable vileness.

At these Sakti orgies devotees of both sexes and of all castes meet and mingle indiscriminately. Vast quantities of food are provided and they stuff themselves with it until they vomit, the same piece of meat being passed from mouth to mouth, each person gnawing off a morsel until it is finished. Indeed, these fanatics regard it as an act of virtue to put into one's own mouth what has been taken, already partly masticated, from another's. When all the meat has been disposed of, fiery native liquors are passed round, every one drinking from the same vessel. Opium and other narcotics are used in like fashion. Then, their passions inflamed by alcohol and poppy, the male and female worshipers pass the remainder of the night together in a saturnalia which, had it been staged in ancient Rome, would have caused the police to padlock the establishment. Modesty, morality, even the most elementary decency, are all forgotten. A husband who sees his wife in another man's embrace has no grounds for complaint, particularly as some other man's wife is probably in his arms, for on these occasions every woman becomes common property.

The Saktas, it should be explained, worship the female energy of Siva as represented by the goddess Bhavani, and may usually be recognized by the *namam,* that unnamable symbol which is painted on their foreheads or suspended from their necks. The mode of celebrating their mysterious and revolting rites varies according to locality—for the sect is not confined to Nepál but also flourishes in India—though all are equally abominable. The ritual usually consists in offering to Bhavani a full-grown girl and a bowl of rum. The former, stark naked, stands before the altar in an obscene posture while priests and worshipers chant their supplications to the goddess, who is supposed to accept the invitation to join in the orgy in her honor by taking up her abode in the jar of rum and in the maiden's body.

Of all the buildings in Bhatgaon, barring, of course, the Durbar Hall, the Temple of Bhavani is perhaps the richest in decoration. Guarding its approach are ferocious dragons of polished brass touched up with blood-red paint. Large bronze bells hang in low belfries on either side of the entrance. The triple doors are incrusted with carvings of religious significance, each story in itself. The window-lattices are wrought from copper instead of wood. Running entirely around the building, immediately beneath the eaves, is a lithic frieze consisting of the heads of beasts and imaginary monsters. Flanking the belfries already referred to are lofty lotus-columns supporting rampant lions, each of which holds in its paws a sort of standard, or oriflamme, of copper gilt. One of the most magnificently adorned religious edifices in the world, this temple is a golden fruit with a rotten core—the seat of a religion so dark and evil, the scene of rites so unutterably foul, as to be beyond the horizon of the Western mind.

Though non-believers are prohibited from entering the Newar temples, it is in many cases possible to obtain glimpses of the interiors from without. The interiors, or at any rate those into which I peered surreptitiously, usually contain a shrine or niche in which stands a large statue, in gilded metal, of the divinity to which the temple is dedicated. Occasionally the figure is serene and reposeful in character; more frequently it is hideous and lewd.

Ranged before the principal idol are a vast number of smaller statues of minor gods, many of them incrusted with gems and jewels but all so thickly coated with the grease and vermilion applied to them by the pious that their original outlines are almost indistinguishable. Scattered about promiscuously in the prevailing gloom, adding to the atmosphere of untidiness and confusion, are votive offerings in many forms—lamps, candlesticks, ewers, bells, rice-bowls, perforated incense-burners, sometimes sculptured portraits of the donors themselves. The place stinks with grease, incense, putrid fruits, decomposing flowers. The visitor has an uncanny feeling of oppression and revulsion. Lurking in the gloom amid the leering idols he seems to sense the presence of something monstrous, horrible, unclean.

Five miles or so to the south of Khatmandu is Patan, the third largest city in the kingdom and the second in artistic importance. Its glory has largely departed, however, there being here none of the bustle and activity observable in the streets of its larger and more prosperous neighbors, for Patan has never fully recovered from its sack in 1768 by the invading Gurkhas. On that sanguinary occasion the king, the nobles and the members of the aristocracy were all put to the sword; the priests were murdered on their own altars; the people, being mainly Buddhists, were subjected by their Hindu conquerors to the most revolting cruelties, thousands having their noses cut off. The royal palace was partially destroyed; the residences of the wealthy were looted of everything of value; not even the temples were spared. But the great Durbar Square, with its public buildings and sanctuaries, though inferior to that of Bhatgaon, still speaks in no uncertain voice of the city's one-time wealth and grandeur.

The sky-line of Patan, surpassingly beautiful at any time, is unimaginably glorious toward sunset, when the rippling roofs of the pagodas, the carved and columned temples, the monumental pillars, the finials in the form of umbrellas, the towers and pinnacles and spires, are silhouetted against a rose-and-crimson sky, mysterious and enchanting as the back curtain of a dream.

Here, in endless profusion, cast from bronze or chiseled from stone, are the fabulous creatures of Hindu mythology, a whole menagerie of them—the *garuda,* a gigantic bird of prey (in reality the Malabar eagle) which bore Vishnu between its wings; the *makara,* the dolphin which was the vehicle of Varuna, god of the sea; Hanuman, the monkey-god; Basava, the bull with its belly to the ground which is the favorite deity of the Sivaites; and the *naga,* a huge cobra with expanded hood, emblematic of eternity, which is the commonest of all.

The frequency with which the cobra appears in the Hindu religion and in Hindu art calls to mind certain curious stories I heard while in the East of a mysterious malady known to the natives as *mar-ashakh,* or serpent-love. Have you heard about it? No? I thought not. Whether it is found in Nepál I cannot say, but there are numerous well-authenticated instances of its occurrence in India, particularly in the Punjab. It appears that the victims of the disease—perhaps complex would be a more fitting word—periodically suffer from attacks of morbidness and depression which can only be alleviated by the man or woman thus afflicted being bitten by a snake. I was told by a physician on the staff of an Indian hospital, a graduate of the University of Edinburgh, that he had knowledge of persons who, in order to keep their health and mental balance, had to be bitten by serpents at fairly regular intervals, say every two or three months, very much as people at home are inoculated against colds. He did not attempt to explain this curious pathological condition, merely stating it as a fact, but here is the native explanation. The first time the victim is bitten by accident, and the snake which inflicts the bite is a female. The poison which she injects produces some chemical reaction in the blood which causes the person bitten periodically to exude the odor of a female snake. (Any one accustomed to handling snakes will tell you that the males and females have different smells.) It is this subtle exhalation which attracts the male serpents, who, disappointed at finding a human being instead of a reptilian lady-love, and doubtless enraged at the deception unwittingly practised on them, bite the victim again, without, apparently, causing any serious ill-effects. The second bite serves, in fact, to alleviate the restlessness and general discomfort caused by the first one. Somewhat painful momentarily, perhaps, but so is the needle of a hypodermic syringe. After this the victim's desire to be bitten at more or less frequent intervals becomes habitual, like a craving for cocaine. You can take this naïve explanation for what it is worth, which is not much from a scientific standpoint. But that does not mean that there is no such thing as serpent-love. I could tell you far stranger things than that about what happens in these mysterious lands, and probably shall before I finish.

But to return to Patan. Radiating in all directions from the Durbar Square are narrow, noisome alleys which lead eventually to temples, shrines and pagodas, many of which are almost hidden by the tumble-down buildings surrounding them. One of the most remarkable of these sanctuaries, tucked away in an evil-smelling gully, is plated from pavement to pinnacle with sheets of copper, elaborately embossed, so that, when the sun strikes upon it, it appears to be of solid gold. Close by is a shrine to Ganesha, the elephant-headed god, its entrance flanked by two granite pedestals on which crouch colossal bronze rats.

Ganesha, the god of obstacles, is venerated by all Hindus, irrespective of sect, his cult being universal. No Hindu dreams of beginning any serious undertaking without first seeking to propitiate him. Hence one comes across his idol everywhere—in temples, schools, roadside shrines, beside tanks and wells—in short, wherever people congregate. He is represented in a hideous form, with an elephant's head, misshapen limbs, an enormous belly, and always with a rat at his feet, the rat, like the elephant, being regarded as emblematic of prudence, cunning, sagacity and forethought. In making offerings to Ganesha there is always placed on the altar a small, conical heap of fresh cow-dung.

Ganesha was a son of Siva and his consort Kali, the goddess of destruction. Kali, like Medusa, had the power of the withering glance, and the first time she set eyes on little Ganesha she reduced his head to ashes. Not an auspicious start in life for any child, you must admit. Siva, being informed of this unfortunate occurrence, was distinctly irritated, for he did not relish the idea of having a headless son seated opposite him at the family table. It is said that he rebuked Kali sternly for her carelessness in looking at the baby. After devoting considerable thought to the matter, he sent out his servants with orders to decapitate the first living creature they found sleeping with its face toward the north, and bring the head to him. Coming upon an elephant dozing in the prescribed position, they cut off the unfortunate beast's head and bore it back to Siva. The latter, though exasperated at his servants' lack of judgment, deftly fitted the elephantine top-piece on his son's shoulders. So young Ganesha grew to manhood, half-human and half-jumbo. He never married, doubtless because he could not find a goddess who wanted an elephant's head resting on the next pillow. So, there being in those days no side-shows or museums in which he could find employment as a freak, he made the best of a bad job by spending the rest of his life in meditation. No wonder that they call him the god of obstacles with such a head to tote around!

On the banks of the Baghmatti, a short distance to the northeast of Khatmandu, is Pashpatti, next to Benares the holiest city in the Hindu world. The situation of this famous place of pilgrimage—a Hindu Lourdes—is singularly eerie and awesome, for it stands at the mouth of a narrow, gloomy defile, from which the sacred river, descending from the heights of the Himalayas, the home of the gods, issues solemnly, a broad stream of molten, dark green glass.

So venerated is the Baghmatti that it is the dearest wish of all Hindus to die upon its banks, their feet laved by its sacred waters. To realize this pious aspiration thousands of the diseased and dying make their laborious way hither, those who are too feeble to walk being carried in litters or on the backs of coolies. Hence, the temples and monasteries are always filled to the doors with those who are approaching the Valley of the Shadow. Tortured in body, they are happy in mind because they have been spared to gasp out their lives within the precincts of the holy city. When a pilgrim dies his body is burned on one of the stone ghats lining the river, into which his ashes are cast to be washed southward to Mother Ganges.

Pashpatti is a place of pilgrimage not only for the sick and dying, but for a vastly greater number, sound in body, who visit the sacred spot in fulfilment of vows, to cleanse themselves of sin, to win salvation. When we were there the great annual *mela* was about to begin, and the pilgrims whom we had passed upon the mountain trails were pouring in by the tens of thousands, the temple courtyards being literally carpeted with recumbent forms in the last stages of fatigue.

Several of the more striking figures we recognized, and some of them waved to us and shouted greetings as though we were old friends. A *guru,* clad in a coat of cow-dung and an antelope skin, who had sullenly refused to let me take his picture on the trail, now so far unbent as to pose before my camera quite willingly. I kept an eye out for the pretty girl whom I had surprised bathing beneath the little waterfall in the Vale of Chitlung, but she was not to be seen. Perhaps she had gone for a stroll up the gorge with a gentleman friend. I suspect that her life was not irrevocably dedicated to religion. She was too good-looking.

Pashpatti stands astride the Baghmatti, as it were, the stream here being spanned by two ancient and picturesque bridges of lichened stone. The more important of the temples, shrines and monasteries are crowded heterogeneously together on the west bank, apparently without any preconceived plan, being built on various levels and connected by flights of stone steps worn deep by the feet of countless pilgrims. Viewed from the river, the town is a chaos of masonry, a conglomeration of terraces, arches, arcades, stairways, passages, and buildings of stone or semi-glazed red brick. Rising above the terraced ghats is a long row of square stone structures, alike in size and design, with fluted pyramidal roofs whose gilded finials are reflected in the smoothly flowing waters. Before the great sanctuary is the colossal figure of a bull in gilded copper, recumbent upon a pedestal, three of his legs doubled under him and the fourth extended straight out beyond his head.

Bordering both banks of the river are stone-flagged terraces descending to the water's edge, and by these the pious go down to bathe and drink, while projecting into the stream at frequent intervals are the burning-ghats on which the funeral pyres are laid. As soon as one corpse is cremated the ashes are swept into the river in order to make ready for the next, so that the pilgrims have the inestimable privilege of wallowing in and drinking water which is covered with a thick black scum—the cinders of the dear departed. In their haste to get the day's work over with, the cremation crews sometimes grow careless and dump into the stream bones and other portions of the human anatomy which have not been entirely consumed by the flames—it is asserted that the navel never burns—but the pilgrims unconcernedly continue their bathing and drinking, happy at the prospect of salvation. As might be expected, disease in every form, both imported and indigenous, is rife in Pashpatti, for the conditions under which the pilgrims live are unsanitary beyond belief. But why worry about disease in a place of such surpassing sanctity that the soul of one who is fortunate enough to die there is borne straight to the Abodes of Bliss?

The pilgrims rise with the dawn, and before the rim of the sun has shown itself above the eastern wall of the Himalayas the ghats are crowded with bathers of both sexes, stark naked, their bodies the color of chocolate, *café au lait* or weak tea, immersing themselves in and lapping up the ash-incrusted waters. (Yet athletic clubs in America insist that their members shall take shower-baths before entering the swimming-pools!) Others, too near death to undergo the exertion of bathing, are borne on stretchers to the ghats, where they are laid so that their feet at least may rest in the sacred stream. Priests chant their orisons. Snake-charmers, fire-eaters, conjurers do their hackneyed stuff, each the center of a little ring of gaping onlookers. Holy men whine for alms, invoking on those who withhold their charity the maledictions of all the gods in the Hindu pantheon. Bells boom. Conch-horns groan. Sacred cattle wander about at their own sweet will, scattering their dung. Swarming everywhere are hundreds of big gray apes, scampering along the lofty ridge-poles of the temples, frolicking on the parapets of the bridges, swimming the river, playing leap-frog with the idols. And over everything hangs the horrid smell of searing human flesh.

With the solemn setting provided by the gloomy gorge out of which the sacred river sweeps so majestically, the dark forests which cloak the encircling hills and, in the farther distance, the Himalayas rising skyward, range on snowy range; with its bizarre temples, mysterious monasteries, sinister idols, fantastic figures in bronze and stone; with its golden forest of roofs, towers, dagobas, spires and finials; its milling throngs of priests and monks and pilgrims in their colorful, outlandish garbs, Pashpatti presents one of the most extraordinary spectacles which this world has to offer.

While returning from Pashpatti to Khatmandu we encountered a singular little procession which aroused my curiosity—a detachment of soldiers, half-a-dozen coolies bearing a stout length of bamboo from which was slung a basket containing a man trussed up like a chicken, and, bringing up the rear, a brawny Gurkha carrying an unsheathed *kukri*. It was an execution party and the poor wretch in the basket was to be the victim. He would be made to kneel beside the river, I was informed, so that his head, shorn from his shoulders by a blow of the *kukri*, would fall into the sacred stream, thus assuring him of an enjoyable hereafter. The native official who was our cicerone inquired politely if we would care to witness the execution, but we declined with thanks. Force of circumstances has compelled me to witness executions in many lands and in many forms—hangings, shootings, beheadings—and they are not pleasant sights.

I asked what punishment was meted out to Brahmans who committed crimes ordinarily punishable by death, for in Nepál the Brahmans are a class apart and not subject to the laws which govern the common run of men. In such a case, I was told, the offender, instead of being decapitated, is loaded with chains and placed in a cage so small that he is able neither to sit upright nor to lie down. Around his neck is riveted an iron collar from which is hung a weight so heavy that he cannot lift his head. To add to his misery his food is reduced to the barest minimum which will support life. If, as a result of this gracious consideration, he succeeds in keeping body and soul together for fourteen years—which rarely happens—he is not pardoned. No, indeed. Instead, he is taken to the river bank and beheaded like an ordinary murderer.

In Nepál homicide and bovicide (cow-killing) are capital crimes, while among the Gurkhas adultery is also punishable by death. In the last-named case the adulterer is killed by the wronged husband, though not until his guilt has been proved before a court of law. Indeed, the husband of an adulteress is treated as an outcast by his relatives and neighbors until he has removed the stain on his honor by killing her paramour. The culprit is given a start of a few yards and then runs for his life. If he escapes he is immune from punishment, but this rarely happens, for he is tripped up by the onlookers and the husband then takes the three cuts with his *kukri* which he is allowed by law. One trifling act remains for the husband to perform. He has to cut off his wife's nose to prevent any one else from falling in love with her. After hearing of this custom, I kept a sharp eye out for noseless women, but I must confess that I did not see one. Perhaps they were hiding their shame behind their veils; perhaps Nepálese wives are more moral than those elsewhere; or perhaps—and this seems the most likely explanation—they are more successful in carrying on their amours without detection.

Some of the customs of the Nepálese are curious beyond belief. Among the Newars, for example, every girl, while still an infant, is married with much ceremony to a bel-fruit, which is then thrown into some sacred stream. I was unable to learn exactly what a bel-fruit is, but no matter. As no one knows what happens to the fruit, a Newarin in theory never becomes a widow, thus escaping the unhappy fate of Indian wives who survive their husbands.

This does not prevent her from having a human husband, however, for at the age of puberty a spouse is selected for the girl by her parents, but she can divorce herself at any time by the simple expedient of placing a betel nut under her husband's pillow and leaving his roof. On the death of her husband a Newarin may, if she so chooses, immolate herself upon his funeral pyre, for in Nepál *suttee* is not prohibited; but the privilege, if privilege it can be called, is rarely taken advantage of. The Newars, unlike the Gurkhas, do not take adultery seriously. The woman does not lose her nose nor her paramour his life. Instead, she is merely divorced, and the co-respondent usually gets off by reimbursing the injured husband for the expenses connected with the wedding ceremony.

Polyandry is practised among certain of the hill tribes, where the women are outnumbered by the men, it not infrequently happening that one woman is married to several brothers, the whole family living quite amicably under the same roof, the husbands taking their common wife in turn.

This arrangement gives the woman a diversified life and seems to suit every one concerned. Among the Bhotias, however, who dwell mainly in eastern Nepál, the marriage tie is regarded with complete indifference and most of them are not married at all, their women being looked upon as communal property.

Throughout Nepál murder and the killing of cows are, as I have remarked elsewhere, both capital offenses, though the latter is regarded much more seriously than the former, because it is an offense against the gods. Manslaughter and the maiming of cows are punishable by imprisonment for life, which, under Nepálese penal conditions, is equivalent to a living death. In some cases all the criminal's property is confiscated and he and his family may be sold as slaves, Nepál being the sole independent country in the world where slavery remains a recognized institution. All families of the nobility and the aristocracy own large numbers of slaves, who are employed in the fields or the household, but they are in general well treated and are protected by rigid laws.

Nepál is a physician's paradise, doctors being always assured of a lucrative practice, as every family of position has at least one *baid,* or medical man, in constant attendance, and there are also many general practitioners. This is as well, perhaps, for there are no civil hospitals in the country save the small one at the British legation, and certain diseases, particularly syphilis, goiter, leprosy, rheumatism, cholera and a peculiarly virulent form of typhoid are common. Astrology is also a profitable profession, the services of star-gazers and horoscope-makers being in constant demand by all classes of the population. Indeed, one cannot build a house, set out on a journey, plan a shooting expedition, or even take a cathartic, without first having a soothsayer determine the most propitious moment for the act.

When the Nepálese authorities framed a law rigidly prohibiting gambling they knew what they were doing, for the natives are the most inveterate gamesters in the world. The ban is lifted, for a single week in the year, however, during the festival known as the *Dassera,* a portion of which is devoted to Lakshmi, the goddess of good fortune. During this brief annual period the whole kingdom goes gambling mad. Extraordinary stories are told of the stakes which have been lost and won on these occasions, there having been numerous instances of Nepálese gamblers who played cards or rolled dice for their wives and children. Dr. Wright, who translated the history of Nepál, states that "one man is said to have cut off his left hand and put it down under a cloth as a stake. On winning the game, he insisted on his opponent cutting off his hand, or else restoring all the money which he had previously won."

We could have remained quite contentedly in Nepál for many weeks, for it is a fascinating country with a glorious climate, magnificent scenery, a courteous and hospitable people. But a message had been relayed to us by runner, via Raxaul, that the Nawab of Bhopal, on whose invitation we had originally started for the East, was expecting us to join him in New Delhi for the horse show and polo week. So we reluctantly said farewell to the Kilburnes, whose kindness I shall never forget, and turned the heads of our ponies down the road that leads across the passes to India.

Reining in the ponies at the summit of the Sisagarhi, we turned in our saddles to take a final look at Nepál. Far, far below us spread the valley, grass-green, grain-yellow, beneath the Asian sun. Yonder rose the rosy roofs of Khatmandu and, beyond, the golden spires of Patan and Bhatgaon. In the middle distance, rearing itself from the dead flat plain, was the solitary hill crowned by the great dagoba of Shambu-Nath. The sacred rivers, Baghmatti and Vishnumatti, trailed across the Vale like blue ribbons tossed carelessly upon the ground. And above the templed cities of the plain, above the mighty ramparts which walled them in, the gleaming crest of Everest emerged for a moment from her veil of clouds. The Ice Empress was bidding us a last farewell.

Thence onward the trail was comparatively deserted, for the bulk of the pilgrims had arrived at Pashpatti, where the *mela* had already begun. So for miles on end we rode or walked in solitude and silence, which is good for the soul. It would be well, indeed, if every man could pass a few days each year amid these lonely heights engaged in meditation, in striking a trial balance, as it were, of himself. In these high places one gains a better sense of values; troubles and perplexities, ambitions and disappointments, which bulk large at home, here seem of little consequence. Nor does one need to be religious, in the orthodox sense of the term, to know that a Supreme Being—Providence, God, Allah, what you will—not only exists but is very near.

We had planned to spend the night going out, as we had done coming in, at the rest-house on the Chandragiri, but upon our arrival there we were informed by the custodian that the British envoy, Mr. Wilkinson, and his niece, were expected momentarily, being on their way back to Khatmandu from tiger-shooting in the Terai. There was only one sleeping-room in the bungalow, and, as we were strangers, our presence might have proved embarrassing for the lady, so we pushed on to Bhimpedi, where we found that arrangements had been made for us to spend the night in as filthy and comfortless a hovel—it was called a rest-house only by courtesy—as I have ever seen. The furniture consisted of a deal table smeared with grease, two broken chairs, a pair of camp-beds acrawl with vermin, and nothing more. To make matters worse, our only lantern suddenly went out and the subadar could find no kerosene in the village with which to replenish it. Of our stock of whisky, however, two bottles fortunately remained, and with these we sought to dissipate the gloom, mental and material, in which we were enveloped. Ere the first bottle was finished my cousin, ordinarily the soberest and most sedate of men, insisted that it was "a wild night on the moor" and proceeded to start a roaring fire in spite of the fact that the heat was almost tropical here in the edge of the Terai.

While we were waiting for Julius and the subadar to prepare our evening meal from the inevitable tinned goods, we heard a clatter of hoofs in the street outside. It was the envoy and his niece, with an escort of sowars, returning to Khatmandu. She was a slim and graceful girl, in a smart riding coat and beautifully cut breeches. I couldn't see much of her features, because it was already dusk and she wore a broad-brimmed topée, but I saw enough of them to make me regret that we had not remained in Khatmandu a few days longer. My cousin was for having them in to join us in a drink, and it was all I could do to dissuade him, explaining that they were English and wouldn't understand.

"I've seen ten million coffee-colored wenches in the last few weeks," he grumbled, "and not one of 'em worth taking a second look at. Now a pretty girl who is white and speaks my own language comes along and you won't let me speak to her because we haven't been introduced. I'm going to lie down and go to sleep and let the world go to hell."

We had been told that, by starting from Bhimpedi before daybreak, we could reach Amlekgunj in time to catch the morning down-train for Raxaul, where we could

THE STRANGEST CITY IN THE WORLD

The great Durbar Square of Bhatgaon is not merely crowded but literally jammed with palaces, temples, shrines, pagodas, towers, spires, columns, with figures of gods, men, beasts and monsters in brass, bronze and stone. An incongruous note is struck by the Ford in the foreground—one of the dozen cars in the kingdom

THE PAGODAS OF PATAN

The city, the third largest in Nepál, was a place of wealth and importance until the Gurkha conquest, but the invaders wrecked its glorious buildings, slaughtered the Newar priests, and cut off the noses of thousands of its inhabitants

make connections with the south-bound mail for Muzafferpur and Benares. But when we reached the railhead we found that for some reason there would be no train until late afternoon, which meant missing our connection at Raxaul.

While we were cursing this bit of ill-luck in particular and train service in the East generally, our friend the minister of communications came cantering up on his white pony. When he learned of our predicament and our anxiety to reach Delhi at the earliest possible moment, he suggested that, instead of waiting for the evening train, we go on to Raxaul by motor. The suggestion was excellent in itself, the only difficulty being that no motor-car for the trip was to be had. The drivers who had brought us from Bhimpedi flatly refused to go farther, for reasons which, as we learned a little later, were good and sufficient. But the subadar, a resourceful fellow, finally discovered a pre-war motor-truck, a somewhat decrepit member of the well-known Ford family of Detroit, and a native who agreed to drive it to Raxaul, a distance of twenty-four miles, for the equivalent in rupees of fifty dollars.

"How is the road?" I called to the prince as we started off.

"Well," he replied evasively, "it hasn't been macadamized yet."

For the first mile or so the trail—it could by no stretch of the truth be called a road—was at least passable, but it soon became so bad that the chauffeur abandoned it altogether in favor of the railway embankment. Along this we crawled for a time with one pair of wheels on the ties and the other in the ditch, the truck tilted at such an angle that its failure to capsize was a miracle. Then, when it seemed that the ancient vehicle must jolt itself apart, we struck a stretch of cowpath on which we were able to speed up in places to nearly five miles an hour. But just as we were congratulating ourselves on our troubles being over, the driver misjudged the depth of a mudhole and the truck sank in the mire until its wheels were almost out of sight.

"Well, what are we going to do now?" my cousin demanded, after our united efforts had failed to budge the machine an inch.

"Why don't you telephone to the nearest A.A.A. station," I suggested, "and ask them to send out a trouble car?"

I suspect that he was on the point of indulging in language of which Dr. Cadman would not approve, when across the plain an elephant hove in sight. Its mahout, for a small consideration, tied a rope to the front axel of the truck and with a single heave the leviathan hauled us out of trouble.

It was a wild ride from there on, for, having already lost much time and fearing to miss the train, I told the driver to step on the gas. He complied enthusiastically. The trail had now developed into something vaguely resembling a road and this we took at top speed, with a rattle, bang and roar, like a tank going into action. Then, for no apparent reason, the man at the wheel decided that he could make better time by going cross-country. We dropped with a crash into deep ditches and struggled out of them again, went plunging across plowed fields, tore through a plantation of opium poppies, took off the corner of a brick wall, skidded through a thorn hedge into a peasant's vegetable garden, killed a brace of chickens, ran down a yellow dog, narrowly missed a sacred cow, and finally, making a wrong turn upon entering Birgunge, found ourselves in the courtyard of a temple, with the frightened worshipers scattering in all directions. But at last, with less than ten minutes to spare, we thundered across the rickety bridge spanning the little river which is the frontier and pulled up alongside the waiting south-bound train. Our Nepálese adventure was over. We were back in India again.

CHAPTER XII

AT THE COURTS OF THE PRINCES

NIGHT, the soft and purple Indian night, had descended on the land when the Punjab Mail roared into the station of New Delhi. Awaiting us on the platform was a little group of officials, their sky-blue turbans denoting that they were attached to the court of Bhopal. A slim, soldierly looking man in evening dress introduced himself as Colonel Amir Ahmed, military secretary to the nawab, and greeted us in the name of his Highness. Cars were in waiting, driven by chauffeurs in the royal livery; servants stowed our luggage in a motor lorry; and we were whirled through broad and tree-lined avenues to the Bhopal camp.

For his fortnight's stay in the capital of India the nawab had leased a commodious private residence in the beautiful suburb known as New Delhi, a quarter which has sprung up around the recently completed government buildings. But the house, large as it was, could not begin to accommodate the numerous members of his entourage, for whom a miniature city of tents had been pitched in the spacious gardens. Somewhat removed from the others, a sentry pacing up and down before its entrance, was the tent assigned to us—a canvas mansion.

Those unacquainted with the East can scarcely conceive of the luxury of Indian tent life. It is as far removed from the American conception of camping as the Petit Trianon is from a Canadian log cabin. We were shown into a spacious living-room, perhaps twenty feet square, carpeted with a superb Kermanshah, its walls hung with green silk. Scattered about, as in a club, were huge armchairs and sofas in green morocco, a writing-desk stocked with crested stationery, a humidor with Havanas, a table loaded with the latest newspapers and magazines. Beyond was the dining-room, the mahogany table gleaming with silver and crystal, strewn with flowers. On the sideboard was an imposing array of bottles bearing the old, familiar labels—Buchanan, Haig & Haig, Dewar, Gordon, Martini & Rossi, Château Yquem, Irroy, Veuve Clicquot, Pères Chartreuse. What a sight for American eyes! Opening from the dining-room were suites for my cousin and myself, each consisting of a bedroom, dressing-room and bath. The whole tent was lighted by electricity; there were even reading-lamps beside the beds. Nothing that would add to our comfort had been overlooked. And, mark you, this canvas mansion had been erected solely for our occupancy and was taken down within an hour after our departure.

The staff of highly trained, silent-footed servants, their long white garments set off with sky-blue cummerbunds and turbans, was under the supervision of the nawab's own steward, a highly efficient Englishman named Babcock. Babcock was a sort of general factotum, a walking compendium of useful information, and to him we turned for anything and everything—my favorite smoking tobacco, medicines when I had a touch of the "flu," hints on the complicated etiquette observed at the Indian courts, advice as to whether we should wear white ties or black ones.

As I surveyed the amazing establishment which had sprung into being in a few hours, as at the wave of a magician's wand, I caught myself humming a once popular but now forgotten song:

> In our castle on the River Nile
> We will live in elegant style,

Eating terrapin all the while
In our castle on the Nile.

Our tent was not a castle, it is true; the near-by river was the Jumna; and terrapin are not procurable in India—had they been we assuredly would have had them—but during our visit to the nawab, both in Delhi and later in Bhopal, we certainly lived in elegant style, to put it vulgarly.

Though the Nawab of Bhopal is the ruler of the second most important Mohammedan state in India, he is as simple and modest a young man as you would find anywhere, being wholly free from the extravagance and passion for display which characterize many of his fellow-princes. His home life, indeed, is so unpretentious as to verge on the austere. Yet he is a reigning sovereign and travels in the state which is expected of Eastern rulers.

He was accompanied on this occasion by his mother, the famous octogenarian Begum of Bhopal, his wife, his three daughters and several nephews and cousins. For a stay of only a fortnight he had also brought with him from Bhopal, three hundred miles away, twoscore cabinet ministers, court officials, A.D.C.'s, and secretaries, upward of a hundred servants, a detachment of household infantry for sentry duty about the camp, thirty-odd motor-cars and some sixty polo ponies. I might add, in this connection, that the nawab is regarded as perhaps the foremost polo player in the peninsula, the Bhopal team, of which he is the captain, having won the championship of India in 1928. His pet project, and one which he discussed with me on several occasions, is to take an All-Indian team to the United States in an attempt to capture the Meadow Brook Cup.

As every moment of our host's time was occupied with political conferences, state dinners and official functions of one sort or another, we did not meet him until the afternoon following our arrival, when one of the equerries brought word that the nawab would receive us at tea-time. Changing into white flannels, we strolled over to the house at the appointed hour to find that his Highness had not yet returned from the session of the Chamber of Princes. While we were chatting with members of the staff a bugle sounded shrilly, the guard turned out, and a big gray touring-car tore into the grounds at top speed, narrowly missing one of the gate-posts. From the tonneau sprang briskly a slender, dark mustached, strikingly handsome young man wearing the light gray frock coat and white drill jodhpurs which comprise the day dress of all Indian gentlemen; his beautifully wound turban was the shade of light blue which is the national color of Bhopal. His clear complexion, alert eyes and air of suppressed energy showed that he was in the very pink of physical condition. Though his demeanor was modest almost to the point of shyness, he possessed the poise and ease of manner which seem to be characteristic of sovereigns.

"So sorry to have kept you waiting," he exclaimed, shaking hands cordially and throwing himself into a cane chair, "but I simply couldn't break away any sooner. The debates in the chamber never come to an end. Do have some tea. Milk or lemon? One or two sugars? I hope my people have made you comfortable. If there is anything you lack don't hesitate to ask for it. Now tell me about your visit to Nepál."

Remembering that the fasting month of Ramadan had begun the night before, and that his Highness was reputed to be an exceptionally devout Moslem, I was not surprised to note that he himself refrained from eating, drinking and smoking. Though he is said to be the most indefatigable worker in his kingdom, and plays polo as hard as he works, he never permits food or drink to pass his lips between sunrise and sunset during the annual thirty days of fasting prescribed by the Koran. His example, I noticed, was followed by all the members of his entourage save only Colonel Amir Ahmed, who, though a Moslem, did not appear to bother himself about religious observances. But I have known most respectable Catholics who ate meat on Fridays, and Jews who ate pork at any time.

Babcock told me in confidence that the nawab's insistence on the strict observance of Ramadan by himself and his household was something of a trial, for it meant turning night into day for the whole establishment. A heavy dinner was served immediately after the firing of the sunset gun; there was a light luncheon at midnight; and every one partook of a hearty breakfast before the crash of the sunrise gun indicated that the day's fast had begun. The nawab's private physician, Dr. Rahman, a brilliant young man who holds a degree from the University of Edinburgh, asserted that the excellent health enjoyed by Mohammedans was largely due to this annual fasting period, which is of particular benefit to the human system in a climate like that of India. It is scarcely necessary for me to remark that my cousin and I were not expected to do any fasting out of courtesy to our host. The royal cooks, in fact, having nothing else to do, seemed to take pride in seeing how many tempting dishes they could devise for our table. Our meals were, of course, cooked and served in European fashion, but Babcock saw to it that there was always one native dish in order to provide a touch of local color.

I regarded our host with undisguised interest, for he has the reputation among English and Indians alike of being the most progressive and the most capable of the native rulers. His Highness Sikander Saulet Nawab Iftikharul-Mulk, Mohammed Hamidullah Khan Bahadur, B.A.,

C.S.I., C.V.O., to give him his full style and titles, is now in his early thirties. He succeeded to the throne of Bhopal in 1926 upon the abdication of his mother, her Highness Nawab Sultan Jahan Begum, now an octogenarian, who ruled the state with great energy and ability for many years.

The nawab does not look like an Indian, nor is he, racially speaking, for the ruling dynasty of Bhopal was founded by an Afghan chieftain, Dost Mohammed Khan, who was granted extensive territories in central India by the Grand Mogul. Upon the disintegration of the Mogul Empire Bhopal developed into a independent state, ranking next to Hyderabad in importance among the Moslem states of India.

Bhopal long enjoyed the unique distinction of being the only Indian state to be ruled by a woman, its destinies having been for three generations, from mother to daughter, in feminine hands. As all three of the nawab's children are daughters, it is to be assumed that upon his demise the throne of Bhopal may for a fourth time be occupied by a woman. The heiress apparent, now in her middle 'teens and reputed to be as charming as her photographs show her to be beautiful (I say reputed because, like all Moslem women in India, she is in *purdah*), is engaged to the youthful ruler of a neighboring state. She is as devoted to sport as her father, and, a few days before our arrival, had shot her first tiger.

Life in Bhopal camp was never dull, yet we were not bound to one of those set programs with which well-intentioned hosts frequently make the lives of their guests miserable. Indeed, we were as free to come and go as though we had been staying at a country club. After an early breakfast we usually motored out to the polo-field, where ponies were awaiting us, and, while the dew was still on the grass, rode for an hour or so along the Ridge, rich in its monuments and memories of the Mutiny. Racing back to camp, we would bathe and change into flannels and spend what was left of the morning visiting the places of historic interest in the one-time capital of the Mogul Empire, or making purchases in the Chandni Chauk, which is the Bond Street of Delhi. At the fascinating shop of a Hungarian, famous from one end of India to the other as a connoisseur of Asiatic *objets d'art,* I bought a pigeon's-blood ruby for my wife, a turquoise bracelet for my daughter, and three Persian rugs for myself, and would have bought more had not my cousin dragged me away in spite of my protests.

After tiffin, the warm weather being already at hand, we took a siesta. But by mid-afternoon the heat had abated, and from then until the dinner-hour our time was fully occupied with race meetings, polo tournaments, tennis matches or garden parties. Dinner was usually a somewhat formal affair, for the nawab made it a point to see that we always had interesting companions—on one evening a cabinet minister, a dignified old gentleman who turned out to be the most amusing raconteur I have ever met; on another the nawab's British chief of staff and his charming wife; on still another the distinguished editor of a widely read vernacular newspaper, who explained that he could not do justice to the very excellent food because he had forgotten to bring his false teeth, but who did more than justice to the champagne. After our guests had taken their departure we would light our pipes and go for a stroll beneath the stars; then to bed to sleep soundly beneath four blankets.

Among my recollections of Delhi is that of the viceroy's garden party at Viceregal Lodge. All official India was there, for the Chamber of Princes was still sitting, and the members of several political commissions just arrived from England also attended the function. There must have been quite a thousand guests in all. In the extensive but not particularly beautiful gardens at the back of the great white palace which is the official residence of the viceroy and governor-general, hundreds of tea-tables had been set upon the sweeping lawns. From the standpoint of sociability it could hardly have been called a success; the annual reception at the White House for the justices of the Supreme Court was a riot in comparison. Though the Indian guests were almost without exception quite at ease, the English were as stiff and self-conscious as only English can be.

Sikh troopers of the body-guard cavalry, gigantic fellows in skirted scarlet coats, white leather breeches, polished jack-boots and blue-and-gold turbans, stood like statues, leaning on their pennoned lances, and through the lane thus formed the viceregal party majestically advanced. Massed bugles sounded a fanfare, the red-coated band burst into the ponderous strains of "God Save the King," the women curtsied, the men bowed or saluted, and the one-armed viceroy, Lord Irwin, who in his gray flannels and soft hat looked more like an English country squire than the ruler of King George's three hundred million Indian subjects, smiled and nodded affably to every one.

When the viceregal party, in which our host, the nawab, was included, had been seated within a cordon of lances, the guests engaged in a wild scramble for chairs and tables. I kept possession of a table by the simple expedient of sitting on it, while my cousin, with much difficulty, succeeded in commandeering a single chair. We spent the rest of the afternoon in changing places, my cousin sitting for a spell and then surrendering his seat to me. At length we spied a vacant chair and I made a dash for it, but a choleric looking field marshal reached it first. My cousin made the next attempt, but a brocaded and bediamonded chieftain from the Shan states beat him to it by inches. At length the situation became so ridiculous that we burst into roars of laughter, to the utter scandalization of the English and the polite astonishment of the Indians.

Considered purely as a spectacle, a pageant of Eastern aristocracy, the garden party could hardly have been surpassed. Conspicuous among the guests by reason of his great height was the Maharajah of Patiala, whom we were to visit later on, a splendid figure of a man, his black beard braided and tied up under his chin, Rajput fashion. There was the Maharajah of Alwar, his smooth, saturnine countenance recalling those portraits of the Borgias which hang in the galleries of the Pitti Palace in Florence. His coat of purple velvet and the great star of diamonds which shone in his turban gave no hint that he was one of the most dashing polo players and perhaps the most brilliant orator in all India, and that his eloquence had often thrilled the meetings of the League of Nations.

There, too, was the Gaekwar of Baroda, a smiling, cherubic old gentleman, turned out as though for Gold Cup Day at Ascot, though instead of a gray topper he wore a head-dress which was a cross between a turban, a bonnet and a deep-dish blackberry tart.

Strolling about democratically, shaking hands and chatting with every one, was the Maharajah of Nawangar, Sir Ranjitsinhji Vibhaji, usually referred to as the Jam Sahib. I ventured to remind him that we had first met twenty-odd years before in London, at a dinner given by Edna May, the star of "The Belle of New York," when "Ranji," as he was popularly called, was the greatest cricketer in England and the darling of the fans at Lord's.

Amid the glittering throng were princes in brocades and velvets, with strings of pearls about their necks, and other princes whose garments bore the stamp of Savile Row; bearded Rajput chieftains with jeweled swords at their waists and jewels flashing in their turbans; rulers of obscure states along the Chinese border, with huge fur caps and long coats of quilted satin; British civil officials in braided morning coats and striped trousers; British generals in khaki, on their breasts multicolored patches of medal-ribbons; youthful A.D.C.'s, very stiff and haughty in their tight blue uniforms; Englishwomen in frocks which bespoke the Rue de la Paix and others in frocks which had palpably been made at home; and Indian women, with gems in their ears and in some cases in their noses, wearing gracefully draped *saris* of the most beautiful and varied colors, so that when a group of them collected on the lawn they looked like a garden of flowers.

At the table next to ours sat a party of English officials and their wives. Two of the men, I gathered from the conversation, were advisers to petty princes and had accompanied their royal charges to Delhi in order to keep a paternal eye on them.

"How's your maharajah chap coming along?" I heard one of them ask the other.

"He's going to make me gray before my time with his extravagance," was the answer. "Only last month I let him buy a silver-plated Hispano-Suiza because I was fed up with his whining for it, and now he wants to buy a fleet of tanks. Tanks! My word! He wouldn't know what to do with the bally things if he had 'em, unless it was to use 'em as road-rollers; but once he sets his mind on a thing, there's no arguing with him. But I told him he can't have the tanks. One really has to draw the line somewhere, y' know."

"My chap," remarked the other, "got mixed up with a French dancer he met last holiday-time in Calcutta. She was deucedly good lookin', too. Had things all fixed up to marry the gel secretly, but the priests got wind of it—I saw to that—and kicked up such a row that he jolly well had to break the match off. He's more damn trouble than a pet monkey. I'm always worried when he's out of my sight for fear he's hatchin' some new devilry or other."

It was fascinating, these surreptitious side-lights on those who sit in gilded howdahs, but my eavesdropping was abruptly interrupted by the strains of the anthem. The viceroy was taking his departure. The party was over. We pushed our way through a milling throng of maharajahs, nawabs, sultans, sahibs and thakurs, of cabinet ministers, governors, generals, political officers and smaller fry, to present the numbered ticket for our car to the gold-braided starter.

"The car of his Highness the Nawab of Bhopal!" that functionary bawled.

The sky-blue limousine rolled up, we climbed in, the door was slammed behind us.

"How would you like to be a prince?" I asked my cousin as we settled back luxuriously on the cushions.

"Hell!" he replied, "I don't want to live in a circus *all* the time."

One morning, at Colonel Amir Ahmed's suggestion, we drove out to Raisina Hill, on the southern edge of Delhi, where, at an estimated cost of more than 1300 lakhs of rupees—upward of forty-four million dollars—the new government buildings are going up. The transfer of the seat of the government of India from Calcutta to Delhi was announced at the Delhi durbar in 1911, when the foundation stone of the new capital was laid by King George. Comprised in this ambitious scheme is the vast palace which is to be the official residence of the viceroy, known as Government House; two huge Secretariats, in which are already housed most of the various branches of the administration; and a large group of parliamentary buildings. The latter is an imposing pile, circular in shape and colonnaded, consisting of three horseshoe-shaped structures for the Chamber of Princes, the Council of State and the Legislative Assembly respectively, a central library serving to connect all three wings. Though vastly larger, and of pinkish-red stone, this building suggests the Pantheon in Rome.

With the inception of the scheme there arose a violent controversy over the architectural style to be followed in the construction of the new buildings, and, though most of them are now completed, the "battle of the styles," as it is called, has not abated. It was the aim of the architects, Sir Edwin Lutyens and Mr. Edward Baker, "to express, within the limits of the medium and of the powers of its users, the ideal and the fact of British rule in India, of which the New Delhi must ever be the monument." The inspiration of the designs is manifestly Western, as is that of British rule, but they combine with it distinctive Indian features without doing violence to the principles of structural fitness and artistic unity. Yet I met no one who was satisfied with the result. And I must confess that I was not particularly enthusiastic myself. There is massiveness, yes, and a certain majesty, and the scale of everything is enormous, but there is nothing, or next to nothing, which suggests that this is the seat of government of India, the most picturesque, colorful and romantic country in the world. As might be expected, the bitterest critics are the Indians, who resent the dominancy of the Western *motif* as much as they resent Western rule. Criticisms are perhaps not seemly from a guest and an outsider, but it seems to me that the French have been much more successful in the government buildings they erected at Rabat, the capital of Morocco, for, though on a far less pretentious scale than those at Delhi, they are frankly Moorish and hence are characteristic of the country.

In a land where servants are cheap and abundant, perhaps communicational difficulties do not greatly matter, but it struck me that at New Delhi little thought had been given to convenience, and that, as a consequence, the business of government must be considerably slowed up. The distances are enormous—one should really have a wheeled chair to get about in comfort—and the corridors and stairways of the vast buildings form a bewildering labyrinth. It took me the better part of half an hour, for example, to make my way from the offices of the Royal Air Force to those of the Political Department, and even then I had to enlist the services of a chuprassi as guide.

The Chamber of Princes was in session when we were in Delhi, and the display of royal cars which were awaiting their owners rivaled that at the New York Automobile Show. All the most expensive makes were represented—Rolls-Royces of course, Renaults, Mercedes, Fiats, Isotta-Fraschinis, Hispano-Suizas, though I did not see a single car of American make. There were cars which were gold-plated and cars which were silver-plated, cars with hoods of polished aluminum and bodies of costly woods, cars in purple, lavender, sky-blue, orange, emerald-green, vermilion, cars upholstered in satins, velvets, brocades. One had mounted on its roof a searchlight as large as those used on destroyers; another was fitted with steel shutters, presumably to save its owner from assassination; a third had on its running-board a small pipe organ on which an attendant played his master's favorite airs.

The English chose wisely when they settled on Delhi as

the capital of their Indian Empire, not only because of its central location but because of its traditions. Delhi is the empress of Indian cities. Its history goes back into the dim and distant past. Eight hundred years before the Latins settled on the plains of Latium and Campania a band of Aryans drove from here the savage aborigines and founded on the left bank of the Jumna the city of Indrapastha, which grew into a mighty kingdom. Then the Moslem came, and Hindu civilization disappeared in smoke and ruin. From the materials of the infidel temples the Mohammedan conquerors erected mosques and palaces and mausoleums which are among the wonders of the world.

Though the wave of Moslem invasion that eventually swept the country first touched India less than a hundred years after the death of the Prophet in 632, Delhi did not become the capital of a Mohammedan empire until 1206, when Kutb-ud-Din, originally a Turki slave, made it his seat of government and erected the great mosque whose majestic ruins still rise above the plain. Between his rule and that of the Moguls, which began in 1526, many kings reigned and fought and built beautiful buildings, and died and have been forgotten.

Just as the sixteenth century had passed its first quarter-mark, Baber, the outcast prince of a central Asian khanate, swept down from the passes of the north, overwhelmed the king of Delhi on the field of Panipat, and made himself the first Mogul emperor of Hindustan. He was succeeded by his son, Humayun, who died and is buried on the banks of the Jumna. The mausoleum which was erected over the grave of Humayun by his son, the Great Akbar—an octagonal mass of white marble and rose-colored sandstone, crowned by a gleaming marble dome—has never been surpassed for chastity of design and delicacy of execution.

During the reigns of the first three emperors, Agra was the capital of the Mogul Empire, but Shah Jehan—a contemporary of Charles I of England—transferred the seat of government to Delhi. This was the golden age of Mogul rule, and to the genius of Shah Jehan, who likewise built the Taj Mahal, are due the two chief architectual glories of Delhi—the palace of the Mogul emperors and the Jumma Musjid.

In the center of Delhi, on the highest eminence, stands the Jumma Musjid, or Great Mosque, one of the most impressive places of worship in the world. Five thousand workmen were employed daily on it for six years. It is to all intents and purposes a sanctuary without a roof, only a small portion, containing the *mihrab,* being covered, so that the worshipers say their prayers under the open sky. It consists, in the main, of a vast platform, surrounded by high walls broken by two graceful gateways. On the eastern side rise three domes of white marble striped with black, and at each angle of the walled inclosure towers a gigantic minaret of alternate stripes of marble and red sandstone from which the muezzins summon the faithful to prayer . . . "*Allahu il Allah! Allah Akbar!*"

Opposite the Jumma Musjid is the palace built by Shah Jehan which was the home of the Mogul Cæsars. Surrounded by lofty granite walls with frowning battlements, it was a fortress-residence worthy of the descendants of the immortal Tamerlane. Entering the palace by the impressive Lahore Gate, you drive through a narrow, arcaded bazaar to the inner entrance, the Naubhat Khana or Royal Drum House. Thence on foot to the open courtyard in front of the great Hall of Public Audience, the Diwan-i-'Amm. This is a vast pillared hall of red sandstone, open on three sides. In the center of the back wall there is a raised recess, paneled in marble, inlaid in jade, agate, lapis lazuli, cornelian. This was known in the old days as "The Seat of the Shadow of God," for here the emperor sat.

A little beyond the Diwan-i-Amm, separated from it by a garden fragrant with flowers, a pile of white marble, its carvings as delicate as the finest lace, overlooks the winding Jumna. It is the Diwan-i-Khas, or Hall of Private Audience, world renowned because of the proud boast which appears above it in letters of gold upon a white marble background: "If there is a paradise upon earth it is this—it is this—it is this!"

In the center of the pillared terrace, where jets of water constantly rose and fell, stood the emperor's judgment seat, the famous Peacock Throne, so called from the figures of two peacocks which formed its back, their outspread tails set with sapphires, rubies, emeralds, pearls and diamonds. The Peacock Throne stands to-day in the dingy treasure-room of the shah's palace in Tehran, where I once journeyed to see it.[1] Though its finest jewels have long since disappeared, though of the canopy of pearls which once covered it no vestige remains, its historic value is beyond computation.

The Mogul Empire attained its widest limits under Aurungzebe, the traitorous son of Shah Jehan. But with his death in 1707, after a reign of half a century, the decline of the Mogul power began. In 1729 the Persian soldier of fortune, Nadir Shah, descended from the Afghan passes, overran Hindustan and sacked Delhi, among the loot which he carried back to Persia being Shah Jehan's Peacock Throne. Then followed a tempest of invasion by the Afghans. Delhi was again taken and again plundered. And in 1788 a Rohilla chieftain dealt the capital of the Moguls its *coup de grâce* by capturing the city, seizing the emperor and putting out his eyes with a dagger. Though Mogul

[1] See Colonel Powell's "By Camel and Car to the Peacock Throne."

emperors sat on the throne of Delhi until the middle of the nineteenth century, they were rulers only in name. The last act came in 1857, at the high tide of the Mutiny, when British soldiers carried the palace-fort by storm, bivouacked in the Diwan-i-Amm, and raised above it the flag that has never since come down. A new race of conquerors had come to Delhi. And now, after a lapse of more than half a century they have made the ancient city once more the capital of Imperial India.

If there is a more perfect climate in the world than that of Delhi in the cold weather I have yet to find it. But it is of brief duration. It begins about the first of January—crisp, clear days, radiant with sunshine, often with the tang of frost in the air—and for perhaps ten weeks the gardens are a riot of color. Ere the Ides of March have come, however, the hot weather is at hand; the flowers wither and die before the blast of dust storms; around midday the mercury in the thermometer creeps up toward the 100 mark; the viceregal court and every one else who can get away seek refuge in the hills; and Delhi is left to stew in its own juice until another cold season rolls around.

Our host, the nawab, was anxious that we should meet as many as possible of his fellow-princes and see as much as possible of the states over which they rule. Accordingly, he made arrangements for us to be received by a number of those who were attending the Chamber of Princes and, convoyed by the suave and capable Colonel Amir Ahmed, who appeared to be upon terms of intimacy with every one in India, we called upon the Jam Sahib, the Maharajah of Patiala, the Gaekwar of Baroda and various less important rulers. All received us with a cordiality that was not simulated for politeness' sake; all insisted that we visit them in their own dominions. Indeed, had we accepted half the invitations which were showered upon us we should be in India still.

But business demanded my cousin's presence in America, and personal affairs required my return to Europe ere long, so we regretfully compromised with our desires by accepting invitations to the courts of Patiala and Gwalior and promising the nawab that we would spend a few days with him in Bhopal en route to Bombay. It had been our intention, I might mention, to make at least a flying trip to Kabul, the government of Afghanistan having sent me an invitation some months previously to visit that country. But the weather and the Bolsheviki were against us. For when I called upon the Afghan consul-general in Delhi to make inquiries regarding the journey, he informed me that the mountain roads between the Khyber and the capital were still deep in snow, even the mails having great difficulty in getting through. He urged us, therefore, to postpone our visit until spring, adding that, as King Amanullah was in Europe, we could not be entertained at the palace, and that every available room in Kabul had been taken by agents of the Bolshevik Government and by Russian concession hunters. So I reluctantly abandoned the idea of visiting Afghanistan, at least for the time being. It is no longer a difficult country to enter, however, provided one obtains permission from Kabul in advance, for Afghan visas are now honored by the British military authorities on the frontier, and from the Khyber to Kabul is a matter of only two days by motor-car.

Patiala is the premier state of the Punjab. Though not a large state, being about the size of Connecticut and Rhode Island put together, geographically it is a jigsaw puzzle, for its territory is scattered and interspersed with petty states and even single villages under the rule of other princes, while certain British districts form enclaves in Patiala territory.

Its present ruler (take a long breath), Major-General His Highness Farzand-i-Khas Daulati-Inglishia Mansur-ul-Zaman Amir-ul-Umra Maharajah Dhiraj Rajeshwar Sri Maharaja-i-Rajgan Sir Bhupindra Singh Mohinder Bahadur, G.C.S.I., G.C.I.E., G.C.V.O., G.B.E., A.D.C., was born in 1891 and succeeded to the throne when only nine years old.

He is a stanch and valued friend of the British, as his numerous grand crosses indicate, he and his predecessors having rendered help to the raj on numerous critical occasions. Upon the outbreak of the World War the maharajah placed the entire resources of his state at the disposal of the king-emperor, the 28,000 troops which he furnished for the Indian army being employed in Egypt, Gallipoli, Mesopotamia and Palestine. He himself saw active service on the western front, contributed generously to the allied cause in money and materials, and was decorated by a number of European governments. A brilliant and forceful orator, he is chancellor of the Chamber of Princes and in 1925 represented the rulers of the Native states at the meeting of the League of Nations.

Patiala, the capital of the state, is a night's run by sleeping-car from Delhi. At the station, officials were waiting to welcome us in the name of our host and we motored through broad and shady avenues to the guest-house, a large and rambling structure, vaguely reminiscent of an English country house, standing amid park-like grounds. Indeed, the entire residential quarter is suggestive of a park, with its winding, beautifully kept drives, its stately trees and sweeping lawns, its flowering hedges and gorgeous gardens. Within a short radius of the guest-house is the Sports Club, with a golf-course, tennis courts, billiard tables and a bar;

the rectangle of emerald velvet which is the polo-field, the Patiala team being one of the best in India; a menagerie which contains, among numerous other animals, the only Indian lion I have ever seen; the Purdah Club, a new and pretentious building with a blind entrance, where the women of the court and the aristocracy may put aside their veils and lunch, swim, play bridge or tennis without fear of being seen by men; *and* a roller-skating rink. Not far away are the royal kennels, the largest in the East, containing two hundred and fifty dogs representing nearly every known breed of canine, including such characteristic Asiatic types as Chinese chows, long-haired Tibetans, Arabian greyhounds and Afghan deerhounds. We visited too the elephant stables, where a score or so of pachyderms, their massive heads elaborately frescoed in many colors, were paraded for our inspection; and the royal garage, which, as I have remarked elsewhere, contained upward of three hundred cars, including forty-two Rolls-Royces.

Our host, who was motoring up from Delhi, did not reach the capital until some hours after our arrival. We were out for a drive with a member of his staff when we heard in the distance the rising crescendo of a siren. "His Highness is coming!" exclaimed our companion, and ordered the chauffeur to pull over to the side of the road and stop. A moment later the largest touring car I have ever seen, its hood of burnished aluminum gleaming in the sunlight, hurtled past us in a cloud of yellow dust. At the wheel was a big, black-bearded man who waved a greeting to us—the Maharajah Dhiraj himself. He was traveling at such terrific speed that it needed two men to tell about it: one to say "Here he comes!" and the other "There he goes!"

The day after our arrival we were invited to lunch with the maharajah at the Motibagh Palace, *moti* meaning pearl and *bagh* garden. The palace is an enormous structure, containing hundreds of rooms, with a façade nearly a quarter of a mile long, built in the ornate but not unpleasing Indian style of carved pink sandstone. Running along its entire front is a balustraded terrace of tesselated marble which overlooks the gardens. These, with their broad expanses of velvety greensward, masses of flowers and shrubbery, marble kiosks and pavilions, numerous statues and fountains, water-channels lined with turquoise tiles, and lotus-covered lagoons, form an Indian fairyland. At the far end of the gardens, set on the shores of a picturesque lake, is a small but beautiful temple reserved for the use of the ruling family, for the maharajah is an orthodox Hindu.

We were received at the palace by his Highness' military secretary in an enormous reception room with a very lofty ceiling. Covering the floor were a dozen superb tiger-skins; on the tables were silver-framed photographs of European and Indian royalties; the walls were adorned with trophies of the chase. The adjoining room contained the maharajah's collection of medals, said to be one of the finest in existence, and the walls of the library, beyond, were lined from floor to ceiling with beautifully bound books.

I remarked on the number and beauty of the crystal chandeliers, of which there were an extraordinary number in the palace, whereupon the military secretary told us an amusing story. Some years ago the present maharajah's father, while staying in Calcutta, sauntered one morning into the show room of a great electrical fixtures house. He was quietly dressed and unattended and the clerks paid him scant attention. At length, unable to get any one to wait upon him, he accosted the manager of the establishment.

"How much," he inquired casually, "do you want for the contents of your shop?"

Then some one recognized him. There ensued apologies, explanations, a hasty consultation among the members of the firm.

"Nine lakh of rupees, your Highness," was the deferential answer. (About $300,000.)

"Very well. I will take the lot. Ship everything to me at Patiala."

They do things in the grand style, these Indian princes. There is nothing picayune about them.

We had waited but a brief five minutes when the Maharajah Dhiraj strode briskly into the room, profuse in his apologies for having kept us waiting. In another five we felt as much at home as though we had known him always, for, like most rulers, he has the knack of putting his guests quickly at their ease. He is a very Hercules of a man, close to six feet six, I should judge, in his stockings, and his turban makes him appear even taller. He has a chest like a barrel and the shoulders of a wrestler. His full black beard was braided and tied up under the chin, as is the fashion among the Sikhs, and he wore in his ears a pair of perfectly matched black pearls, as large as marbles, for which he had paid a quarter of a million dollars. Incidentally, his collection of jewels is among the finest in India, including, among other items, the famous diamond necklace, once belonging to the British crown jewels, which James II took the precaution of slipping into his pocket when he fled from England and which eventually passed into the possession of the Empress Eugénie of France.

His Highness is an excellent and amusing conversationalist and the talk at the luncheon table touched on many subjects—shooting, polo, horse-breeding, President Coolidge, Roosevelt, Mussolini, Henry Ford, irrigation, railways, the League of Nations and, of course, the American prohibition laws. The chief of staff, General Chanda Singh, a magnificent type of Sikh aristocrat and, despite his advanced age, a famous polo player, had been in the United States and played at Meadow Brook, and we found many mutual friends and many subjects of common interest.

Learning that we were fond of shooting, the maharajah gave orders that a hunt should be arranged for the following day, for roaming the plains in the vicinity of the capital are vast herds of nilghai, sambhur and black buck. I had expected that we would shoot from blinds, and that a vast number of beaters would be employed to round up the game, and I had hoped that we might even get a glimpse of a form of sport peculiar to India—hunting with trained cheetahs. I was mildly disappointed, therefore, when, early the following afternoon, there drew up before the guest-house a light American touring car, of a type noted for its speed, stripped of running-boards, top and wind-shield, with a pair of Mannlicher sporting rifles resting in the tonneau. At the wheel was the maharajah's principal A.D.C., a most companionable and amusing colonel of cavalry, who was also captain of the Patiala polo team.

"We always shoot from cars here in Patiala," he explained. "It's much more sporting than using beaters, because the game has a better chance, and, as I think you will agree with me after you have had a taste of it, it is much more exciting."

It certainly was. The only wonder was that we came back alive, for the colonel drove the car as recklessly as he rides his polo ponies.

The game herds, comprising thousands of animals, range over vast and comparatively level plains, which, however, are by no means as free from obstructions as the plains of the American Southwest. On the contrary, they are dotted with clumps of thorn-scrub and mimosa, broken at frequent intervals by stony watercourses, irrigation ditches, groves of trees, patches of dense jungle, and occasionally by the low mud walls surrounding the fields of peasant farmers.

We had driven scarcely half-a-dozen miles along the Simla highroad before we spied, some distance to the right, a large herd of black buck. There must have been several hundred in all. As long as we kept to the highway the beautiful animals, the color of dark Jersey cows with white markings, paid no attention to us, but the moment the colonel swung the car on to the open prairie they took alarm. Long ere we could get within range they were off in a mad stampede. I did not know that any animal could cover ground at such speed, could jump so high or far. They progressed, indeed, in a series of amazing bounds, some of the bucks seeming to go fully ten feet into the air. A beautiful and thrilling sight.

"Are your rifles loaded?" called the colonel. "All ready? Hang on, then. Here we go!"

He jammed his foot hard upon the accelerator and the speedy little car leaped forward, almost from under us, like a race-horse at the rise of the starting-gate. Straight across the plain we tore, our pilot shaping a course which would eventually converge with the line taken by the fleeing game. Our speed was increasing with every revolution of the wheels. I glanced at the speedometer needle. We were doing fifty-five miles an hour.

Suddenly a low wall of sun-dried bricks rose squarely athwart our course. "Look out!" I cried instinctively, my fingers dug deep into the leather cushion. But our pilot, forgetful of everything save the thrill of the chase, paid no heed to my warning. *Crash!* We went through the flimsy wall as though it were made of cardboard. We wallowed across a plowed field, the car rocking and rolling like a motor-boat in a heavy sea, threatening at every instant to go over. Then out upon the open plain again, with smoother going before us. Now we were abreast of the thundering herd, though the panic-stricken animals were still beyond the effective range of our rifles. The speedometer needle was hovering between sixty and sixty-five. And that's going some even on a paved highway, let me tell you.

We splashed through the shallow bed of a stream amid a smother of spray; took an irrigation ditch in our stride as a hunter takes a fence, all four wheels of the car leaving the ground; plunged into a patch of forest, our hubs missing the trees by fractions of inches; burst through a screen of thorn-bush, one of the spines laying open the back of my hand, though I failed to notice the wound in the excitement, and emerged into the open again to find ourselves racing parallel to the leader of the herd. The animal, a magnificent buck with a splendid pair of spiral horns, was perhaps a hundred yards distant.

"Now's your chance!" the colonel shouted over his shoulder.

"Go ahead! Shoot!" I urged my cousin.

"Shoot yourself," he shouted. "Don't waste time being polite."

The terrain was for the moment comparatively smooth and the car was traveling at the pace of the Twentieth Century Limited when it is making up time. The buck, which the colonel had skilfully cut out from the herd as a cow-puncher cuts out a steer, was covering the ground in thirty-foot leaps, bounding across my field of vision like an animal target in a shooting-gallery.

I braced myself as well as I could in the swaying tonneau, brought the Mannlicher to my shoulder, caught a glimpse between the sights of a slender pair of horns, a straining neck, a sleek black shoulder . . . and pressed the trigger. *Whang!* With the crash of the rifle the buck gave a convulsive bound and crumpled in its tracks with my bullet through its heart. It was a magnificent head—even the old shikari who shared the front seat with the colonel admitted that—and one of these days, I hope, it will fill the space over my great fireplace at Journey's End.

A little later my cousin brought down another fine buck and our hunt in Patiala was over, for I have no patience with those game-hogs who turn shooting parties into massacres. When we drew up before the guest-house, our trophies lashed to the fenders, I stepped in front of the little car and gravely raised my topée.

"What are you doing?" my cousin asked curiously.

"I'm lifting my hat to the car," I answered. "I'm proud of its being an American."

Nothing would have pleased me better than to have stayed on in Patiala indefinitely, for I liked our courteous and hospitable host, his people and his country. But we were expected at Gwalior, and later at Bhopal, and we had booked our passages on the next steamer sailing from Bombay for the Persian Gulf and Basra. And, as Mr. Kipling has remarked, "the steamer won't wait for the train."

Gwalior, which is in Central India, its borders reaching northward almost to Agra, is the principal fragment of the great empire of the Marathas. In area it is nearly twice the size of Switzerland, with only a slightly smaller population. The founder of the dynasty was one Ravoji Scindia, who at the beginning of the eighteenth century was slipper-bearer to the Maratha emperor, the Balaji Peshwa, who granted him the territory which has been ruled by princes of the Scindia family ever since. During the French wars Gwalior played an important part in shaping the destinies of India, and in 1782 was recognized by the British as an independent state.

Sir Madho Rao Scindia succeeded to the throne in 1886. An able and enlightened ruler, an honorary lieutenant-general in the British army, holding the honorary degrees of LL.D. from Cambridge and D.C.L. from Oxford, his just and beneficent reign lasted for nearly forty years. Upon his death in 1925 he was succeeded by his son, George Jivaji Rao Scindia, then a lad of nine. The administration of the state is carried on by a council of regency under the presidency of the senior maharanee until her son attains his majority.

We were met upon our arrival at Lashkar, the capital of Gwalior, by a member of the youthful maharajah's civil cabinet, a Mr. Felose, whose family has served the state for many generations.

"I know about you, or, rather, about your family, if I am not mistaken," I remarked when he introduced himself. "Are you not a descendant of that Neapolitan soldier of fortune, General Felose, who, late in the eighteenth century, purchased from the American, General John Parker Boyd, the army of mercenaries which the latter had raised and which under his leadership played such a brilliant part in the wars in Hindustan?"

"I am," he exclaimed in astonishment. "The General Felose to whom you refer was my great-grandfather. But how does it happen, pray, that you, an American, should be so familiar with the history of our family?"

"It's really quite simple," I replied. "I once wrote a book,[2] or, rather, I devoted a chapter in a book to the exploits of General Boyd—I called the chapter, if I remember rightly, 'For Rent: An Army on Elephants'—and in the course of my researches I became acquainted with the remarkable career of your distinguished ancestor."

At the other Indian courts at which we had visited we

[2] See Colonel Powell's "Gentlemen Rovers."

had been met by motor-cars, which, despite their speed and luxury, were incongruous and spoiled for me the picture. But at Lashkar station there was awaiting us a great landau, reminiscent of the old-time "open-faced hack," ornate in red and gold, drawn by a beautiful pair of white horses, with two servants in orange and turquoise-blue liveries clinging to the rumble behind. As we drove in this magnificent equipage through the streets of the city, with a couple of turbaned lancers clattering in the rear, I felt as though I were a king on the way to my coronation. Or did until I glanced at my cousin. He, with his helmet drawn low over his sun-burned face and a pipe clenched between his teeth, certainly bore no resemblance to a queen.

The royal guest-house of Gwalior is one of the most beautiful residences I have ever seen. Though not connected with the palace, it is separated from that immense white building only by a broad walled garden, dotted with fountains and abloom with flowers. It is built of white marble, dazzling in the brilliant sunlight, and the broad gallery on which the bedrooms open is shielded by a series of the most beautiful marble screens, their carving as delicate as the finest lace, no two alike in design. Everywhere, alert to obey our slightest wish, were chuprassis in liveries so colorful and picturesque that I could not wholly rid myself of the feeling that we had gotten into a theater by mistake and that a comic opera was going on.

Each evening, before retiring, a servant handed us cards, which, beneath the emblazoned arms of the house of Scindia, bore a legend which ran something like this: "It is requested that the guests of his Highness the Maharajah have the kindness to indicate on the form below what mode of transportation they desire for to-morrow, and the hour at which they wish it." Then followed a list which included motor-cars, carriages, saddle horses and elephants. You can guess which one we chose. And, sure enough, when we emerged on to the terrace at the hour we had indicated, there, kneeling at the foot of the steps, was a bepainted elephant, gorgeous in trappings of green and crimson velvet, with a mahout astride its neck and an attendant holding the ladder by means of which we ascended to the howdah. What a pity, as I have remarked elsewhere, that all this splendor should be wasted on those to whom it was a commonplace!

Lashkar, or "the Camp," is the modern capital of the state, and merges imperceptibly into the old city of Gwalior, which is built around a massive octagonal tower dating from the Middle Ages. In a little plaza at the foot of the tower is an ancient cannon—I think it is a relic of Portuguese rule in India—with a sculptured barrel nearly forty feet in length. Hard by is the huge Durbar Hall, not unpleasing without but rather garish within. Enormous crystal chandeliers depend from its lofty ceiling; lining its walls are life-size portraits of the various rulers of the Scindia line—dark-skinned, black-bearded, arrogant-looking men for the most part, with diamond aigrets in their turbans, jeweled simitars at their waists, strings of pearls festooned about their necks, the breasts of their brocaded coats ablaze with orders.

The capital is well laid out, scrupulously clean—at least as cleanliness is interpreted in India—and architecturally is extremely interesting, for the houses of the wealthy are built of the lovely pale sandstone peculiar to the country, in color a creamy white, their façades from ground to eaves covered with the beautiful and delicate carving for which the craftsmen of Gwalior are famous. The bazaars resemble those of other Indian towns, though I saw few objects of much artistic value. The principal square of the city was alive with small boys running up and down in pairs holding between them lengths of brilliantly dyed muslins—turquoise, emerald, cerise, saffron, pale rose, heliotrope, magenta—while other lengths fluttered from every balcony and window. I assumed that some sort of a festival was in progress, but Felose explained that Gwalior is celebrated for the beautiful colors of its muslins, and that the pieces displayed in such profusion had been freshly dyed and were being dried in the sun.

Standing in a vast park is the palace of the maharajah, an enormous structure of white stone embowered in crimson bougainvillea. To me it appeared amply large enough for the purposes of any ruler, let alone a twelve-year-old one, but hundreds of workmen were engaged in the construction of an immense wing. Within it is a palace of glass—glass chandeliers and candelabra, glass banisters, glass fountains, even glass furniture, with mirrors set in the walls and ceilings. One room was filled with the mechanical contrivances for which the late maharajah had a passion. Among the innumerable toys and novelties was a miniature train for use at state dinners. It was composed of an engine and seven cars, all made of silver and perfect to the minutest detail, and ran around the table on a little track. Its freight consisted of cigars, cigarettes and various liqueurs and it was operated electrically, the maharajah stopping it before each of his guests and starting it again by means of a botton.

A short distance from the palace, overlooking a little stream, is the Chhatri, a small pavilion of white marble, exquisite in design and execution, which was erected by the late ruler in memory of his mother. It is in reality a cenotaph. A devout Hindu, the body of the maharanee was cremated on the banks of the Ganges and the ashes cast into the sacred river, but she still lives within these snowy walls in the form of a life-size statue, said by those who knew her Highness to be a speaking likeness. The marble maharanee has a retinue of women to wait upon her, just as she had in life, and the statue is daily bathed, dressed and adorned with jewels. Meals are set before it, there is an electric fan to keep the image cool, and a couch for it to rest upon. To Western ears this doubtless sounds bathetic and ridiculous, but in reality it is pathetic and beautiful, as is always a son's devotion to his mother.

Two or three miles from Lashkar the rock-fortress of Gwalior rises abruptly from the plain. The citadel is built on the level summit of an isolated table-land, nearly two miles in length, its immensely steep sides rising to a height of a thousand feet above the level of the surrounding country. The face of the rock is perpendicular and where it is naturally less precipitous it has been scarped. Long a stronghold of the Marathas, the fort was taken by the British during the Mutiny and held by them until 1885, when it was restored to Gwalior, though in the interim its ancient monuments had been seriously mutilated by the military. Bordering the edge of the precipice are massive ramparts of rose-red sandstone, broken at regular intervals by beautifully sculptured turrets and bastions, from which may be obtained an entrancing view of the city below and the far-flung plain.

The area within the ramparts is crowded with very impressive and interesting Jain and Hindu temples and monuments, and here also is the great fifteenth-century palace of Rajah Man-Singh, which is unequaled for picturesqueness and interest by anything of its sort in Central India. The wilderness of courts and chambers, the beauty of the lustrous tiles with which they are adorned, the window-screens of fretted marble, the magnificently carved ceilings, all remind one of the Alcazar and the Alhambra, all speak of the splendor amid which these Eastern potentates lived when

America was still unknown. The outer face of the palace, three hundred feet long and eighty high, is a continuation of the sheer cliff, so that, were a man to be hurled from its roof, as doubtless happened more than once in the bad old days, his body would hurtle through nearly a quarter of a mile of emptiness before it struck the ground. Beneath the palace may still be seen the dungeons and torture chambers, cut so deep into the solid rock that the screams and groans of the unhappy inmates could not disturb the ruler's peace of mind. In them happened dark and evil things.

In ancient times the summit of the rock was a famous seat of Jain worship. Two of the Jain temples in particular, long unoccupied and now in a sad state of disrepair, are tremendously imposing, the blocks of sandstone used in their construction being of such enormous size that one wonders how they were brought to this inaccessible spot without the aid of modern machinery.

The Jain sect, which was founded by the Prophet Malhavira in the sixth century before the Christian era, has its roots in Hinduism, though the Hindus regard the Jains as atheists, in spite of the fact that they worship many of the Hindu gods. There are only about a million Jains in India, localized mainly in Rajputana, but they control a large part of India's wealth and trade. The primary principle of Jainism is the doctrine of *ahimsa,* the sparing of every form of life in however early a stage of evolution. A Jain, for example, would never dream of killing a mosquito or harming a fly, while birth control is about as common among them as ice in Hades.

There are two ways of gaining access to the citadel of Gwalior. A road which can be toilsomely ascended by carriages or motor-cars climbs to the summit of the plateau by devious twists and turns through the gloomy, rock-walled gorge known as Happy Valley. Happy, in this case, has a purely spiritual significance, for the road leads through a sort of pantheon, colossal figures of Jain deities and pontiffs, one of them fifty-seven feet in height, having been hewn in long-past days from the perpendicular face of the rock. When Baber invaded and conquered India, he, being a devout Mohammedan, ordered these idolatrous images to be destroyed, but they escaped with minor mutilations, perhaps because of their enormous size.

The only other entrance to the fort is through the Hathi Paur, or Elephant Gate, a portal of great beauty and impressiveness. The road which leads to it is so steep, however, that it can be ascended only afoot or on the back of an elephant. Provided elephants are available, I should advise visitors to use them, for they can go where wheeled vehicles cannot, as we discovered in Nepál, and they fit into the Indian picture.

An acute politico-domestic crisis had arisen in the royal family of Gwalior a few days before our arrival, it having been precipitated by the arbitrary action of the British resident. Concerned for the physical and moral well-being of the young maharajah, then twelve years old, the representative of the raj had given orders that the boy, accompanied only by his mother, the senior maharanee, and a small suite, should be removed from the palace in Lashkar to the citadel and there remain under the supervision of European and Indian tutors until he was old enough to enter one of the colleges which have been established by the Indian Government for the education of princes. This drastic step had been made imperative, I was informed, by the intolerable conditions prevailing in the palace, where the youthful ruler was surrounded by hundreds of women-folk and servants. One always hears various versions of such affairs, but, from all I could gather, a palace clique, headed by the younger of the two widows left by the late maharajah, bitterly jealous of the influence exerted by the senior maharanee, had deliberately set out to debauch the boy-ruler.

Save in very rare cases, as I have explained in an earlier chapter, the British residents at the native courts scrupulously refrain from interfering in the domestic affairs of the rulers, but here was a case where prompt and energetic intervention was amply justified, for the health and morals, perhaps the life, of a small boy who is destined to rule over three millions of people, were at stake. Those who are intrusted with the upbringing of the princes have to be constantly on the alert, for India in many respects still lives in the atmosphere of the Middle Ages, and dark and sinister things still happen behind the jealously guarded walls of her palaces.

Our arrival in Bhopal was like a home-coming, for Colonel Amir Ahmed and the other members of the nawab's staff, whom we had come to know and like, were waiting to greet us. One and all were as cordial, as eager to hear of our experiences, as though they had been old friends. And the guest-house, Lall Kothi, though not as large as the one at Patiala, or as impressive as the one at Gwalior, was far more cozy and comfortable than either, like a country house at home. The building was a long, low bungalow—it might have been in California instead of Central India—with deep verandas, and broad terraces covered with hundreds and hundreds of flowering plants in pots. Within there was a billiard-room, a library lined with books (did it ever occur to you that books make the finest tapestry in the world?), a dining-room in English mahogany, with some fine old silver on the sideboard, and bedrooms gay with hangings of flowered chintz.

I was glad to reach Bhopal and be among friends, for, just before leaving Gwalior, I had come down with the "flu," complicated with an attack of sinusitis, and felt about as miserable as one well can and still be able to take nourishment. Some one must have telephoned the nawab that I was ill, for within half an hour after our arrival his private physician, Dr. Rahman, a most entertaining fellow, with a delightful bedside manner, came tearing over from the palace in his car, ordered me to bed, and sent a chuprassi to the hospital for medicines. I might mention that the Prince of Wales Hospital in Bhopal, built and maintained by members of the reigning family, is one of the finest institutions of its kind in India, as up-to-date in its methods and equipment as any in the United States. I know, because I went there daily for treatment.

Bhopal, though no larger than a Texan county, is one of the most progressive and best governed states in India. It occupies the great Malwa Plateau, a region of rugged hills and fertile valleys, of forest, jungle and plain, with delightfully mild winters and summers, which, though hot, are not insufferably so. It is bisected by the Great Indian Peninsula Railway; has excellent roads; possesses an admirable educational system; and financially is in a flourishing condition.

The capital, Bhopal City, with fifty thousand inhabitants, stands on the northern bank of an extensive lake, a lovely, irregular shaped sheet of water, blue as the skies which are mirrored in it and dotted with the sails of pleasure craft. There is a suggestion of Italy in the white bridge which spans an arm of the lake and in the white walls, covered with flowering vines, which border it at one end. The houses, all of unpretentious design, are white, pink and pale blue, very charming amid the verdure, and there are purple hills beyond.

The city itself contains nothing of outstanding interest, whether from an architectural or historical point of view.

There are several rather imposing old brick gateways, dating back to Mogul days, though the wall which once connected them has long since disappeared. Fronting on a spacious square is a group of palaces which look as though they had been made by a confectioner from icing, so sugar-white are they and so elaborate their decorations. The town palace is no longer used as a place of royal residence, however, the nawab as well as his mother, the begum, occupying an extremely modest establishment, scarcely more than a group of bungalows, set on a lofty ridge a mile or so beyond the city. The residence of the nawab—one can scarcely dignify it by the name of palace—is indicative of its owner's simple tastes, having nothing in common with the huge, ornate, magnificently appointed establishments maintained by his fellow-princes.

A member of the staff took us one morning to visit the penitentiary, a short distance from the town. Were I a criminal I should be tempted to conduct my nefarious enterprises in Bhopal, for penal life there is delightful compared with other prisons I have seen. The convicts live in small bungalows, very neat and clean, and do their work—rug-weaving appeared to be the principal prison industry—in the open, under the shade of banyans and palms. The atmosphere is far from being grim or depressing, for the whole place is gay with flowers, the walls are hidden by vines, and there is sunlight everywhere.

An equerry brought us word one morning that we would be received in audience at the palace that afternoon by her Highness the begum, whom we had already met in New Delhi. I rose from a sick bed to keep the appointment, for the invitations of royalty are commands.

The Queen Mother of Bhopal, now well past the four-score mark, is one of the most fascinating women I have ever met, and this in spite of the fact that I have never seen her face. I have mentioned elsewhere that in 1926, after a reign of many years—the only woman ruler in India—she abdicated in favor of her youngest and only surviving son, the present nawab. Notwithstanding the limitations imposed by the *purdah,* she has led a life of extraordinary energy and usefulness. She took an active part, and still takes an active interest, in every phase of the state's administration; she has built hospitals and orphanages; has rendered immense services to the causes of child welfare, education, public health and the amelioration of social conditions. She has paid several visits to England; has even made the pilgrimage to Mecca, the wish nearest to the hearts of all devout Mohammedans; and has found time to write a number of books. A woman of wide sympathies and vision, she has consistently stood for progress in everything save the emancipation of women. The suggestion that the veil be abolished in India, as it has been in Turkey, is to her anathema.

The *purdah* system, which prevails throughout the greater part of India, at least among women of rank, is, of course, of Islamic origin. In the old days, before the Moslems came, the Hindu ladies went about unveiled and enjoyed an honored position. The adoption of the veil was due in part to a desire to copy the fashion set by the Mogul conquerors, who were Mohammedans, and in part to dictates of safety, the Hindus deeming it prudent to hide the faces of their women-folk from the eyes of the invaders. The custom is general, as might be expected, in the Mohammedan states of Hyderabad and Bhopal; it is common in those parts of India which came under Mohammedan influence during the ascendancy of the Moguls; but it is weaker in the south, while in Bombay, owing to the influence of the Parsees, it is hardly apparent at all. Emancipation from the tyranny of the veil must come eventually, however, for education is spreading rapidly among Indian women of the upper classes and is bringing with it a demand for greater freedom.

The begum received us in a small reception room, its furnishings simple to the point of bareness. It was in striking contrast to the barbaric magnificence surrounding the other veiled woman ruler whom I have met, the Empress Zauditu of Abyssinia. The Queen Mother is a woman of slight stature, and, I should guess, of slender figure, though of this it was difficult to judge because she was completely enveloped in a voluminous garment, a sort of Mother Hubbard, of gray-green gabardine. As is the custom of all Mohammedan women in the presence of men who are not members of their immediate families, she wore the *burkha* —a muslin covering, something like a bridal veil, which is gathered round the head into a close-fitting cap and has a narrow, lace-covered slit before the eyes. Surmounting the *burkha* was a little turban of white crêpe, somewhat resembling the bonnet worn by Queen Victoria.

Her voice is low and pleasing and her command of English is astonishing, particularly in view of the fact that she is self-taught. It was a remarkable experience to chat with this extraordinary old lady, whose mannerisms constantly reminded me of my own grandmother, and hear her speak quite casually of "my government," "my ministers," "my people," "my army." She is extremely well informed in regard to American conditions, particularly those relating to public health and education, for she is an assiduous reader of American women's and educational magazines. She is, indeed, so impressed with our educational methods that she is desirous of engaging an American governess for her grandchildren.

"I admire and like the English," she remarked, "but you Americans are more energetic, more progressive, you have a broader vision. That is why I should like to have my granddaughters brought up by an American, if I can find the right one."

I thought of half-a-dozen young women of my acquaintance who would jump at such an opportunity, but when her Highness enumerated her requirements for a royal governess I began to wonder whether I knew any one who could fill them all. The successful candidate for the post must, of course, be highly educated—a college woman; she must have a fluent command of at least three European languages; she must ride, shoot, play tennis, and do all three superlatively well; and, above all else, she must possess tact, poise and social experience to an extraordinary degree. And—I almost forgot this—she must be an accomplished dancer and musician. Should you know of any young woman who can meet these specifications, I have no doubt that the Queen Mother would like to hear about her. It would be an interesting job, governess at the court of Bhopal.

When I went to meet the begum I was feeling as thoroughly miserable as only one suffering from an acute attack of influenza can; my head throbbed and fire coursed through my veins. Her Highness did not fail to notice my condition, and after half an hour's conversation she leaned over and tapped me on the knee.

"You are too sick, my boy," she said, "to sit here gossiping with an old lady. You ought to be at home and in bed. Go straight back to the house and lie down and I will send my physician to see you."

As we were making our adieus she excused herself for a moment, returning shortly with two sets of books, beautifully bound, which she had written herself. Inscribing her name on the fly-leaves in a firm, delicate hand, she presented a set to each of us. We bent low over her outstretched hand.

Then she turned and disappeared like a white wraith behind the draperies.

The night before our departure from Bhopal the nawab gave a farewell dinner for us at the palace. All the members of his cabinet were present, the hard-riding English colonel who is his chief of staff and the latter's pretty wife, and, of course, Colonel and Madame Amir Ahmed. It was a warm and fragrant night, the sky streaked with star-dust, and the table, set with great rose-filled bowls of silver, was laid upon the terrace. In the purple distance the lights of Bhopal City gleamed like diamonds. Behind the chair of every guest stood a servant resplendent in the nawab's blue-and-silver livery, and from a balcony came the strains of hautboy, zither and flute. It was a fitting finale to a delightful visit and I shall carry the memory of it with me always.

Our departure from Bhopal was a distinct anticlimax, supremely ridiculous in retrospect, though it did not strike me as being laughable at the time. Through an oversight on the part of some subordinate, no reservations had been made for us on the Bombay Mail, and when the train pulled into the station we found to our dismay that every compartment was taken. Not even an upper berth was to be had.

"You must come back to the guest-house," Colonel Amir Ahmed insisted, "and wait over until to-morrow. We will wire to Delhi for reservations on to-morrow's train."

"It's out of the question," I told him. "Our boat sails day after to-morrow for Basra, and if we were to wait until to-morrow we would miss it. We must take this train even if we have to stand up all the way to Bombay."

Meanwhile my cousin and Julius, followed by a dozen servants laden with our luggage, had been running up and down the train in quest of accommodation.

"Come on!" my cousin shouted. "I've found a place for us."

The place he had found was the compartment at the end of the goods van (which corresponds to an American baggage-car) used for the storage of ginger ale and mineral waters, of which enormous quantities are consumed by travelers in India. Fully half of the compartment, which was no larger than the drawing-room of an American Pullman, was filled with cases of bottled water; in the corner was a rude sink for washing glasses; and along one side was the attendant's seat, an uncushioned plank barely eighteen inches wide. Despite the protests of Colonel Amir Ahmed, to the astonishment of the palace servants and the utter scandalization of Julius, we jammed ourselves and our luggage into the narrow space that was left. For a monetary consideration the attendant betook himself elsewhere. The guard slammed the door, the whistle shrieked impatiently, and as the train pulled out we leaned from the windows to wave Bhopal farewell.

The twenty-hour journey to Bombay was a nightmare. Not even when I crossed Arabia by caravan—nineteen days on a camel—have I been more thoroughly uncomfortable. Our quarters were directly over the truck, and it seemed as though the vibration must eventually shake loose our teeth. Through the unscreened windows the dust swirled in suffocating clouds and brought on violent paroxysm of coughing. The bottles made such a racket that we could converse only by shouting. I ached in every bone and muscle, for the "flu" had not entirely disappeared, and I think I had a touch of fever. It was impossible for both of us to lie down on the single narrow plank at the same time, so we took turns. My cousin, however, can sleep anywhere, any time, and the clatter of the bottles was drowned by his snoring. At length, sitting upright in my corner, I too fell asleep from sheer exhaustion. And I dreamed . . . of the soft beds in the marble guest-house at Gwalior . . . of elephants caparisoned in gold and crimson . . . of state carriages with resplendent servants . . . of our luxurious tent life in New Delhi, with Babcock serving the cocktails . . . of the viceroy's garden party . . . of dinners on moon-drenched terraces. . . .

I was brought slowly back to consciousness by some one plucking at my sleeve. I drowsily opened my eyes. It was broad daylight. The train had come to a stop beneath the glass roof of a great, reverberating station. Julius, immaculate as usual, was standing by the open door.

"Come, marster," he said. "Time to get up. We have arrive in Bombay."

CHAPTER XIII

ARABIAN NIGHTS AND MAGIC CARPETS

FOR those who come out from Europe in the traditional way, by P. & O., Bombay is the gateway to India, the vestibule of the East. It has a population of not far from a million and a quarter, some extremely broad streets and numerous spacious squares, a splendid harbor which is really a great arm of the sea, a number of beautiful gardens, and an insufferably hot and humid climate. It is the sort of a place where a person should carry two handkerchiefs—one for the nose, the other to wipe away the perspiration.

Its architecture is for the most part atrocious, in the very worst style of the Victorian era, meretricious in design and wholly unworthy of the third largest city in the British Empire. Facing the bay is a row of public buildings, imposing enough as a whole, but too suggestive of nineteenth century mediocrity and conventionalism. The main features of the Secretariat, a massive pile in which the government offices are housed, were borrowed from Venice, but all that makes Venetian architecture beautiful was lost on the way. The High Court is of Gothic construction, huge, ugly, and totally unsuited to tropical conditions. The towering campanile of the university evidently had its inspiration in Giotto's Tower in Florence, but it is incongruous in an Indian setting. The library of the university might be a town hall in England. Indeed, the architecture of the whole city displays a deplorable lack of taste, sentiment and imagination. Nowhere have the architects made any serious attempt to suggest that this is the threshold of the glittering East, the home of romance and splendor. Their chief aim, instead, seems to have been to transplant as much as possible of Europe to the Orient.

The city has one fairly good hotel, the Taj Mahal, whose architecture has the merit of being at least a hybrid sort of Indian; two which are not so good, and several which are not good at all. They are nearly always crowded, however, and those desiring rooms at the beginning or end of the cold weather, when great numbers of tourists and officials are arriving or departing, should make their reservations weeks in advance. The Taj Mahal has a blue-and-silver grill-room which overlooks the bay and has numerous electric fans, so that even in the hottest weather it is a pleasant place to dine, but the best food in the city is to be had at the Royal Bombay Yacht Club—that is, if you are partial to mutton chops, underdone roast beef and highly seasoned curries.

Bombay is the stronghold of the Parsees, descendants of the ancient Zoroastrian fire-worshipers, who emigrated from Persia to India upon the conquest of their country by the Arabs in the eighth century. Adherents of the faith known to antiquity as the religion of the Magi, they brought the curious rites of their cult with them, still keeping up the sacred household fire, still building their grim Towers of Silence, where the corpses of the dead, which may not pollute the earth, contaminate the sea or be consumed by fire, are exposed to the voracity of the birds of the air.

With his portly form, singular headgear and suave, ingratiating manners, the Parsee is a familiar figure east of Suez. He is essentially a trader, rivaling the Jew in his flair for making and keeping money, but he is nearly always generous and open-hearted, freely affording assistance to the poorer brethren of his faith and contributing munificently to philanthropic causes. His prosperity is dependent on the stability of British rule in India, and hence the Parsee community forms the most loyal element of the native population, for under its protection he can traffic and flourish. Were the British to go, however, his lot would be as hard as was that of the Jews in Palestine under Moslem rule. Many of the Parsees are bankers, and—at usurious rates of interest—finance impecunious Eastern rulers; a number of them have been knighted for their philanthropies or for their services to the British Crown. In Bombay the Parsees control the banking business, they own the best residential properties and many of the larger office buildings, in fact, have a finger in nearly every form of lucrative enterprise. Their shrewdness and acquisitiveness have given them a prominence in the financial and industrial life of India wholly out of proportion to their numbers, for there is only one Parsee to every three thousand Indians.

Set on the summit of the lofty and beautifully landscaped ridge known as Malabar Hill, commanding an entrancing view of the city, the bay and the volcanic peaks of Mahratta land, is a group of squat, circular, windowless structures, hundreds of vultures perched upon their lofty walls. These are the Towers of Silence, where the Parsees dispose of their dead according to the curious method which they have practised from time beyond reckoning. Inside each roofless, whitewashed tower, which in shape and size resembles a gas-house or an oil-tank, are three circular stone shelves or platforms. These slope from the sides to the center, where there is a well covered with an iron grating. The bodies of the dead, stark naked, are laid on these shelves—men on the upper tier, women on the middle one, children on the lower. No sooner have the priests and attendants deposited a body and turned their backs, than

THE GARDEN OF EDEN

If, as tradition asserts, this canal-pierced paradise of palms near Basra was the home of Adam and Eve, then the forbidden fruit which caused the fall was in all likelihood a large and luscious date instead of an apple

WAITING FOR THE NEXT ONE TO DIE

Buzzards on the wall of one of the Towers of Silence, where the Parsees of Bombay leave their dead to be devoured by birds

the waiting vultures—huge birds with a five-foot spread of wing—swoop down and strip it to the bones, commonly beginning with the eyes, which they pluck out with their long, sharp beaks. It is said that a man is kept on duty for the express purpose of noting which eye of a corpse is plucked out first, this betokening the spiritual state of the deceased. If the right eye is the first to go the relatives take it as a sign that the dear departed is happy in the Parsee paradise.

The skeleton is left for a few days to bleach in the sun and wind. Then the carriers of the dead, who are of a separate class and may not have any intercourse with other Parsees, come gloved and armed with rakes and tongs—a dead body being regarded as an unclean thing—to break up the skeleton and cast the bones into the central well, where they are decomposed by lime and running water.

The Towers of Silence, surrounded by beautifully kept gardens of their own, stand in the heart of the most fashionable residential section of Bombay. On one occasion, a good many years ago, I was having tea in a friend's garden on Malabar Hill when a vulture, flapping overhead, dropped something upon the lawn. My host's fox terrier retrieved the object and deposited it beside the tea table. It was a baby's hand.

Because the Red Sea attains the temperature of a baking-oven by the end of March, and because I have traversed that historic body of water so many times that I know by heart every port, island and promontory between Suez and Aden, I had determined to return from India to Europe by the overland route, or rather, by a portion of the overland route. This meant by sea from Bombay up the Persian Gulf to Basra, by rail or river to Baghdad, by the motor-cars of the Overland Desert Mail to Damascus, by a narrow-gage mountain line over the Anti-Lebanon range to Rayak, by the Baghdad Railway through the Cilician Gates to Konia and by the Anatolian Railway across the steppes of Asia Minor to the Bosporus and Constantinople. My cousin, who by this time was fed up with the smells and discomforts of the East and was anxious to get back to his window in the Union League Club, was all for taking the Red Sea route and the luxurious steamers of the P. & O., but I finally succeeded in persuading him to accompany me. He was not enthusiastic, however.

The time had now come to part from Julius, for he spoke no Arabic and would have been of little use to us in the Arab lands. So we presented him with our tropical clothing, our bedding-rolls, and a case of tinned goods which we had left over, together with a hundred rupees apiece by way of backsheesh, and bought him a third-class ticket to Colombo, where, I have no doubt, he is now a figure of considerable importance in the Buddhist community by virtue of his pilgrimage to the shrines in Nepál. He was a good bearer, as bearers go, but I was not wholly sorry to be rid of him. To tourists who wish to follow the traveled routes I can highly recommend him, but for trekking across wild and little known lands he was not an unqualified success. Shortly after my return to Europe I had a letter from him. In it he mentioned that the cost of living in Ceylon had gone up during his absence, and that, if his late marsters could spare another hundred rupees or so, he could find use for them.

On a glorious golden morning toward the end of March we sailed out of Bombay harbor aboard the *Vasna,* a four-thousand-ton British India oil-burner, immaculate as a yacht, bound for Karachi and the Persian Gulf ports. From the taffrail we watched the spires and towers of the great city, the wooded slopes of Malabar Hill, the purple peaks of Mahratta land, drop behind the horizon's rim. For my cousin it was, I think, a last farewell, but for me it was only *au revoir*. One of these days I shall go back to India again.

There were only about a dozen first-cabin passengers aboard the *Vasna,* but all had traveled far and hence were, in their respective ways, interesting. There was a titled Englishman, accompanied by his aristocratic-looking wife, who was bound for the oil-fields of Abadan on a tour of inspection. An enormously stout and very jolly American woman who, after many years spent in the interior of Asia Minor, was on her way to Persia to write a book on some subject which I have forgotten. A youthful and enthusiastic American, Becker by name, sent out by a great New York dry-goods house to purchase rugs in Shiraz and Ispahan. A Dutch merchant who, after a lifetime spent in the Indies, where he had made his pile, was returning to Europe with the intention of dividing his remaining days between Paris and Monte Carlo. An itinerant American evangelist and mission worker, Dr. Jones, author of "The Christ of the Indian Road," who enthralled us with tales of his experiences along Indian byways. And, finally, the two attractive American girls whom we had met in Madura months before and whom we had not expected to see again. All in all it was a very congenial little party, and the days which we had feared would be monotonous slipped by almost before we realized they had begun. In the mornings we played deck tennis violently in order to get into a perspiration; then a cold shower and tiffin. Reading, talking and naps in the long cane chairs served to pass the time until the cocktail hour came round. In the evenings we played bridge at a rupee a hundred or formed a little circle on the deck and swapped stories of adventures in many lands. For between us we had seen the earth and all that is thereon.

Our first port of call was Karachi, the entrepot of Sind, the gateway to Beluchistan and the northwest frontier country, and the third city of India in commercial importance. In the waters near Karachi are found extensive beds of window-pane oysters, the pearls which they produce being largely exported to China for medicinal purposes. In these waters the true pearl oyster is also found, the two principal fisheries being carried on by the Maharajah of Jannagar and the Gaekwar of Baroda, which doubtless accounts for the magnificent strings of pearls with which those princes bedeck themselves on occasions of ceremony.

We remained at Karachi only for part of an afternoon and an evening, but judging from what I could see of the city from a motor-car I should say that the best thing about it is the weekly steamer for Bombay. A few miles behind the city begins the Thar, or Indian Desert, and in the dry season, when the wind is from the east, Karachi is almost buried in sand. Karachi has gained considerable prominence in the newspaper date-lines of late as the place of voluntary exile chosen by Colonel Lawrence of "Revolt in the Desert" fame. After an amazing career as a leader of Arab armies during the World War, that strange and erratic young genius, tiring of the monotony of a world at peace and eager to escape from the spot-light of public attention, enlisted as a mechanic in the Royal Air Force, under the name of Shaw, and is stationed at Karachi, or was, the last I heard of him.

After another two days of steaming across a mirror-like sea we passed through the Straits of Ormuz and entered the Persian Gulf. Now we were in waters of mystery and romance, rich in history and tradition, dotted with dirty British oil-tankers, graceful Persian feluccas, lumbering Arab dhows. Twice or thrice we caught sight of a lean, swift craft, scudding across the gulf under full steam or canvas, bound on some errand which would not bear too close investigation, for in these waters slave- and gun-running persist in spite of the vigilance of the British patrol.

Ah, those never-to-be-forgotten nights on the gulf, when the *Vasna* plowed her way through a sea as smooth and dark as melted amethyst, with phosphorescent ostrich-feathers curling from her bows and her foretruck grazing the stars. To starboard, though there was only an occasional light to betray its presence, stretched the low Persian shore-line; somewhere off our port quarter was the pirate coast of Oman; dead ahead lay the pearl islands of Bahrein. At night, when the passengers had turned in and the ship was silent save for the steady throbbing of the engines, we would perch ourselves in the bows, with scores of blanket-shrouded natives sleeping on the planks at our feet, and listen expectantly for the sound of the lookout in the crow's-nest hailing the quarterdeck. From the bridge would come at last the muffled notes of the ship's bell—one . . . two . . . three . . . four . . . five . . . six . . . seven . . . eight . . . Then, a moment later, a long-drawn musical wail from the sailor at the foretopmast-head—"Eight bells . . . starboard an' port lights shining bright an' all's well-l-l-l-l. . . ."

At daybreak one morning we dropped anchor four miles off Bushire. With my glasses I could make out a line of low white houses, a fringe of palm-trees, a stretch of white-hot sand. Here Becker, the young American rug-buyer, disembarked to make his way by such conveyances as he could obtain—horse, carriage or car—across the wild, sparsely inhabited regions of the Bakhtiari country to the marts of Shiraz and Ispahan. He left us in a dhow with a kicker at the stern, loaded to the guards with fur-capped Persians, turbaned Arabs, frightened Hindu immigrants, and slovenly customs officials in conductors' caps and light-blue uniforms. It was a motley, noisy crew. I slipped into my dressing-gown and went out to the rail to bid him farewell, for he was setting forth on a long and perilous journey. He was already in the dhow, his white helmet conspicuous amid the sea of lambskin caps and turbans.

"So long! Good luck!" he called cheerily as the dhow shoved off and headed for the distant shore.

"Good luck to *you!*" said I.

The following night, I think it was, we put in at Abadan for fuel, for here the petroleum of the South Persian oil-fields is brought down to the coast by pipe-lines. The little stream which bisects the town is a barrier between civilization and barbarism. On one side is the British concession, all spick-and-span, with well-laid-out streets and the trim white bungalows of the employees of the Anglo-Persian Oil Company, a group of administration buildings, and along the waterfront a row of huge iron oil-tanks. There is a considerable colony of English in Abadan, and the night we were there they were putting on an amateur musical comedy—"The Pirates of Penzance," if I remember rightly.

But cross the rickety bridge which spans the little stream and you find yourself in the native town, a fragment of old Persia at its worst. Here you can obtain a glimpse of the Wild and Woolly East, for in it foregather the scum and offscouring of coast and hinterland—English and American oil-drillers, Chinese gamblers, Arab slave-traders, 'Iraqui gun-runners, Indian pearl-buyers, Bakhtiari bandits, Kurdish ruffians.

The girls insisted that they wished to get a glimpse of Persian night life, so we formed a little slumming party in spite of the warnings of the ship's officers that the native quarter of Abadan was "a damned tough town." Before I had been ashore ten minutes I was more than willing to agree with them and regretted that I had not brought my automatic along. I had no need for it, as things turned out, but its presence in my pocket would have been distinctly reassuring.

The gin-shops and coffee-houses lining the single unpaved street were crowded with sallow, black-mustached, fierce-faced men in skirts and turbans; Bakhtiari chieftains with bandoliers of cartridges slung across their chests, and high caps of black lambskin; bearded Arab sheiks from the opposite coast, very dignified and aloof, their keffiehs held in place by camel's hair agals, their broad sashes bristling with weapons; Chinese gamblers, bland of countenance and dexterous of finger; Indian money-lenders, cringing and furtive-eyed; sallow-faced troopers of Riza Shah's new army in unkempt, faded uniforms; bepainted women of easy virtue hailing from all the ports between Basra and Muskat and from the hinterlands beyond. Lamps smoked and guttered; gramophones blared raucously; from the gambling dens came the clink of coins and the sound of voices raised in altercation; from the dance halls the wail of pipes and the throb of drums; the night patrol passed by with clinking weapons.

We had now entered the Shat-el-Arab, the broad, swift-flowing stream, sixscore miles in length, through which the Tigris and the Euphrates, from their confluence at Korna, gain the Persian Gulf. The shores gradually converged as we steamed northward and the scenery of lower Mesopotamia unrolled itself before us as on a motion-picture screen—low banks green with date palms; charming vistas opened up by the irrigation canals which penetrate deep into the plantations; cubical mud houses; occasional mosques of sun-baked brick with domes of turquoise tiles, like beautiful bonnets on the heads of shabbily clad women; slender, white-washed minarets from whose lofty balconies muezzins chanted their shrill call to prayer; long strings of camels laden with the golden dates for which this region is famous; Arab dhows with high bows and tawny sails; toothpick-shaped canoes hewn from single palm-logs, with swarthy boatmen at the paddles.

We found Basra in a frenzy of excitement and alarm. There had been a battle in the near-by desert the day before between 'Iraq levies and Wahabi tribesmen. A British scouting plane had been brought down by rifle fire and the pilot had been cut to pieces by Arab knives. Ibn Sa'ud, the overlord of Arabia, was about to take the warpath again and rumors were rife that the tribes were mustering in force to attack the town. Measures for defense were being hastily taken. Trenches were in course of construction, barbed-wire entanglements were being set up, the streets were filled with marching men, batteries, machine-guns.

Every sort of alarmist rumor was in circulation. There was a report—which proved later to be not wholly without foundation—that an overland convoy had been attacked by Bedouins near Rutbah Wells and wiped out to the last man. We were assured that desert communications had been interrupted indefinitely; that the military authorities had issued orders that no further convoys should set out on the desert run until things had quieted down; and that, the Damascus route being closed, we would be faced by the alternatives of remaining in Baghdad perhaps for months or of returning whence we had come. And, by way of lending substance to the rumors, Dr. Jones, who was on his way to Jerusalem to attend a conference of churchmen, received a radio message advising him not to take the desert route. But I have heard so many alarming rumors in the course of a long and adventurous career that I no longer pay any attention to them. Had I given heed to the calamity-howlers during the past thirty years I never should have gotten far from home.

Basra, a modern city for Mesopotamia, for it was not built until the beginning of the seventh century, is situated some two miles from the Shat-el-Arab, with which it is connected by a broad tributary known as Ashar Creek and by a fine macadam road. Though it has a pleasant winter climate, and in the European suburb of Ashar a fine residential club whose rooms, when vacant, are open to visitors, it is otherwise an uninviting place, its unpaved streets, deep in dust during the dry season and almost impassable from mud during the rains, being bordered by nondescript, ramshackle, mud-walled buildings which have no single architectural feature to recommend them. But in one respect Basra is unique among Arab towns, for it is intersected by a perfect network of canals and natural waterways along which ply great numbers of slender, gaily painted, gondola-like boats known as *bellums,* so that the place has an atmosphere distinctly Venetian—a Venice of the East.

There is next to nothing of artistic merit to be purchased in Basra, but in a hole-in-the-wall shop near the Governorat we found an old Arab craftsman who does the most beautiful etching on silver I have ever seen. Framed on the wall was a letter of commendation from the Prince of Wales, who was one of his patrons. My cousin gave him a silver tobacco box and a flask of the same material to be engraved. I suggested that it would be highly appropriate for the flask to bear a likeness of Mr. Andrew J. Volstead, but, as we had no picture of the author of the act which made America thirsty, we compromised on a desert scene with a camel in the foreground. The camel, as you know, can go an astonishingly long time without drinking.

It is three hundred and sixty miles from Basra to Baghdad, and the weekly mail train, which runs in connection with the steamers, makes the journey in about twenty hours. A first-class ticket costs twenty-three dollars, and there is a dining-car of sorts attached to the train. Or, if you have several days to spare, you can make the trip in more leisurely fashion by river.

The scenery is dreary and monotonous—a vast stretch of tawny desert, broken at infrequent intervals by sand hills, groves of date palms, miserable mud towns. But it is the most stirring journey in the world for the traveler who has any imagination in his soul, for here, according to tradition, the human race began, this semi-fertile strip of land being generally identified with the Garden of Eden.

Tradition aside, every mile of the journey is haunted by the ghosts of ancient history. Shortly after midnight the train came to a halt beside the platform of a small station. The single guttering light enabled me to decipher the legend on the sign-board: "Ur Junction." On the low and barren hills which I could vaguely discern in the moonlight once stood Ur of the Chaldees, the capital of the Sumerian kingdom, the site of the great temple of the moon-god Sin, and the home of the first Jew, Abraham. The inscribed bricks recently discovered by American and English archæologists on the summit of the mound prove conclusively that the city was built in 2400 B.C., the century which witnessed the Deluge.

By breakfast time the next morning we were at Hillah. Drawn up alongside the station platform was a line of dilapidated American cars, each bearing the sign "Taxi for Babylon." By this token I knew that we were now in the domains once ruled by Nebuchadnezzar, King of Assyria; that over there, four miles away across the desert, had stood the city that in Old Testament times was famous for its splendor, its hanging gardens, its corruption; that here

> *The Assyrian came down like the wolf on the fold,*
> *And his cohorts were gleaming in purple and gold.*

The excavators have made the Old Testament figures live again by laying bare the foundations of Nebuchadnezzar's palace and the banquet hall of Belshazzar. It was during a great feast in the latter, you will recall, that there appeared on the wall, written by ghostly fingers, the ominous warning, *Mene, Mene, Tekel, Upharsin,* which foretold the doom of the last of the Babylonian kings.

Half an hour by motor-car from Hillah station is Birs Nimrud, the great mass of fused brickwork which crowns the little eminence being, according to tradition, the ruins of the Tower of Babel. The supporters of this theory point to the shattered structure as evidence that God struck it down in his wrath, as described in Isaiah, but history as recorded on bricks found at Babylon shows that, twenty-two centuries before the Crucifixion, Birs Nimrud was the shrine of the god Nebo. Scientists are always taking the romance out of things.

At forty-five minutes past noon, the train being by a miracle on time, we pulled into Baghdad, the city of the Califs, of the Thousand and One Nights, of Haroun-al-Raschid and the lovely Scheherazade.

Though I had not been in Baghdad for half-a-dozen years, and though in the interim the Government has had ample time in which to make much-needed municipal improvements, I could detect no striking change in the appearance of the 'Iraq capital. Upon second thought, there was one sign of progress, however, for nearly every street in the business district was torn up by paving gangs. Concrete mixers, steam-rollers and the smell of tar made me homesick. But the city was as filthy as ever, the buildings as dilapidated, the hotels as badly run. Gertrude Bell, whom I had known well, was dead, but Feisal, the young Arab from Hedjaz whom she had put upon the throne of 'Iraq, still reigned.

We put up at the Hotel Maude for old time's sake and because we could get a room with a balcony overhanging the Tigris, for I never tire of watching the round black *goufas* wallowing across the stream, and the lights from the houses on the opposite bank dancing on its waters at night. The Maude is run on a sort of hit-or-miss plan. It is not really expensive according to American standards, but the management puts on all that it thinks the traffic will bear and then adds some more for good measure. The bartender chalks up the drinks you order, and you are astonished to find how many you have had when you get your bill. There is not a bell in the place, but when you require a servant you summon him by the simple expedient of going to the door and clapping your hands. Despite its shortcomings, I rather like the place, however, for there is a friendly, happy-go-lucky, help-yourself-to-anything-you-want atmosphere about it.

Spring was now at hand, and toward midday the heat became too great for perfect comfort. We were none too early in the season, as in another fortnight or so the people would be taking to their cellars, for during five months of the year the unfortunate Europeans who are condemned to live in Baghdad have to spend their waking hours in subterranean apartments, called *serdahs,* where they live and eat and carry on their business. The American consulate is particularly fortunate in this respect, for it has the deepest *serdah* in the city, thirty feet beneath the surface. Shortly after my return from Mesopotamia I met in

Washington a young man who had just been assigned to Baghdad as vice-consul. He told me that he welcomed the assignment because he had heard so much about the romance of life in the city of the Califs and was eager to taste it. I imagine that most of the romance evaporated, however, after a few months spent in the consulate's damp and gloomy cellar.

Baghdad is a modern city. By that I do not mean that it is distinguished for its modern conveniences, for it is not, but that virtually nothing remains of the city depicted so alluringly in the Thousand and One Nights. The only reminder of Haroun-al-Raschid, indeed, is the pineapple-shaped tomb of the philandering calif's favorite wife, Zobeideh, which still stands in the outskirts of the city. I know nothing of that lady's history; perhaps she died from heart-break over her husband's amours with the beautiful Scheherazade, who, if all the stories one hears are to be believed, kept the ruler in her apartment until a scandalously late hour telling naughty bed-time stories. Douglas Fairbanks's film, "The Thief of Baghdad" was being shown in one of the local picture-houses, but the Arabs could make nothing of it. They marveled at Fairbanks's agility, but Hollywood's conception of the ancient city of the califs puzzled them sorely.

A mile or so outside Baghdad, on the banks of the Tigris, is the Alweyah Club—at least, I think that is the way to spell it—which is the rendezvous for the city's European society. It has deep verandas, which are usually cool even in the hottest weather, and is a pleasant place at which to dine and spend the evening. Here I was introduced to three cocktails of which I had never heard before—the Desert Dream, the Sheik's Breath and the Lion Tamer. After sampling each of them, I decided that they ranked with the Tarantula Bite and the Whisper of Death, two highly potent drinks with which I had become acquainted in British North Borneo. To concoct a Desert Dream, all you need is the yolk of an egg, a small cup of fresh cream, a jigger each of port wine, crême de cocoa and brandy, some cracked ice and a shaker. The Lion Tamer is made of . . . But what's the use? It would only exasperate you to hear about it, and you couldn't get the ingredients in America anyway. It is enough to say that, after taking three of them, I had no more fear of lions than had the Prophet Daniel.

The bazaars of Baghdad, though not as large as those of Tehran, nor stocked with as fine goods as the marts of Ispahan, are world-famous. Carpets from Persia, Anatolia, Kurdistan and the Central Asian khanates; pearls from Bahrein; silver wrought and curiously inlaid by a secret process known only to the Amara Chaldeans and jealously guarded by them; hammered brassware from Damascus; ivory-hilted simitars and razor-bladed yataghans made by the Kurdish tribes; Samarkand tiles of the beautiful "lost blue"; lambskins out of Turkestan; smooth and soft as velvet; amber from the shores of the Caspian; hand woven silks from a thousand villages in which the women still use primitive looms and home-made vegetable dyes—all these may be bargained for amid an interesting throng more polyglot than may be found perhaps in any other mart in the world.

I had had it in mind to pick up a few rugs if opportunity offered, for the idea of buying a carpet of Baghdad in Baghdad appealed to me, but I hesitated because I wanted to be certain of what I was buying. For they have a saying in the East that it takes two Greeks to get the better of a Jew, two Syrians to get the better of a Greek, two Armenians to get the better of a Syrian, and that a Persian can get the best of them all. And the rug merchants of

Baghdad are Persians. But, while in the consulate one morning, I chanced to meet an American rug-buyer, Mr. H. H. Orahan, of Brooklyn, who, the consul informed me, is one of the foremost authorities on Oriental rugs in the world. Having been waylaid and robbed the day before in the desert by Bedouins—an episode which I shall describe later on—Orahan found himself compelled to remain in Baghdad until he could communicate with his bankers. Learning that I was interested in rugs, he courteously offered to place his services at my disposal—an offer which I accepted promptly and gratefully. It was like having Mr. J. P. Morgan offer to go down to Wall Street with me and help me pick out a few good stocks. At the rug khan we happened to meet Air Vice-Marshal Sir E. L. Ellington, who commands the British forces in 'Iraq and is himself a well-known rug collector. He was as eager as Orahan to aid me in making my selection. That is always the way with experts, I have found. Once they learn that you are intelligently interested in their particular line they will put themselves to any amount of trouble to assist you.

I had the good judgment to leave the selection and bargaining to my two self-appointed mentors, while I sat back and watched them. It was a liberal education in all that pertains to wool-growing, dyeing, designing, weaving and bargaining. At a glance they could tell the period of a carpet within a decade or so, and that is more than can be said for ninety-nine out of every hundred so-called experts.

Before the war, rugs could be purchased comparatively cheaply in Baghdad, but that condition no longer holds true. It is open to question, indeed, whether rugs cannot be bought as cheaply in New York or London as in the East, particularly when the freight and the 55 per cent. *ad valorem* duty charged by the American customs are added to the price. If, however, one is in quest of rare and unusual pieces, such as hunting carpets, as I was, he will have in the Oriental markets a wider range to choose from.

We spent a long half-day in the rug khans, and when we left it took three porters to carry my purchases to the hotel. They included an eighteenth century Mushkabad hunting carpet which had been made to the order of Nadir Shah; a superb Royal Bokhara; a Golden Samarkand, interesting because of the Arabic and Chinese motifs combined in its design; a superb old Shiraz, which glows as though made from rubies crushed in claret; a Sarouk which, when the light falls upon it, leaps into flame and which by rights should be in a museum. These magic carpets now cover the floor of my library at Journey's End, and in the evenings, when the great room is illumined only by the open fire, I amuse myself by flying back to Baghdad in imagination upon them.

CHAPTER XIV

WITH THE OVERLAND DESERT MAIL

UPON our arrival in Baghdad we found the papers filled with sensational accounts of the hold-up of the east-bound Overland Desert Mail, rumors of which had reached us in Basra. The details of the affair I learned from Orahan, the American rug-buyer whom I had met at the consulate.

The onset had come suddenly, at dawn, in a region dotted with low hills, only a few miles from the fort at Rutbah Wells, which is midway between Damascus and Baghdad. Instead of attacking on their swift riding camels, as has been their custom since time beyond reckoning, the Bedouins introduced a startlingly modern note by sweeping down upon the straggling convoy in a fleet of Buicks. It was a tremendously thrilling spectacle, said Orahan, the Deadwood coach episode of Buffalo Bill's Wild West brought up to date and Orientalized, for the cars were driven at reckless speed, the turbaned tribesmen standing in the tonneaus, their keffiehs and burnouses streaming in the wind, pouring in a hail of lead as they came. Most of the bullets went wild, for the Arabs are notoriously poor marksmen, but one passed through the body of a passenger, a young Armenian.

The heavily laden cars of the convoy were easily overhauled by the raiders' speedier machines, whereupon the drivers, realizing that resistance was useless and escape out of the question, halted and put up their hands. Crews and passengers were bruskly ordered to get out and line up, the tribesmen going through their garments in true road-agent fashion. Nothing was left to the victims save the clothes they stood in. But the desert drama had its touch of comic relief. Orahan was wearing a massive gold ring engraved with a Masonic device. It fitted so snugly that the ruffian who was relieving the American of his possessions was unable to pull it off. The Arab had drawn his knife preparatory to amputating the finger as the most expeditious means of removing the circlet, when the leader of the band, catching sight of the mystic emblem, intervened.

"Mason?" he demanded in English, addressing Orahan.

The frightened American admitted that he was a thirty-third degree member of the great fraternal order, whose lodges are found throughout the East.

Whereupon the sheik, evidently a desert Robin Hood, ordered his henchman to sheath his knife and leave Orahan in possession of his ring.

"Did you give him the grip and high-sign?" I asked Orahan.

"I did not," he replied emphatically. "The fellow may have been a Mason—there are lodges in Damascus, Aleppo and Baghdad—but he was no brother of mine, for, though he left me my ring, he took my watch, my money, my letter of credit and my baggage."

It is in the neighborhood of seven hundred miles from Baghdad to Beirut, and in normal times, when the tribes are quiet, the cars of the Overland Desert Mail make the journey from the Tigris to the Mediterranean in twenty-eight hours, which even on paved highways is fast going. This, of course, necessitates running day and night, with only a brief halt at Rutbah Wells for refueling and overhauling.

The remarkable system known as the Nairn Transport Company, which operates the Overland Desert Mail, is due to the initiative and energy of two young New Zealanders named Nairn, who came to Palestine with the Anzacs early in the war and remained on after peace with the Turks was concluded. At first the brothers found it hard sledding, for there was little employment in that distracted country for Europeans, but they finally succeeded in scraping together enough money to purchase a couple of touring cars, and with these they established a motor service between Beirut, Haifa and Jerusalem. When, in the spring of 1922, I with three companions traveled overland from Paris to Persia, the elder Nairn was our chauffeur during the Syrian section of the journey.

They finally succeeded in interesting in their project a number of English and French capitalists and, financed by them, purchased a small fleet of cars, all American built, including several six-wheel, sixteen-passenger buses specially equipped for desert travel. Within a year the daring enterprise, for which the wiseheads had predicted failure, was an assured success, for it cut the journey from the Mediterranean to India nearly in half (it takes only eight days by the overland route from London to Baghdad) and reduced by at least ten days the time from Europe to Tehran. For oil operators, rug-buyers, diplomatic officers, Indian potentates, and others to whom time is money, this saving was of enormous value. By 1924 the Nairns had obtained mail contracts from the governments of Syria, Palestine, 'Iraq and Persia, and in 1927 they sold the enterprise outright to an Anglo-French syndicate for a price which, it is reputed, has made them independent for life, the elder brother retaining the managing directorship of the reorganized company.

The buses are driven by former pilots of the Royal Air

Force, tireless young men with frames of rawhide and nerves of steel, who travel in pairs, one driving while the other sleeps. As there are no roads in the desert, only the broad, straggling trails made by centuries of camel caravans, the cars are pointed by the sun by day and by the stars at night, the steering wheel is lashed and the throttle set for a speed of fifty miles an hour. Shortly before our arrival in Baghdad Major Nairn had made a wager with Sir Arnold Wilson, the Anglo-Persian oil magnate, that he would drive him from the Tigris to the Mediterranean in seventeen hours, Nairn to have advantage of the hour's difference in time. If he accomplished the feat he was to receive double the usual fare, which is £20; if he lost, Sir Arnold was to have the ride for nothing. Nairn won with twenty minutes to spare.

Though, owing to the precautions taken by the Syrian and 'Iraq governments, which patrol the routes on their respective sides of the frontier with *méharistes* of the Camel Corps, armored cars and airplanes, the trans-desert journey is reasonably safe—as safe, certainly, as rail travel in many parts of Mexico—unfortunate episodes occasionally occur. Several of the Nairn drivers have been killed or wounded, and in 1926, during an attack by Bedouins, the wife of the French consul at Baghdad lost her life. The danger of fatalities has been materially reduced, however, by Nairn's orders that neither his employees nor his passengers shall carry firearms, thereby making resistance impossible, and by the generous subsidies which, it is generally understood, he pays to the sheiks of the various tribes in order to secure immunity. The only really dangerous section of the journey is within the salient of Arab territory to the west of Hit which here separates 'Iraq and Syria. This is a sort of no man's land, where British and French writs do not run, and it is here that attacks, whether from

Ibn Sa'ud's warriors, nomad tribesmen or bandits from the Fringe, are most likely to come.

The Overland Mail is a service which requires for its maintenance men of extraordinary endurance, courage and daring. It is, in fact, a counterpart of the Pony Express or the Wells Fargo stage-coaches which carried mails and passengers across the plains in Indian days. About the only differences are that the vehicles, instead of being drawn by four galloping mustangs, have the power of fourscore horses beneath their sloping hoods; that they carry rug-buyers and oil-drillers instead of prospectors and cattle-men; that they are in danger of attack from Bedouins on racing dromedaries instead of feathered warriors on painted ponies. I should advise any one heading East, who is willing to face a little risk and undergo some discomfort for the sake of romance, to take the desert route, for here, and here alone, may one taste the thrill of travel in stage-coach days, of life on the old frontier.

Owing to the recent attack on the convoy and the increasing restlessness of the desert tribes, the 'Iraq authorities were reluctant to let the semi-weekly mail depart, and for a day or so it looked as though we would have to remain in Baghdad indefinitely or else retrace our steps through the Persian Gulf, the Indian Ocean and the Red Sea, for the only alternative route to Europe, through Russian territory, was closed to us. The waiting and uncertainty finally got on my cousin's nerves, for he was already considerably behind the schedule he had set for himself and had pressing business awaiting him at home. So I was not wholly surprised when he announced at dinner one evening that he had booked passage to Cairo by the mail plane which was leaving Baghdad the following morning at daybreak.

"But you are missing out on the best part of the whole trip," I argued. "Have you no longing for adventure? No desire to sleep in a desert fort, like the one described in 'Beau Geste,' and perhaps be attacked by Bedouins? You might even be captured and carried off to Nejd and held for ransom. Think what a story that would make to tell your friends at home! Even if you had no such luck as that, you would see Arabia and Syria and Anatolia and the Baghdad Railway and Constantinople. Come on! Have a heart! Change your mind."

"Absolutely nothing doing," he replied firmly. "I'm in a hurry to get home and I'm fed up with the East. I've had enough of sun and sand, of flies and fleas, of discomfort and dirt, to last me the rest of my life. By taking the plane I can reach Port-Saïd to-morrow night in time to catch the P. & O. boat for Marseilles, and while you are still wondering when you will get a bath and a decent meal I shall be dining at Voisin's and sleeping at the Crillon."

His westward trip was in a way as remarkable as mine. The big British army plane in which he was the only passenger took off from the Baghdad field at break of dawn and had crossed above the frontier of Palestine by noon. He caught a glimpse of Jerusalem from an altitude of four thousand feet, lunched at the Royal Air Force mess at Gaza, had tea on the terrace of Shepheard's in Cairo, caught the evening train for Port-Saïd, and before midnight of the same day on which he had left Baghdad was aboard a P. & O. liner anchored in the canal, with passengers in evening dress playing bridge on the deck and stewards hurrying about bearing tall glasses with ice tinkling in them. That is what I call rapid transit.

The delay which my cousin had prophesied did not materialize, for the day after his departure the local representative of the Nairn company sent me word that the authorities had given permission for the convoy to depart the following morning. We were to have a strong escort of armored cars, he assured me; the route would be patrolled by airplanes; and, instead of passing through the stretch of dangerous country after nightfall, we would spend the night in the fort at Rutbah Wells.

It was a great moment when the huge six-wheeler appropriately named the "Babylon," all of its sixteen seats occupied, slowly picked its way through the narrow streets of Baghdad, strings of camels and droves of donkeys scattering at the sound of its siren, lumbered across the creaking pontoon bridge which spans the Tigris, and turned its nose toward the desert and the Mediterranean. No one knew what adventures lay before us, and I don't think that any one greatly cared.

The rickety bridge of boats by which we crossed the Euphrates at Fellujah held exciting memories for me, for, five years before, while crossing it in the opposite direction, a herd of camels had suddenly stampeded and we had had to run for our lives to escape being trampled by the panic-stricken beasts. We reached the 'Iraq custom house at Ramadi, fifty miles from Baghdad but several times that distance from the frontier, shortly after noon, and halted there for an hour while our passports were examined and to wait for other west-bound cars which, under government orders, were to join our convoy for mutual protection. These comprised touring cars belonging to various native transportation companies (for Nairn no longer enjoys a monopoly of the desert traffic), two postal vans and several camions laden with merchandise and luggage.

From Ramadi we struck across the terrible alkaline wastes to the south of Hit and by mid-afternoon were in the open desert, heading at fifty miles an hour into the setting sun. Contrary to the popular idea, Arabia, at least in the north, is not a sea of sand—indeed, there is scarcely any sand at all—but a limitless, almost dead-flat plain of sunbaked earth strewn with fine gravel which the winds keep nearly as smooth as a parade ground. There is nothing to be seen in any direction—not a house, not a tree, not a shrub over a foot in height, not a sign of human habitation. Later on we glimpsed in the distance several herds of gazelle, which at our approach fled on the wings of the wind; and numbers of the huge storks known to the Arabs as Hadji Lugigi, because their white topknots look from a distance like the turbans of the faithful, and because it is asserted that when winter comes on they make their way toward Mecca. Also several jackals, a lizard the size of a small alligator, and an enormous species of bustard.

At four o'clock to the minute we halted in the desert for tea, without which no Englishman's day would be complete. In little more time than it takes to tell about it our two pilots had split up a packing case, soaked it with gasoline, had a kettle singing over the fire, and had broken open tins of marmalade and biscuits. I imagine that they would have insisted on having their tea had hostile Bedouins appeared on the horizon.

During the day it had been somewhat too warm for comfort, but with nightfall the thermometer dropped forty degrees in little more than an hour. It grew bitterly cold, and despite the heavy greatcoats and blankets in which we were wrapped we shivered. There is no twilight in the desert and darkness fell like the lowering of a curtain, but our speed did not decrease. Our powerful lamps bored a hole in the darkness, and along the lane of light they made we tore with the speedometer needle hovering around fifty.

Owing to the delay at Ramadi and the necessity of keeping our pace down to that of the other cars, it was not far from midnight when, dust-caked, weary, hungry and parched, we came to a halt before the fort at Rutbah Wells. It was a foursquare structure of mud brick, its walls loopholed for rifle-fire, with heavy iron-bound gates opening into a spacious courtyard for the accommodation of cars and camels—a perfect counterpart of the Saharan fort described so graphically by Percival Christopher Wren in "Beau Geste." Garrisoning the fort, which is the westernmost outpost of 'Iraqui power, was a half-company of infantry, sturdy, soldierly looking men muffled in khaki greatcoats and red keffiehs, with bandoliers of cartridges slung across their chests.

The Nairn company had had the foresight to make arrangements for feeding its hungry patrons and we were served a hot meal which was astonishingly good in view of the circumstances. The waiter even tendered me a much-thumbed wine list, evidently brought from Damascus, but the prices were prohibitive because of the excessive cost of transport. For a half-bottle of mineral water I was charged two rupees, or about seventy cents.

The fort was built not for the convenience of weary travelers but to hold in check marauding Bedouins, and, as a consequence, the accommodation was extremely limited. The four women passengers were assigned cots in the guard-room; the rest of us were forced to sleep wherever we could find space to spread our blankets. The difficulty with this was, in my case, that I had brought no blankets along. A British cavalry officer, who had been serving with 'Iraqui levies in Kurdistan, and I finally discovered a tiny cubicle, unoccupied save for numbers of the voracious little insect known to science as the *Cimex lectularius*. From a soldier we obtained the loan of a piece of tarpaulin and, with our bags for pillows, snuggled down for a cold and cheerless night on the floor.

Before turning in I lighted my pipe and climbed the

steep stairs leading to the platform which runs around the interior of the fort. Sentries, muffled to the eyes against the piercing cold, paced up and down or stood motionless in the embrasures of the ramparts, seeking to pierce the night. There was no moon, but the stars were exceptionally bright, and I could see for a considerable distance after my eyes had become accustomed to the darkness. Far out on the desert a pin-point of flame flickered for a moment and disappeared. When it showed again I called the attention of a sentry to it.

"Bedawin?" I asked.

"Ya," he replied, and with a grim chuckle drew his finger suggestively across his throat.

When I went below I got out my service automatic, pumped a shell into the chamber and laid it within easy reach. There was no telling what might happen before morning. Then, without troubling to remove my boots, I stretched myself on the floor and in thirty seconds was sound asleep.

We were awakened when it was still pitch dark by a bugle sounding the "Stand-to." We stumbled into the courtyard to find it filled with soldiers, drivers and passengers, for in the desert, as in the trenches, the hour before dawn is the hour of greatest danger. It is then, if at all, that the Arabs will attack. From a soldier I obtained a bucket of water. It was icy cold but I plunged my head in it to the neck and abruptly became awake. Three tin cups of steaming coffee, followed by a vigorous session with the toothbrush, and I was a new man. It is amazing what cold water, hot coffee and a toothbrush can do to bolster up a drooping spirit.

By five o'clock the convoy was ready to start. The armored cars which were to escort us through the danger zone now put in an appearance, but they were not armored at all. They were merely Ford trucks, loaded with 'Iraqui irregulars in scarlet head-cloths, Lewis guns mounted where the wind-shields had been. They and their wild-looking crews were picturesque enough to satisfy the most exacting, but they did not inspire confidence as a means of defense against a well-executed attack. Moreover, they were always too far in advance or too far behind, leaving our flanks exposed. There were a dozen times during our passage through the low sand hills beyond Rutbah when a Bedouin *harka* could have swooped down and wiped the convoy out.

The second day was not as enjoyable as the first, for the novelty of the experience had worn off, the possibility of an attack was decreasing with every mile we covered, it was bitterly cold and the dust was suffocating. I have never seen such dust anywhere, not even during a Saharan sand-storm. It had not rained for months, the desert was as dry as tinder and the wind was at our backs, so that the dust cloud frequently overtook and enveloped us. Sometimes it was so dense that the interior of the car was a yellow haze. We looked like a cargo of mummies, for we had bound handkerchiefs over our faces in order to breathe. At times the wind whipped up whirlpools of dust, so that the drivers could not see at all and had to drive by instinct, but this was not as dangerous as it sounds, for the terrain was flat and the cars of the convoy too far apart to be in danger of collision.

During the second day there was only one moment of excitement. As we approached the low volcanic hills of the Tulul-es-safa a faint cloud of dust rose from behind one of them, such as might have been made by a car driven slowly or by camels. Our pilot, instantly on the alert, put on his brakes and sounded his siren. The other vehicles of the convoy closed in, as sheep draw together when menaced by wolves. The cars of the escort, which had dropped behind in order to repair a puncture sustained by one of them, came tearing up, for all the world like a pack of terriers, and flung themselves before the flank where danger threatened. The crews slapped pans of cartridges upon the breeches of the Lewis guns. The red-turbaned infantry tumbled out, deployed and advanced slowly in skirmish formation. For a few moments we sat expectant and helpless, for, barring the pistols which most of the men carried surreptitiously, we were unarmed. The dust cloud receded, grew fainter, disappeared. The escort cars took up positions on our flanks and we went on.

"What was it all about?" I asked our driver.

"Oh," he replied nonchalantly, "probably a scouting party of Bedouins."

Shortly after noon we came upon a sign-post standing solitary in the desert. There was not trace of a road, but one arm, pointing westward, bore the word "Syrie"; the other "'Iraq." A little later a monoplane with red-white-and-blue circles painted on the under side of its wings droned overhead—the air patrol with which France guards her desert routes. Then, rounding the shoulder of a butte, we came upon a cluster of Arab huts and a small adobe building over which floated the tricolor. We were in Syria.

Dusk was at hand when the "Babylon" came to a halt before the Hotel Victoria in Damascus. Throughout the journey across the desert I had looked forward to a hot bath, a good dinner and a soft bed upon our arrival in the Syrian capital, but none of the three materialized, for three hundred tourists, passengers on a Mediterranean cruise, had arrived that morning by rail from Beirut and every hotel in the city was packed to the doors. Because I had once been a consular officer in Syria, and was known to the manager of the hotel, I managed to get a room of sorts, but I have seen prison cells which were far more comfortable. To complete our discomfort, the supply of hot water had been exhausted by the earlier arrivals, the food was abominable, and, the hotel being inadequately heated, we had to huddle about the one and only stove, in our overcoats, in order to keep warm. The bar was crowded with Americans buying cocktails at a dollar apiece. Every one was disgruntled and irritable. I sometimes wonder why my country-people are so eager to pay exorbitant prices for damp rooms, hard beds and wretched food, when they could be so much more comfortable at home.

The annual influx of American tourists is like manna from heaven for the merchants of these Levantine cities, for the prices of everything are doubled automatically when word comes that a cruising steamer has entered Beirut harbor. The shops of Damascus were crowded with Americans in quest of souvenirs. Callow youths from Wichita and Terre Haute were buying agals, keffiehs and Arab weapons—most of the latter probably produced in Birmingham. Eager-eyed women, as excited as though they were attending a bargain sale at home, were paying fantastic prices for hammered brassware, inlaid boxes, *mushrabiyeh* screens, embroidered table-covers, and such-like junk. Merely to watch them was as good as going to a play. One middle-aged couple from somewhere in the Middle West were in tow of their daughter, a flapper of the most aggravated type, who announced that she was looking for a "sheek." When I left she was carrying on a violent flirtation with the hotel dragoman. She was quite worried, however, for fear that her parents might get into bad company. She caught her father talking to a Church of England bishop, a venerable and distinguished person.

"Now, poppa," she said shrilly, "you know I warned you not to talk with strange men."

I had not been in Damascus since the French bombarded the city during the Druse uprising of 1925, and I was shocked to see the havoc wrought by the shells in the world's most ancient city. The residential quarter, with its fine old Turkish dwellings, including the Azm Palace, recognized as the most beautiful building in the city, was in ruins; enormous damage had been done to the historic Street Which Is Called Straight; soldiers of the Foreign Legion, negro tirailleurs from Senegal, spahis from Algeria, swarmed everywhere; the native population was sullen and depressed. Shell-shattered Damascus is a monument to French administrative methods of which the French have good reason to be ashamed.

At Damascus I said farewell to my fellow-travelers, most of whom were continuing to Beirut, Jerusalem or Cairo, and set out alone on the long train journey across Syria and Asia Minor to Constantinople. The train on the narrow-gage railway leaves Damascus at midnight, climbs the five-thousand-foot Anti-Lebanon range, drops down into the lovely valley on the other side and at four-thirty in the morning reaches Rayak, the junction for Aleppo. It was bitterly cold, the mountain passes deep in snow, and the train unheated, but I managed to keep myself from freezing by wrapping my overcoat about my legs and keeping up my circulation with an occasional sip of whisky. This whisky, which I had bought in Damascus, involved me in serious complications later on.

Rayak was many degrees warmer than Damascus. Here spring was at hand; I caught the pleasant scent of new-turned earth and the fragrance of blossoms. But life in that smiling valley was not as peaceful as it seemed, for on a siding beside the station stood an armored railway truck, grim and menacing. From the steel turret protruded the lean barrel of a long range naval gun on which had been painted the legend "Le Terreur des Druzes." On the sun-drenched hill-slopes could be seen villages, or what had once been villages, dozens of them, which had been transformed into heaps of débris by shell-fire. Yet the French, when they occupied the country by mandate of the League of Nations, assured the Syrians that they came not as conquerors but as friends.

The journey from Rayak to Aleppo is very beautiful and intensely interesting, for this has been a land of milk and honey since history began. The train rambled leisurely up a broad and fertile valley, with tremendous snow-clad ramparts, the Lebanon and Anti-Lebanon, on either hand. White villages clung precariously to the mountainside; the fruit orchards, just bursting into bloom, dotted the green slopes with broad areas of rose-tinted snow; peasants were tilling their fields with implements no different from those used in the days of Solomon.

At Baalbek the marble columns of the great sanctuary of the sun-god rose in majesty against an azure sky. Farther on the mountains dwindled into ranges of bare brown hills and these in turn merged almost imperceptibly into a vast and tawny plain, patched with grass and flecked with scarlet poppies, which rolled away, billow upon billow, to the distant sky-line.

At Homs a huge and ancient fortress, its massive walls showing the scars left by centuries of invasions, dominates the straggling, dilapidated town. Here once stood the famous Temple of the Sun, one of whose priests, Helliogabalus, exchanged his sacerdotal vestments for the purple robes of an emperor of Rome.

Hama is a fascinating place, with a wealth of scented gardens, where huge black water-wheels, fifty feet in height, stand astride the Orontes as it meanders through the town. Beyond Hama the plain for scores of miles is dotted with the curious beehive villages peculiar to this region, the conical dwellings of sun-dried brick, ranged in rows of circles, being strongly suggestive of central Africa.

Now there was more color in the costumes of the people. Congregated on the station platforms to watch the train come in were sturdy, slow-moving Turkish peasants, their tight felt trousers elaborately arabesqued in braid; active, alert-eyed Syrians, their tarbooshes wound about with yellow scarfs; Moslem priests, bearded and venerable, in flowing robes and snowy turbans, some with the green scarfs which showed that they were *hadjis* and had made the pilgrimage to the holy places; Druses from the mountains, tall, slim men, contemptuous and haughty; officers of the Syrian spahis with purple bands about their képis and purple facings on their khaki uniforms; women with tattooed faces wearing short, embroidered jackets and voluminous trousers of lemon yellow, bright green, madder rose. Graceful riders on beautiful Arab horses cantered across the plain. Shepherds who might have stepped straight from the pages of the Old Testament guarded great flocks of fat-tailed sheep. Fierce-looking, filthy nomads emerged from their low black tents to stare at the passing train. Long strings of camels swayed along, bound for the markets of the cities with the products of the Fringe. The bridges and tunnels were heavily guarded; everywhere were wire entanglements and machine guns.

A weekly sleeping-car service, an extension of the Orient Express, is now in operation between Haidar Pasha, on the Asiatic side of the Bosporus, and Tripoli-in-Syria, and at Hama there was attached to the train a long brown car, the European equivalent of one of our Pullmans, bearing in brass letters the familiar legend, *Compagnie Internationale des Wagons-Lits et Grands Express Euro-*

péens. When the maroon-uniformed porter relieved me of my bags and ushered me into a cozy compartment, lighted by electricity and heated by steam, and I stretched myself luxuriously upon the plush divan, I realized that I was nearing civilization again.

The overland journey from Damascus to the Bosporus is a complicated undertaking because of the vexatious and needless restrictions imposed by the various railway administrations in regard to the purchase of tickets over their respective systems. A first-class ticket from Aleppo to Constantinople (in Turkey, by the way, the historic Greek name of the former capital is no longer used; it is now called Stamboul) costs 3520 Syrian piastres, which means about twenty-seven dollars when translated into terms of American coinage. The price of a sleeping-car ticket is 2045 Turkish piastres, or approximately eleven dollars. And the traveler must pay for the former in Syrian currency and for the latter in Turkish. If he has nothing but gold he is out of luck. To quote from the regulations: "No other currency than those designated will be accepted for the payment of tickets. This ruling is strictly observed and, as there is no official exchange bureau at the station, but only individual money-changers, it is advisable for travelers to furnish themselves with the necessary currency."

It took me half a day to do this in Damascus, for Turkish piastres were not obtainable at any of the banks and I had to go out and purchase them from money-changers in the bazaar. But I had been warned that I must have them. Moreover, acting on the advice of the consul, I provided myself with various other forms of legal tender, so that when I left that city my pockets bulged with Turkish gold liras, Turkish paper piastres, Syrian piastres, French francs, English bank-notes and American greenbacks. At

Constantinople, in preparation for the journey across Europe, I supplemented these with Greek drachmas, Bulgarian leva, Serbian dinars, Hungarian penga, Austrian kronen and Swiss francs. The next time I take the trip I shall provide myself with a roll of American bills of small denominations and let it go at that. They are accepted without question everywhere.

Because I had foreseen some difficulty in purchasing my ticket from Aleppo to Constantinople, I had wired the American consul at the former city the hour of my arrival, and awaiting me at the station was the consular kavass. He took charge of getting my tickets, and it was well that he did, for, the regulations having been changed overnight, the Turkish piastres with which I had taken such pains to provide myself were useless, the sleeping-car officials refusing to accept anything save Turkish gold. So that meant a dash to the bazaars, where we obtained it from the money-changers. I have no idea how much I lost on the exchange in these various transactions, but it must have been a considerable sum.

It is in the neighborhood of twelve hundred miles from Aleppo to Haidar Pasha and the weekly express makes the journey in forty-eight hours. We reached Yenidji, the Turkish frontier station, at two o'clock in the morning. I was in bed and asleep when the customs inspector, followed by two soldiers with rifles, invaded my compartment. All three were arrogant and rude. Before leaving Baghdad, however, I had taken the precaution of obtained a *laissez-passer* from the Turkish consul-general, and upon my displaying this document the official's manner became a shade less discourteous. He passed my luggage without examination, but, as he was about to depart, his eye fell upon the bottle of whisky, or what was left of it, that I had acquired in Damascus.

"What's in this?" he demanded insolently.

"About a pint of poor Scotch," I told him, the porter acting as interpreter.

There was a volley of Turkish gutturals.

"He say, sare," translated the porter, "the law it forbid to bring spirits into Turkey. Must get spirits only from government monopole. He say you fined twenty Turkish pounds."

"Tell him," I said sleepily, "that I haven't twenty pounds with me. What is he going to do about it?"

There ensued an animated colloquy, in which a couple of other officials joined.

"He say, sare, if you not have the money then you please consider yourself under arres'."

"All right," I replied. "I'll consider myself under arrest so long as he will get out and let me go to sleep again."

"He say, sare," was the cheerful answer, "you will please dress and get off train. I think he take you to prison."

This was serious, but I tried to laugh it off.

"Nonsense," I said lightly. "He can't put over anything like that. If he tries it I'll keep the wires hot to Angora. Tell him I know Mustapha Kemal and that he won't stand for travelers in Turkey being treated in this fashion."

My mention of the dictator-president's name had a magical effect. The inspector became almost polite, his subordinates positively obsequious. There was another rapid-fire of words.

"He say, sare," said the porter, "he not understan' you a frien' of the Ghazi. That make things quite different. He say please tell you arrest is lift, fine is remit."

"And the whisky?"

"Oh, sare," was the answer, "the weesky is contraban'. It is confiscate."

"Well," I said drowsily, snapping out the light and turning my face toward the wall, "how much like home it all sounds. If they had only made me break the bottle on the pier, then I would have known that I was back in America again."

Shortly after dawn the train plunged into the first of the remarkable series of tunnels by means of which the German engineers of the Baghdad Railway penetrated the mighty range of the Taurus, to emerge eventually into a long and gloomy gorge whose rocky walls rise sheer on either hand—the Cilician Gates, through which invading armies have poured southward into Syria since history began. From this narrow defile we debouched suddenly upon the great Anatolian plateau, a vast rolling table-land, bare and brown, rimmed by snow-clad ranges. It had turned cold again, for we had climbed steadily during the night, and the upland air was as clear and invigorating as that of Switzerland.

About the natives congregated at the stations there was something curiously familiar—or unfamiliar. At first I could not make up my mind what it was. Then I decided that it was their caps. In the old days, when I lived in Asiatic Turkey, the turban and the tarboosh were universal. A hat was the distinguishing mark of a European. But now, as a step in Mustapha Kemal's enforced Westernization of Turkey, the wearing of the old head-coverings is illegal, and any Turk who ventures to defy the law is fined or goes to jail. As a result of this sumptuary legislation the fez-makers have gone bankrupt, while the hat and cap makers are doing a roaring business. Caps of every pattern and material are worn—plaid caps, checked caps, plain caps, caps of tweed, of fur, of leather—but, whereas the tarboosh suited the Turk's physiognomy, the cap does not, making him look like a gangster, an apache. Great numbers of soft hats were also in evidence, but I saw no derbies—doubtless because a Turk in a derby would find it difficult to say his prayers.

The rigidity with which the law is enforced was evidenced by the fact that during the entire journey across Turkey, a distance of more than a thousand miles, I did not see one tarboosh and only a single turban. The latter was worn by an old, old man, white-bearded and decrepit, who peered cautiously around the corner of a freight car at a way station, as though fearful of being observed. He was a *mollah,* I imagine, for his turban was of snowy linen, but, by way of compromising with the law, he had perched atop of it a golf cap of shrieking pattern, holding it in place with a bit of string under his chin. He had good reason to be cautious about showing himself thus bonneted, for the ultra-Nationalist newspapers are constantly calling attention to such evasions of the law and demanding that the offenders be punished.

There were throngs of idle onlookers at all the stations we passed, and red-and-white Turkish flags fluttered everywhere, for it was Grand Bairam, the end of the fasting month of Ramadan and the principal feast-day of the Moslem calendar. Consequently, the shops were closed and the local populations had assembled at the stations, dressed in their holiday best, to see the train come in—a form of recreation which is apparently as popular in Anatolia as it is in some of our own country towns.

In the back-blocks of Asia Minor the old Turkish costumes have not yet wholly disappeared, as is the case along the seaboard, and some of the outfits were amazingly picturesque. At Ula Kishla, for example, there stood in the station doorway an enormously stout and very dignified old gentleman—a pasha, I should guess, from the deference paid him. His baggy blue trousers, terminating in bright red slippers, were girt at the waist by a sash of variegated colors from which protruded the hilts of a miniature armory of weapons. His white felt jacket was braided in elaborate designs and over it he wore a sheep-skin coat with the fleece side out, the whole being topped off by a jaunty pearl-gray fedora.

It was tag-day at Konia, and pretty Turkish girls, with the insignia of the Red Crescent Society (the Turkish equivalent of the Red Cross) on their sleeves, passed through the train, shaking their metal money-boxes and pinning paper flowers to our lapels in return for contributions to some local charity. That, I think, was the most striking evidence I saw of the astounding change that has come to Turkey, for in my time no decent woman ever dreamed of appearing outside her home unveiled, and for one to have addressed a man not a relative was unthinkable. But there was nothing bashful about the good-looking damsel who tagged me.

At Afium Karahissar the train was boarded by a Turkish general of division and his staff—all smart, soldierly looking men with scarlet-faced gray overcoats reaching to their heels and caps of black lambskin. At every station at which the train stopped thereafter the general would descend and stride briskly up and down the platform, while his officers and the soldiers on duty stood rigidly at attention in true Prussian fashion.

Another proof of Mustapha Kemal's insistence on making the Turkish Republic a Western nation was provided by the sight of railway employees painting out the Arabic numerals on the rolling stock in the yards at Eskishehr and substituting European characters. This change has been authorized by the Grand Assembly at Angora and will eventually be extended to include the whole language, though it is estimated that, owing to the need for educating the masses in the new alphabet, a dozen or fifteen years will elapse before it is generally used.

From one end of Turkey to the other there were evidences aplenty that the whole nation is at work, and working hard. Though Asia Minor is a poor country both industrially and agriculturally, and the inhabitants have a hard time wresting a meager living from the soil, I observed few signs of actual want. The people appeared to be well fed and comfortably dressed; I did not see a single beggar. The inhabitants gave every evidence, moreover, of being proud of the progress which the country is making and loyal to the Government at Angora. As for Mustapha Kemal, or the Ghazi, as he is commonly called, his picture is displayed everywhere, invariably with a Turkish flag above it. No other ruler in the world is so worshiped by his people save only Mussolini.

At Konia the Baghdad Railway (now completed to within about fifty miles of Mosul) ends and the Anatolian system begins. Shortly after leaving that city the line began to descend. From a wild and rocky gorge we emerged into a country of well cultivated fields and rolling pasture lands. At Akshehr we skirted the lovely lake of that name and then followed for a time the winding course of a broad, swift-flowing river. Soon after leaving Afium Karahissar we began to see the remains of trenches, rolls of barbed wire, ruined rolling stock, bent rails and twisted bridge-girders—the débris of the Greek débâcle. The land was dotted with graves, Greek and Turkish. Military history contains few more remarkable chapters than that of the defeat and utter rout of the great Greek army, provided with all the paraphernalia of modern warfare, by the miserably equipped forces under Mustapha Kemal. The Greeks in their advance on Angora destroyed the railway line by tearing up the ties, bending the rails and scattering them. But the Turks straightened the rails out again, relaid the tracks, using wooden pegs in lieu of steel spikes, and sent their troop trains crawling over them at four miles an hour in pursuit of the demoralized Hellenes. No defeat was ever more merited, no victory more deservedly won. The Greeks were waging a war of conquest and spoliation; the Turks were fighting for the same cause for which we fought in the Revolution—independence.

After Eskishehr, which is the junction for Angora, the line descended rapidly to the lowlands bordering the Gulf of Ismid. Now we were in the military zone, where photographs may not be taken. Soon we were booming along the shores of the Marmora Sea, with the Isles of the Princes, on one of which, Prinkipo, I once lived, rising in the blue distance. This country I knew well, for twenty years before I had hunted here, and had yachted along its shores with Bucknam Pasha, the American sailor of fortune who was naval adviser to Sultan Abdul-Hamid.

Eight and forty hours to the minute after leaving Aleppo the train rolled out on the quay at Haidar Pasha. Moored alongside was the vedette which was to bear us across the Hellespont to Constantinople. Breasting the terrific current which Leander swam to meet Hero, we crossed the Bosphorus, rounded Seraglio Point, where a great bronze statue of the Ghazi looks down upon the city which he saved to Turkey, and entered the Golden Horn. One of the most sublime panoramas in all the world unrolled itself; before us the minarets of Santa Sophia rose above the clutter of Stamboul; to the right were the white buildings of Péra and, a little lower down, the Galata Tower; to the left the palaces and gardens of the Old Serai.

With much clanging of bells the ferry nosed into its berth beside the Galata Bridge. Brawny hamals descended upon my luggage and bore it to a waiting taxi. Not one of the old-time *arabeahs,* mind you, but a trim American car with a uniformed chauffeur and a taximeter. We roared up the long and winding hill, past the Ottoman Bank, the American embassy, the Constantinople Club, the Péra Palace Hotel.

As we swung into the Grande Rue de Péra a traffic light flashed red and a policeman peremptorily raised his white-gloved hand. My driver failed to stop promptly enough to suit the short-tempered guardian of the law.

"Say," he growled, "who'n hell do yu think y'are anyway, an' where in hell yu goin'?" At least, I assume that such was the import of his words, though he spoke in Turkish.

As we drew up before Tokatlian's a radio loud-speaker at the music store next door burst into the familiar strains of American jazz.

Then I knew for certain that I was back in civilization again.

The palm-fringed seaboard of Ceylon . . . the Indian temples with their hideous Hindu gods . . . the wind-swept Himalayan passes . . . the glittering princely courts . . . the scented nights on the Persian Gulf . . . moonlight on the Tigris . . . the fort in the desert . . . romance . . . excitement . . . adventure . . . all these lay far behind. Yes, the song was ended. But the melody lingers on.

INDEX

MAY WE HELP?

THE PUBLISHERS *of Star books have tried to maintain a high standard in the selection of titles for their list, and to offer a consistent quality of workmanship and material. They trust that the book you have just read has, in part at least, earned your esteem for other titles in their list.*

They are trying to make the Star Library comprehend the best in the literary fields of biography, science, history, true adventure, travel, art, philosophy, psychology, etc.

Believing that you will be interested in other books of a nature similar to that which you have just finished reading, the publishers have reproduced on the following pages a few extracts from other Star books. These are pages picked at random. Although there is no continuity, we hope that they will give you some idea of the style in which the books are written and perhaps the character of the subject from which you may form an opinion as to its place on your personal book shelf.

unaccountable restlessness which is apt to seize us in beautiful surroundings when we have already made up our minds to leave.

Never shall I forget Gong. He is probably dead by now, for he was not in his first youth when I made his acquaintance. His mistrust of me was never completely overcome. He was one of those hill monkeys of India, which are more imposing than their brethren of the jungle. They have different ways, but it would not be true to say that they have better manners.

To this companion of mine during the early morning hours I gave the name of Gong on account of his extraordinarily hideous voice, the tones of which resembled the noise made by throwing a rusty old tin kettle against a stone wall. Fortunately he had not much to say, but he was greatly interested in all my doings. He had obviously made up his mind to enjoy some signal experience before departing this life. Having pitched upon me as the person most likely to put him in the way of such happenings, he came to spend his mornings beneath the tall latania and tamarind trees overlooking the house.

Not wishing to miss the coolest hours, it was my custom to rise as soon as the distant sea began to silver in the twilight. Through the bars of the window grating came this pale light reflected from the waters, hardly distinguishable from moonlight. From the landward side were now heard the first calls of the birds of prey, as they circled round the crags already standing out clear against the dawn. An hour must pass ere the rays of the sun would

Reprinted from Waldemar Bonsels' AN INDIAN JOURNEY *by permission.*

reach our highland. At first, far to the west, I could see the sunlight sparkling on the water. Eastwards, the crags would now show golden edges as they thrust upwards against the pale-blue background of the sky. Morning after morning, their radiant stillness was a fresh delight to me, and the peace with which they filled my soul lasted far on into the day—for here there was nothing to ruffle my tranquillity. Those only can understand nature who learn to know her in such a manner and under such conditions; for, like all that is great, she demands from us a limitless self-surrender before she will reveal herself to us fully.

At this hour, Gong would take up his station in one of the trees close to the house, usually upon a thick branch near the ground. To be ready for any emergency, he would keep one hand upon a higher branch, and if my gun were within reach, nothing at first would persuade him to linger. I do not know when or how he had made acquaintance with this weapon, but I am certain that the monkeys had known me and watched me far longer than I had known and watched them.

At the outset a great troop of his companions was in attendance. It was easy to observe them, for the trees were widely spaced, and the monkeys could only progress from tree to tree by way of the ground. One day, Gong departed from the custom of his tribe, for he remained seated as I drew near. This brought me to a standstill, so astonished was I to notice that he did not immediately make off. He was sitting on one of the thick lower branches, holding on with all four, as if wishing to keep himself from taking to flight. Trembling, and raising his eyebrows, he contemplated me with a mixture of curiosity, spitefulness, and fear.

In general, my experience of animals has convinced me that they do not try to work us a mischief unless we take the lead. Perhaps my conviction depends upon the fact that during boyhood I was never hurt by a dog, a horse, or a cat, although I cannot venture to say that I always refrained from teasing. An additional reason may perhaps be that a sense of superiority is distasteful to me. Of all the sentiments that can be aroused through companionship with other living creatures—men or beasts—the most offensive to me is that sort of exultation. I am ever wont to fancy that those who are most ready to assume such a pose are in reality the most paltry of mortals. The very essence of respect for living creatures is that one should not set oneself apart from them. We must concede rights to others, and we should claim rights only when our leadership is essential to the common welfare. Among all the voices of life which stress our emotions during our brief earthly span, the sighs of the oppressed have ever been, for my ears, the most conspicuous tones—like a clamorous motif in a tempestuous piece played on the organ. Since it is equally repugnant to me to be compelled to give sympathy and to receive it, my only resource has been to regard the life of all living things as a natural expression, and as having rights co-equal with those of my own.

When Gong remained seated on his branch, though his fellow monkeys had fled, I could discern in his face, as I slowly drew near, the tension of one whose heart palpitates as he see-saws betwixt fear and curiosity. Suddenly, however, it occurred to him that there was a third possibility, and he tried to intimidate me, to prove to me that he was a person of importance, with forest rights of his own. First drawing his head down between his shoulders, he then stretched it forwards with a jerk, at the same time shaking the branch on which he was sitting, and swaying his body to and fro with all his might, as if about to make a savage onslaught. From his pouting lips came a sound hard to describe. You can produce something like it by pressing a lamp chimney to your mouth, and by trumpeting through this, in chest notes and with a tone of fierce conviction, "Great Scott!"

The effect was so comical that I burst out laughing, and slapped my thigh resoundingly. For a moment Gong was disconcerted; but then, deciding that my gestures were friendly advances, he imitated them to the best of his ability. His eyes, however, retained their serious expression, and his forehead was still puckered.

On this occasion, and thenceforward, we showed our mutual sympathy by imitating one another as well as we could. Amusing as we doubtless were to one another in this respect, it remains somewhat distressing to me when I recall how greatly I fell short of Gong as a mimic.

In the course of our acquaintanceship it became plain to me that Gong was much vexed whenever I failed to put in an appearance, and that he was honestly pleased by my little attentions. Perhaps he may have thought that I reciprocated this feeling. He was anxious to learn, and was eager to understand anything within his powers. Even though at times he could get no further than outward mimicry, the wish for a neighbourly approximation was manifest on both sides.

It is true that he would never let me come quite close to him on the physical plane. My distance was five or six paces. As soon as I attempted to approach any nearer, he would wave me away regretfully, and would seize a higher branch, as a hint of what would happen were I to come closer.

During the progress of our friendship, Gong learned everything concerning a man's activities which can be learned simply by inspection from a distance. He had put my sun-helmet on his head; he had used my pocket handkerchief: and he knew the functions of a knife. He had fluttered the leaves of my notebooks; he had swung in my hammock: and he could imitate the movements of putting on and taking off a coat so perfectly that the onlooker might have imagined he had worn clothing all his life.

We were not always entirely pleased with one another, for Gong knew no limits to his endeavours to be like me. I was nettled at times by his mimicry, which made my own doings appear ludicrous to me. I felt that he was mocking me. Indeed, it became necessary to consider how Gong could be unschooled of some of his acquirements, for it grew plainer from day to day that he, and his companions as well, no longer took me seriously, and that they failed to show me the respect to which I deemed myself entitled. These monkeys positively laughed whenever I appeared. Sometimes they closed in upon me in serried ranks, in order to make fun of everything I did. They nudged one another to draw attention to me, rubbing their grey hands gleefully, and smacking their thighs. They chattered in all possible tones, while begrudging one another some trifle which an instant before they had been willing to share. All the time their demeanour was so self-important that it would have seriously annoyed a more even-tempered person than myself.

I was never alone now, for my train followed me wherever I went. Respect for the gun lessened as the days passed, for the monkeys had realised that it was used only to shoot birds and four-footed game, and that the great race of quadrumana was quite immune from danger. Whenever some little creature had fallen to my marksmanship, they would wait until I had laid down the weapon, and would then come close to me in crowds, with gestures showing their conviction that I had them to thank for my success.

What annoyed me more than anything else was their forgetfulness. It was really scandalous to see how at one moment they would make a tremendous fuss about something, and a moment later would let it slip from memory as if there had never been such a thing in the world. New whims took hold of them and passed in an instant, and in each fresh pose they would insist on being taken no less seriously than in the last. After a time I came to regard myself as a visitor in some foreign town, an eccentric tolerated by the citizens because he was a source of amusement to them. My observations of animals and the world were confusing my judgment.